TİMAŞ PUBLISHING

İstanbul 2019

timaspublishing.com

THE BOSPHORUS: AN ILLUSTRATED STORY
SEDAT BORNOVALI

TİMAŞ PUBLISHING | 4655
Non-Fiction 8

EDITOR
Neval Akbıyık

TURKISH-ENGLISH TRANSLATION
Gökçen Ezber

PROOFREADING
David Hendrix

COVER DESIGN
Ravza Kızıltuğ

COVER PICTURE
Bosforo Tracio / Vincenzo Maria Coronelli
Private Collection

PAGE DESIGN
Hüseyin Özkan

1ˢᵗ EDITION
May 2019, İstanbul

ISBN
ISBN 978-605-08-3019-4

TİMAŞ PUBLISHING
Cağaloğlu, Alemdar Mahallesi,
Alayköşkü Caddesi, No: 5, Fatih/İstanbul
Telephone: (+90) (212) 511 24 24 Fax: (+90) (212) 512 40 00
P.K. 50 Sirkeci / İstanbul

timaspublishing.com
info@timaspublishing.com
facebook.com/timasyayingrubu
twitter.com/timasyayingrubu

Ministry of Culture and Tourism
Publisher Certificate: 12364

PRINTING AND BINDING
WPC Matbaacılık
Osmangazi Mah. Mehmet Deniz Kopuz Cad. No:17-1 Esenyurt / İstanbul
Telephone: (+90) (212) 886 83 30
Printing Certificate No: 35428

COPYRIGHT NOTICE
© All right reserved. No part of this publication may be reproduced, stored in a retrieval system, or transmitted, in any form or by any means, electronic, mechanical, photocopying, recording or otherwise, without the prior permission of Timaş Publishing.

THE BOSPHORUS: AN ILLUSTRATED STORY

From Prehistory to The Eurasia Tunnel

Sedat Bornovalı (PhD)

Sedat Bornovalı (PhD), Art Historian and Geographer, graduated from the Boğaziçi (Bosphorus) University where he had already started gathering notes about this marvelous piece of landscape.

He always enjoyed sharing what he learnt and worked as a tour guide continuously during his college and postgraduate years, through which he had the chance to present the monuments of his city to many distinguished visitors, including His Holiness the Pope Benedict XVI. Among his former patrons, he misses especially Prof. Umberto Eco.

Now he shares his knowledge more as an Assistant Professor of History of Architecture at Nişantaşı University than as a tour guide for groups. His recent book about the Bosphorus became a local best seller in Turkish and was subsequently translated in English.

Being honored as a Knight of the Italian Republic, Order of Merit, he does not deny that he favors researches that discover unpublished Italian cultural heritage all around Istanbul and mostly on the Bosphorus.

Contents

Preface 7

What Is The Bosphorus And Where Is It? 11
Those Who Have Come and Gone 16
The Persians Built the First Bridge Across the Bosphorus 18
The Dawn of a New Era 26
Passing through the Bosphorus 29

Beginning the Tour 33
What Karaköy Lost 38
Istanbul Modern Formula as an Answer to Istanbul's Need for Art 41
Conflict Among Embassies 50
Hardships That the Dolmabahçe Mosque Survived 53
A Garden Filled with History 56
Dolmabahçe Palace 57
Akaretler and Its Cosmopolitan Residents 63
Barbaros Hayreddin Pasha's Neighborhood Beşiktaş 69
Traces from the Remote Past 71
We Come by Çırağan 76
Küçük Mecidiye Mosque and Yahya Efendi Lodge 84
Feriye Palaces 87
Mosaic of Cultures: Ortaköy 90
A Centuries-Old Dream: Bosphorus Bridge 97
An Art Nouveau Palace: Nazime Sultan Waterfront Mansion 103
New Breath at the Bosphorus 110
Bebek: from Egypt to the Soviet Union 120
Robert College and Beyond 128
Dead poets' 131

Fortress of Rumelihisari; to the Second Bridge 134
Emirgan: a Centre of Attraction in the Bosphorus 150
Yeniköy: Place of Mansions and Cavafy 165
Huber: an Arms Dealer in the Bosphorus 180
Seeing the Black Sea 189
The Asian Shore 201
The Russians are coming 203
Industrialisation and The Hills of Beykoz 205
Çubuklu 212
From Keçecizade Fuat Pasha to Modern Architecture 216
Mansions Laid Together 218
Vegetable Gardens and Mansions in Çubuklu 220
Hekimbaşı Mansion and the Balance in Architecture 225
Amcazade Mansion 227
"Hisar Peçesi" (Veil of Fortress) 231
Mihrişah Sultana Fountain and Küçüksu Pavilion 232
Remembering Cemile Sultana 240
Kandilli High School for Girls as an Alternative to American College for Girls 242
From Eastern Turkey Down to the Bosphorus 245
Great Elegance in Great Size: Kuleli Military High School 248
A Peaceful Dock in Beylerbeyi 257
Beylerbeyi Palace: Resort and Exile on the Bosphorus 259
Kuzguncuk 262
Paşalimanı 264
Dream City Üsküdar 269

Illustration Acknowledgements 274
Bibliography 275

PREFACE

The book you have started reading will talk a lot about the Ottoman history, local topography, major monuments, museums, and mosques but also about many other things; the protestant missionary activity, coups d'état, the Crimean War, Russia, oil trade, Napoleon, Egypt, Shakespeare's Globe Theater, Venetians, Persians, local culture, contemporary architecture, even Johann Strauss, movies, a Ford factory far from home, Ancient Greek and Roman authors, just to mention a few.

While it does not try to be an all-inclusive text about the Bosphorus, it reaches to give a comprehensive view of the Bosphorus as a whole, and, at the same time, tends to surprise even the most ambitious reader with several unpublished and unexpected archival documents and photos.

This book is not a lament; its aim is not to mourn over values "gone forever". It's true that many things went wrong, many historic homes were damaged by oil tankers, many monumental buildings were lost, but the Bosphorus is still beautiful without a match and unique.

This is not one of those books which exposes all the details and monuments of a neighborhood. There are works which do this very well already, and undoubtedly, there will be many detailed publications. It would not be wrong to say, though, that we made mention of some remarkable examples when they sprang to mind.

This book could also not be defined as a book which attempts to describe all the details of some major monuments. Outstanding monographs about many monuments have already been written. However, if we identified details which are not mentioned even in these monographs, we have presented them here.

Is this an academic book? Yes, it is; but it tries to avoid being one of the most boring examples of this genre. It doesn't consider a saturnine style as a prerequisite for being academic in nature.

We could perhaps define it as a book which brings to mind a little bit more of what we think about the Bosphorus when we think of it casually. Another possible definition would make it the exposition of a few details about the places we visit along the Bosphorus to go out to eat, have some fresh air, enjoy ourselves, and, sometimes, attend an event.

It is most probably not a book which reveals a lot of unknown facts about the Bosphorus, but we can say that these pages repeat and sometimes offer a different perspective on many things which are worth remembering.

Besides all these, we can also say that many historical documents, some of which have not been published elsewhere and unearthed in archives, both in Turkish State Archives and in private collections, are being published on these pages. We hope that this will be of some additional value for those who like to remember the good old days.

A preface cannot go without acknowledgments, but the number people to thank is just too many, which would increase the book's volume significantly. Therefore, I would like to content myself only with thanking all those at Timaş Publishing who have contributed to the making of this book at every stage; if Samet Altıntaş had not come up with such a suggestion unexpectedly, this book would not have existed in any case. If Neval Akbıyık and Zeynep Berktaş had not embraced this work, we would not be able to finalize it. If Hüseyin Özkan had not touched every inch of the book, it would not have been this pleasant to hold it in our hands.

Numerous people and institutions have contributed to saving the book from mediocrity a little bit by providing information and materials. Among all those, I am thankful to Saffet Emre Tonguç, Gökçen Ezber, PhD, Erhan Ermiş, PhD, for their friendly support and owe particular gratitude to Mr. Erol Makzume and Architect Mr. Sinan Genim, PhD, for generously sharing their own living spaces, collections and even information and documents that they could not yet publish themselves.

I will be more than happy if the end result could loosely resemble what they expected.

Sedat Bornovalı
May 2019, İstanbul

What Is The Bosphorus And Where Is It?

While locals tend to associate the Bosphorus with songs, poems, paintings and scenes from films, along with their own nostalgic memories, the main determining factor behind its entire cultural heritage is the region's physical geography. Accordingly, it is crucial, at the risk of boring the reader, to define and clarify its borders at the outset. The Bosphorus, as the famous Straits of Istanbul are known internationally, is the name of the waterway between the Çatalca and Kocaeli peninsulas, part of the ancient Thracia and Bithynia, where they are the closest to one another. The name Bosphorus is used as a general designation of the open and settled spaces on both shores of this waterway. Both peninsulas are peneplains, vast plains with a slightly uneven surface close to sea level. The surrounding hilly areas (made, for example, of quartzite) are more resistant to erosion. Such elevations (inselbergs or monadnocks, as they are technically called) are known as "witness hills" in Turkish. Taksim (110m), Çamlıca (262m), Kayışdağı (438m), Alemdağ (442m), Aydos (537m) and Altunizade (110m) on the eastern and western banks of the Bosphorus are some notable examples. The nearby Princes' Islands have the same characteristics, as can be seen, for

A map of the Bosphorus, (1715)

instance, with the Aya Yorgi Hill (202m) on Büyükada.

Situated further to the south of the Çatalca peninsula is Istanbul's historic center and the Golden Horn (known as "Haliç" which means "gulf" in Arabic and "Estuary" in Turkish) just north to it. All these areas are, geographically speaking, part of the Bosphorus. Even though the locals visiting along the Golden Horn do not usually call it the Bosphorus; neighborhoods along the Golden Horn are, strictly speaking, part of the geography of the Bosphorus.

The boundaries of the Bosphorus have not always been drawn in the same way, as different definitions limited or extended what is meant by the Bosphorus. There is, nonetheless, an area which most have agreed upon: the Strait of Istanbul (as the locals call) will continue to exist as long as Kocaeli peninsula on the Asian continent in the east and Çatalca peninsula on the European continent are located in proximity to one another; and once they move away from one another for good, it will cease to exist. The Anadolu and Rumeli lighthouses in the north are generally accepted as the northern boundaries of the Bosphorus, while it is commonly held that the line between Seraglio Point (Sarayburnu) and Salacak, near the Maiden's Tower, form its southern border.

The length of the Bosphorus, between the northern and southern ends, is about 30 km (around 17 mi.). Its eastern shoreline, on its Asian side, is about 35 km long, while its western shore on its European side nearly 55 km. The reason for the significant difference between the lengths of the two shores is that the Anatolian shoreline is relatively straight in comparison to the European side, which has the Golden Horn (which, as stated above, is officially part of the Bosphorus) along with a large number of coves.

As a side note, the terms "north" and "south" will be used through this book, even though the Bosphorus has a slight northeastern and southwestern axis. Furthermore, it does not run in a straight line, but rather winds between the Black Sea and Marmara. As a matter of fact, except when one is near to the Black Sea and Marmara, it can feel like you are passing from one lake to another.

While most of the references around the Bosphorus (including the ones in this book) are about the monuments on the shores of the Bosphorus, it is important to bear in mind that it is essentially a waterway. It is for this reason that the waters of the Bosphorus deserve to be mentioned first and foremost; it is where the waters of the Black Sea meet the rest of the world.

There are several well-known, large rivers flowing into the Black Sea. These include the Kuban, Dnieper, Don and the Danube outside Turkey and the Kızılırmak (Halys), Yeşilırmak (Iris), Sakarya (Sangarios) and Çoruh (Akampsis) rivers in Turkey. The amount of the freshwater carried by all these

The first oceanographic measurements in history, by Luigi Ferdinando Marsili (Bosphorus, 1681)

rivers and the limited evaporation due to low average temperature, unsurprisingly, result in the low salinity of the Black Sea.

As mentioned, the waters of the Black Sea "encounter" the rest of the world – meaning that there is a current flowing from the Black Sea through the Bosphorus. While there is a current on the surface of the waters of the Bosphorus that visibly and continuously flows to the Sea of Marmara in the south, at the same time there is actually an undercurrent – invisible to the common observer – flowing in the reverse direction towards the Black Sea. The amount of water flowing in the undercurrent is more limited. Although it is not easy to observe these currents, they were the subject of scholarly interest even centuries ago. In the 17th Century, the Italian Count Luigi Ferdinando Marsili demonstrated for the first time that the currents of the sea could be measured scientifically, and he thus had the honor of initiating the science of oceanography in the very waters of the Bosphorus.

These currents, however, do not flow smoothly like a river: sometimes the southwestern wind is so strong that the surface water cannot flow southward and instead flows north. This phenomenon has a specific name: the Orkoz current. Additionally, the surface current sometimes turns towards the north when it hits the capes so one may observe two surface currents in opposite directions.

Those Who Have Come and Gone

With its natural beauty and strategic location, the Bosphorus has never had the problem of being uninhabited. It has long been desired as it has been the site of wealth, both in terms of commercial interest, and also for it strategic position, both in its own right and for the city of Istanbul to the south, one of the most important cities of human history; at other times, as a dream location for habitation or as a place desired for its natural beauty.

Until very recently, when talking about the history of the Bosphorus, we used to only be able to rely on historical sources which went back to antiquity. Since 2017, however, our knowledge of the area changed significantly: during the subway constructions in Beşiktaş, thanks to the salvage excavations carried out by Istanbul Archaeological Museums, the existence of at least one settlement on the shores of the Bosphorus, belonging to a much earlier period in history, was ascertained. The layers of a necropolis, proven to belong to the Iron Age and most probably even to the Chalcolithic period, were unearthed at the site.

During the Antiquity, when the Greeks and Romans dominated the region, there were many mythological and historical references to the Bosphorus. Almost none of the monuments belonging to this period have survived to this day even in ruins.

What is most important, though, is that two colonies of Megara were founded on the southern entrance of the Bosphorus in the 7th century BC. Their names are very familiar: Byzantium (now Fatih, the historical peninsula of Istanbul) and Chalcedon (modern Kadıköy). Generally speaking, most of the monuments from the Antiquity, whose ruins are not visible today and mainly consisted of sacred areas, would have belonged to these two settlements.

Due to the central trade ports on the shores of the Black Sea, those who left major cities to the south founded colonies here during antiquity. The most ambitious and active of these were the Milesians. Among the new colonies of Miletus beyond the Bosphorus, a city of philosophers south to the Meander River, İnebolu (Ionopolis), Ordu (Cotyora), Giresun (Cerasus), Sinop and Trabzon were founded along the Black Sea coast.

Because there were numerous colonies along the Black Sea in antiquity and the Bosphorus was the only means of access to these colonies, we can state with high confidence that it must have been aa much busier hub than records show.

Not far from here is another strait - the Dardanelles, which is also along the route from the Black Sea down to the Mediterranean. We do not have mythological references to Istanbul which could be compared with the story of Troy, but even Troy itself, located near the Dardanelles clearly testifies to the significance of these waterways as early as the 13th century and even before. Most probably, in antiquity the landscape of the Bosphorus was not determined by its monuments but mainly by nature. If there were particularly monumental buildings, no tangible proofs of them have in any case survived.

The concept of crossing the Bosphorus, however, should not only be viewed as passing through the waterway. As a matter of fact, the etymology of the Bosphorus means 'cattle-passage' or "ox-ford". A mythological narrative attached to the Bosphorus refers to the passage of a bull, which swam across the waterway, passing from Europe to Asia.

Beyond myth, the Bosphorus is an important passageway not only for the bull in the myth or for humans in recorded history, but also for birds as one of the most important and dense migration routes. The migration of storks is just one of the most impressive events of the region that also hosts hundreds of thousands of water birds, predatory and singing birds during periods of migration.

The Persians Built the First Bridge Across the Bosphorus

In an account by the historian Herodotus we are told that 2500 years ago the Persian Emperor Darius built a pontoon bridge across the Bosphorus by tying boats together and they used this bridge, their historic landmark, to cross between two continents. We even know the architect of this temporary bridge: Mandrocles of Samos. With what was left from the substantial sum of money paid to him, the architect commissioned a painting that would celebrate his work. He donated this painting to the Temple of Hera on the island of Samos (just across Kuşadası in Western Turkey), and he thus was able to immortalize his own name as well.

Speaking of temples, the shores of the Bosphorus were not densely settled in antiquity. Monuments that marked the view were most probably temples appealing to passers-by. We know about numerous locations related to such monuments thanks to the writers of the period including a temple which Jason and the Argonauts supposedly built around İstinye.

The prominent points of the Bosphorus geography, starting from the present Sarayburnu, which was Byzantium's acropolis, and to the Pillar of Pompey (which built on the Clashing Rocks mentioned in the myth of Jason and the Argonauts) in Rumeli Kavağı, were likely adorned with monumental structures honoring gods of the period. To visualize the Bosphorus during that age, we could perhaps imagine that monuments like the Çanakkale Martyrs' Memorial, the *Abide*, on the Dardanelles were scattered along the shores of the Bosphorus.

It is clear that the region during the Byzantine period, even if not as much as the present day, was somehow populated. Fishing and agriculture activities that fed a great capital along with numerous monasteries built in beautiful rural areas would have left their mark on the Bosphorus. However, there were still not many reasons to think that the Bosphorus was something more than scattered villages that were largely distinct from the capital Constantinople. We can imagine a series of shore villages and some monasteries on the hills with minimal connections to the City. Villagers would travel the capital only to sell their goods in the markets.

Another noteworthy moment from earlier periods of Byzantium is when Emperor Heraclius crossed a pontoon bridge built with boats tied together while he was marching for the Persian Campaign. The building of this bridge is a striking incident, because the design was aimed at lessening Heraclius' fear of water.

It is also recounted that the Pechenegs, during one of their raids against the Turks in 1048, crossed to the Anatolian side across a bridge built with boats. It must have been another unforgettable moment when they decided not to continue this journey and swam back across the waters of the Bosphorus with their reserve horses.

Another noteworthy crossing of the Bosphorus belongs to the Holy Roman Emperor Frederick Barbarossa following an agreement with the Byzantine Emperor during the Third Crusade.

Since the emperor lost his life near Seleucia (now Silifke), drowning in the river Calycadnus three months after his landing on the Anatolian shores in the March of 1190, he was unable to make it back to the Bosphorus.

In the aftermath of the Fourth Crusade, which resulted in the conquest of Constantinople in 1204, the dominance of the Bosphorus was passed on to the Latin powers. Even after the reconquest of Constantinople by the Palaiologos dynasty, the Venetian and Genoese maritime powers continued to dominate the area.

Genoese trade was focused on the Black Sea during the Byzantine period resulting in efforts to control the Bosphorus. The monumental Yoros Castle situated on the northernmost point of the Bosphorus on the Anatolian side is living witness to this period.

It was precisely during this period when the Turkish presence in the Bosphorus started to be felt. The entire Anatolian side of the Bosphorus, including the Yoros Castle, came under Ottoman control during the reign of Orhan Gazi, the empire's second sovereign in the first half of the 1300s, when the Ottoman state, which was merely one of many Turkish principalities of Anatolia, was just founded. The Ottomans were virtually invincible in and around the Bosphorus, and they were the ones who would determine the rulers of the surrounding geography. Thus, one of the battles of the Second Venetian-Genoese War was held on 13 February 1352 in the Bosphorus, and it was only through an alliance with the Ottomans that Genoa won the war against Venice in the Naval Battle of the Bosphorus between the two Italian states.

Afterwards, just as the colonies of Miletus earlier, the Genoese colonies, allies of the Ottomans dominated the Bosphorus, but not much longer because the only ruler of the Bosphorus passage would be Sultan Mehmet the Conqueror and he would turn the Black Sea into an Ottoman lake. Following this, the Genoese colonies fell to the Ottomans one by one: Amasra in 1459, Sinop and Trabzon in 1461, Caffa, the largest of the Black Sea colonies, in 1475 and Kopa and Anapa, other ports on the shores of Crimea in 1479. Around the same time the Genoese brought the plague to Europe from Crimea through the Bosphorus.

SEDAT BORNOVALI

WHAT IS THE BOSPHORUS AND WHERE IS IT?

The Long History of Crossing and Passing Through the Bosphorus

While history is full of interesting stories of crossing the Bosphorus, it has in fact not always been that easy to cross. During Byzantine rule, the crossing of this waterway was possible by the permission of the emperor in Constantinople. The 12th century historian Niketas Choniates even mentions another chain (in addition to the one at the mouth of the Golden Horn) between Seraglio Point (Sarayburnu) and the Maiden's Tower to control ships passing through the Bosphorus.

The most glorious and most famous of the buildings that represent the end of the Byzantine era is again along the Bosphorus. Built a year before the fall of Constantinople, the fortress known as Rumelihisarı represents the final stages of the conquest of the Bosphorus both literally and symbolically. In

Istanbul and a part of the Bosphorus, engraving from Hartmann Schedel's Liber Chronicarum (1493)

addition to considering who could pass through the Bosphorus, it is also important to bear in mind those who were not allowed to pass. Those who did not heed the rules of passage established by the Sultan Mehmet the Conqueror after the construction of the Rumeli Castle were not allowed to pass.

On November 26th in 1452, for example, "The first cannonball shot from the castle sank Antonio Rizzo's ship, because the ship, bringing barley to help Constantinople, refused to lower sails."

Following the Conquest, the Bosphorus for nearly two hundred years continued to be a series of rural settlements close to the capital. Surely, by then, the Ottomans, who ruled almost all the Black Sea as well, had no particular concern for defending the Bosphorus. Hence, there was no reason for dense settlement to emerge along here, and the pre-existing ones were developed as centers for agricultural production. Populations from the coastal towns of the Black Sea, especially from its eastern provinces like Rize and Trabzon, were settled in the villages of the Bosphorus. Since less populated areas were more in danger of pillage, villages were established, and new populations were brought in so as not to leave them uncontrolled.

Furthermore, the coastal areas, especially the southern parts close to Istanbul, were allocated to high state officials and elites. The mouths of streams and surrounding areas were preserved as agricultural lands and rural settlements sprang up around them.

The historian Naima narrates one of the most traumatic moments in Ottoman history: on July 20th in 1624 the northern parts of the Bosphorus down to Yeniköy were raided by the Cossacks, (yes, like those mentioned Sholokhov's "And Quiet Flows the Don" and Gogol's "Taras Bulba"). They raided with boats known as *chaikas* that each had 50 rowers. Large fleets were not able to move fast when there was no wind, whereas these boats could maneuver very well and could harm an opponent. Naima's History mentions that the Cossacks arrived with 150 *chaikas*. These Cossacks went ashore in Tarabya and Yeniköy and pillaged the land. They escaped by sea and disappeared when the soldiers arrived.

Ottoman traveler Evliya Çelebi (1611-1682) refers to the incident as well: "They have come from the Black Sea Straits (Kerch Strait) with 300 chaikas and captured one thousand men as slaves and stole five Egyptian treasures and the same amount of valuable goods. They soon easily left for their hellish homeland fearlessly and recklessly." Interestingly, it mirrors a similar incident, centuries earlier when the Rus, Vikings from what is now Ukraine and Russia, suddenly attacked the Bosphorus in 860.

Undoubtedly, such an unexpected attack on the Bosphorus, an indispensable part of Istanbul, triggered an inexpressible terror in the city. Hence, a new defense perspective was adopted for the Bosphorus in the aftermath of this attack. Just after the raid of 1624, firstly the villages of Anadolu and Rumeli fener, and then Garipçe and Kilyos were turned into settlement areas. It was thus possible to see possible raids beforehand and prepare an initial defense against them.

New defense components were added after this date, and there was a transition from mostly medieval structures to the defensive principles of the Modern Era. During the reign of Mustafa III, the French Hungarian architect Baron de Tott built the Garipçe and Poyrazköy castles in line with the principles of modernity.

The ongoing struggle for dominance over the Bosphorus then was felt in other areas as well. The Treaty of Küçük Kaynarca signed with Russia in 1774 granted Russian traders the right to pass through the Bosphorus, which was a significant blow to Ottoman prestige and interests. Fortunately, at the time Russia's internal problems increased and its diplomatic leverage was weakened. The Russian insistence on granting the right of free pass to warships as well could not be sustained. The relations between the Russian and Ottoman empires were not unidimensional, but rather also involved all of the Great Powers of the time. Although war was never-ending, wheat began to be imported from Russia for the first time at the end of the 19th century during the reign of Abdülhamit I to answer Istanbul's increased need for bread.

Since Napoleon referenced the strategic significance of the Bosphorus in sustaining global balance against Russia, it has often been claimed that he was the source of the quotation "If the world were only one country, Istanbul would be its capital". As a matter of fact, it is reported that a vast crowd applauded the Russian fleet passing through the Bosphorus in September 1798 to cooperate with the Ottomans in the Mediterranean against France who occupied Egypt.

As Ottoman industrial initiatives were being implemented during these years, the Bosphorus emerged again as a focal point. The area around Beykoz, in particular, emerged as one of the major production centers for goods like paper, leather, and glass. Some key elements for sustainable industry are actually the more important natural beauties (e.g., river sources and ports) that need protecting. Therefore, the choice of Beykoz for the first industrial initiatives of this early period should come as no surprise. Fortunately, we have started feeling sorry for the risk of losing even these relatively recent but beautiful buildings by considering them as a sort of industrial archeology.

When the army at the command of Muhammad Ali of Egypt's son Ibrahim Pasha left Egypt, a source of dispute with Napoleon, and reached around Kütahya, many people inside and outside the Ottoman Empire began worrying about a possible occupation of Istanbul. When the Russians came for help from the north as a solution, the Bosphorus once more played a central role in history.

The landing of Russian soldiers so close to the capital, in the area where the current Beykoz Shoe Factory (not in use anymore) is located, and their staying there until the Ibrahim Pasha's troops retreating behind the Taurus Mountains, should have certainly raised concern for Istanbul's security, even when the Russians were deemed as saviors at the time. Russians should have reacted in a friendly way, not because of their fondness for Sultan Mahmut II, but because they preferred that the weak Ottomans remained in power rather than a strong enemy like Muhammad Ali. Furthermore, a long stay on the Bosphorus was a great opportunity to learn and document the zone in detail. After all, with the signing of the Treaty of Hünkar İskelesi in 1833, the Russians gained a great advantage in Bosphorus, and the Ottoman State had to enter an agreement that allowed the Russians use the Bosphorus.

Britain, of course, was in no position to celebrate in this state of affairs. Hence, worked hard on a different front and only five years later, having increased their pressure within the Ottoman state, the British also signed the Baltalimanı Trade Agreement in the Bosphorus (at the waterfront mansion of Reşid Pasha) in 1838. The British have thus gained significant privileges, and this paved the way for granting new rights to other European states as well. The Ottoman State lost its monopoly in foreign trade and the extraordinary power of taxes and limitations, including the customs duties.

During the last year of Abdülmecit's reign in 1861, other series of trade agreements were signed with Western states on the shores of the Bosphorus (again at the Keçecizade Fuat Pasha's waterfront mansion that no longer exists). These are known as the Kanlıca Trade Agreements. Even the fact that the agreements then signed with the Great Powers at were named after the neighborhoods of the Bosphorus indicates how it became a focal point once more.

In the meantime, the establishment of *Şirket-i Hayriye* ferry company and the first regular ferry lines on the Bosphorus made this waterway as virtually a central part of the city. It should also be noted that since Beşiktaş was the center of court life starting with Mahmut II in the same era, the Bosphorus became even more central to the political and social life of the city.

The Crimean War (1853-56), which had decisive outcomes for the Ottoman State, and left a lasting mark: the British, French and Italians, this time, passed through the Bosphorus together against the common enemy of the time, the Russian Empire. This is how Cevdet Pasha describes what happened in his own words: "They got used to the pleasant way of living and attempted renting waterfront mansions in the Bosphorus. No corner has been left empty; finding a four-room house in Büyükdere was equal to a victory one could very rarely obtain".

The Dawn of a New Era

Many European states during these years strengthened their positions with the ambassadorial summer houses built along the northern Bosphorus. The US first appeared on this waterway, which had already been a significant point for Russia around the same period. The development of a country's influence through educational institutions was also general practice at the time.

A Protestant-based American religious institution was already teaching a small number of students in Bebek since 1840; later it began to look for a new plot of land in Kuruçeşme. After this search, the school, with the name Robert College, acquired Ahmet Vefik Efendi's land in Rumelihisarı in 1863 and leading to the establishment of what is known today as *Boğaziçi* (Bosphorus) University.

As revealed above, the Bosphorus was a miniature of the empire, especially during the last years of the Ottoman state. It offered many beauties to enjoy, yet also grappled with many troubles.

The German Goeben and Breslau (renamed Yavuz and Midilli) warships, which are among one of the most important examples of ships passing through the Bosphorus, should certainly not go without mention. These two ships passed through the straits of the Dardanelles and Bosphorus and attacked the Russian cities Odessa and Novorossiysk, leading to the Ottoman entrance into World War I. After staying moored in İstinye for a short period of time, the two ships started off for the Black Sea leading to an irreversible course of events.

After the World War I, during the occupation of Istanbul, with the British fleet anchored just in front of Dolmabahçe Palace, the Bosphorus has once again revealed that it had symbolical meaning as well as posing an actual threat.

The far-reaching reforms of the Republican era were reflected on the shores of Bosphorus as well. During the early years of the Republic, there was a significant transfer of property ownership. The deported members of the Ottoman Dynasty sold their personal properties on the shores of the Bosphorus in the very short time given to them. Many of the waterfront mansions were declared to be public property and were given new functions by the state.

Magnificent waterfront mansions during these years were mostly allocated to educational institutions, though some of them were used as warehouses. Since the educational function is less harmful to the buildings, many of the mansions assigned to schools could survive to this day after generations of graduates, whereas the ones used for industrial purposes gradually fell into ruin. Even the most splendid ones of their kind, such as Nazime Sultan and Hüseyin Avni Pasha mansions, were not saved from falling into ruins; they totally collapsed or burned.

Fire was a constant tragedy that affected waterfront mansions used as residences during both the Ottoman and Republican eras.

Furthermore, it was even argued that those who were no longer interested in their timber mansions chose to destroy them by setting them on fire, only to later erect concrete apartment buildings in their plot However, perhaps it is wiser not to prematurely accuse anyone with such a crime, as the nature of timber building material is prone to being engulfed with fire with the slightest spark, destining them to be ultimately replaced by concrete buildings..

The year 1973, by the way, was the year during which the most prominent man-made structure added to the Bosphorus was constructed. The two continents were connected with a bridge and the ease of transportation that the bridge provided, also resulted in an uncontrolled building activity on the Asian side. The relatively greener part of this city also fell prey to an ever-increasing density of concrete.

The uncontrolled construction period lasted up to 1983. With the Bosphorus Law enacted by the Turkish Grand National Assembly in November, it was decreed that the period brand new constructions in the Bosphorus basically had come to an end. The parliamentary system in the country was just being rebuilt at the time, and a parliament's ability to enact such a decisive law with such strong will and with the necessary instruments only a very short while after a military coup (12th September 1980) is an indication of how effectively the institutions were running. Thus, the Bosphorus we have inherited today is the Bosphorus given to us during that period.

Passing through the Bosphorus

All those who want to sail to and from the Black Sea have to pass through the Bosphorus; it is the only seaway that connects the Black Sea and its surroundings to the entire world. This makes it a route of high-volume trade. Oil is its most important trade good, partly due to Russia, which is a major oil exporter, relying on this route. While there are other oil routes, they are somehow problematic for Russia, which for instance, exports 3 million tons of oil from the Port of Murmansk, but the port can only be reached via the Barents Sea north of Norway. The Barents Sea, as expected, is a cold sea and the ice acts as an obstacle for traffic for most part of the year.

Russia can also export its oil through the Baltic Sea. However, the narrow entrance of the sea is rather shallow, making it difficult for large vessels to use this route. Reaching high volumes requires an extraordinarily high number of small tankers to pass here, which is not a desired setup. Since there is no freedom of passage through the Danish straits, as there is in the Turkish straits, the Bosphorus emerges as the only practical water way, the right of passage being guaranteed by international agreements. Therefore, huge tankers loaded with oil frequently pass through the Bosphorus. Not only oil but also imports of the Black Sea countries are brought by huge container carriers through the Bosphorus as well and each type of vessel is subject to different rules of passage. Sometimes military ships, and even submarines, pass through the Bosphorus; and although their numbers have decreased recently, a significant number of cruise ships, too use the straits.

The "rules" referenced above are a form of legal acquis that has emerged over the course of the centuries. The rules took their most recent shape in the Montreux Convention in 1936. The rules, described in broad strokes in the convention (and not so easy to follow in practice), have been made applicable through regulations. If the range of vision drops below 1 mile, for example, traffic becomes unidirectional. If the range of vision is below 0.5 miles, the Bosphorus is closed to traffic. Military ships can pass without paying any fees and do not need to be escorted by maritime pilots. Aircraft carriers are not allowed to pass. Submarines can pass from the surface and only during the daytime. However, ships not belonging to the Black Sea countries need to weigh less than 45 thousand tons, and they should give notice 21 days beforehand to benefit from exemptions.

Passage for merchant ships is for free in theory, but they have to pay health and lighthouse duties. If they don't stop between the Black Sea and the Aegean Sea, they are not obliged to use a pilot. However, even if they will stop at only one place in Marmara, their exemption is lifted. Almost 60% of the ships do not stop between the Aegean and the Black Sea, thus they often do benefit from the exemption. Tugboats are also decisive for traffic security in the Bosporus: they are not obligatory under normal conditions, except for tankers measuring more than 250 meters long. As a matter of fact, these extraordinarily large vessels are subject to some special technical constraints, such as passing in company of even 2-5 tugs. Recently a pilot went to the port of departure of a particularly large vessel and spent several weeks aboard it for training and it was only after this that the ship was permitted to pass through the Bosphorus, under the guidance of the same captain.

These large tankers not only transport oil; they are often loaded with water so as not to lose balance. It is through this "ballast" water that some foreign fauna from distant geographies is brought to the Bosphorus. These sea creatures cause much greater harm than what one might expect, as they are invasive species that can damage the environment and harm local species in these waters. The amount of these ballast waters is quite substantial. It is calculated that billion tons of water travel from distant seas in this way every year. The International Maritime Organization, a specialized agency of the United Nations, fortunately, decided to implement regulations on ballast waters before the impacts become more severe. An international convention was recently put into force. Accordingly, the problem will be solved by 2024, however, the cost of these new regulations for the ship owners will be billions of dollars.

The waters of the Bosphorus, with its narrow passages, sharp turns and many challenging currents, have been the site of occasional accidents. Some of these incidents were near misses, whereas some others caused disasters. In 1979, the 300-meter Romanian crude oil carrier Independenta on her way from Libya to Romania exploded when she was waiting for a pilot to lead her during the passage through the Bosphorus. The ship was on fire for weeks causing the death of tens of people on its board; it was one of the most tragic accidents that occurred on these waters.

In 2009, a ship hit and demolished half of the Yeniköy Şehzade Burhaneddin Efendi waterfront mansion. After the accident, the media focused more on the fact that the tenant of the mansion at the time was an actress and the tabloid press published many pieces about the accident (discussing mainly about the choice of a luxury mansion of a left-wing artist).

Only a few days before this book was written, another ship was involved in an accident, hitting the Hekimbaşı waterfront mansion and caused considerable damage. The owners used to rent the property for social events like weddings and other ceremonies, and they were also trying to host activities like classical music concerts. The antique pieces and documents owned by the family were also preserved and exhibited in the waterfront mansion. Since the accident occurred on a day when there was no event, there was no loss of life, but the unprotected pieces of art were surely heavily damaged. Fortunately, these timber mansions can easily be rebuilt as needed. Although the accident caused severe damage, a great part of the building can still be saved if the intervention is not too late.

An even more unusual crash was between a Lebanese and a Philippine ship that caused the death of more than 21 thousand sheep. Several of them floated on the Bosphorus waters for a long time.

BEGINNING THE TOUR

So now it is time for us to embark on our virtual tour of the Bosphorus. This book, which is based on the itinerary of the actual tours given, will proceed as if you just joined a tour, which sets off from the Yemiş Pier in Eminönü. This is a appropriate place to begin, as everything started here for the famous Ottoman traveler and travel writer, Evliya Çelebi as well. The small mosque (Ahi Çelebi Mosque) is the very place where *Seyahatname*, a huge travelogue, was first inspired by a dream. This will be the best spot to start our journey along the Bosphorus, described as a "miniature of the empire." The pier is located on the Ragıp Gümüşpala Street's shore, a name that will appear again on the Bosphorus.

We set off from the Ahi Çelebi Mosque. The first building nearby is ITO (Istanbul Chamber of Commerce) University. The project that was chosen with a contest in 1963 belongs to the Architect Orhan Şahinler.

We will pass under the Galata Bridge and take our exit from the Golden Horn (known in Turkish as Haliç or the "Estuary"), an important port for the Romans and Ottomans alike. We will thus start our journey along the Bosphorus. At this moment we can see the Galata Tower, that dominates the landscape to our left.

We know that previously the Galata Tower was not alone, but rather was accompanied by the Genoese walls of Galata where it rose up as the most magnificent of their towers. There used to be a line of fortifications close to the sea between Azapkapı and Tophane. The walls used to go up on both sides of the hill and reached the tower. There were other sections of fortifications within the neighborhood. The walls were demolished in the 1860s with the Şehremaneti (Ottoman Municipality) decisions and roads were built instead.

When the decisions were primarily driven by financial considerations, authorities did not reflect upon what Istanbul was losing and how its heritage was damaged. It was calculated that

Galata Tower and surroundings, Florentine School, 19th century

with the demolition of 3500-meter long walls and the 30 towers, 2,5 acres of land would be gained. This new patch of land would ease the traffic, and also dead ends would no longer pose a problem during fires. The moats in front of the walls were filled, and more land was obtained (evidence of all these live on in the names of *Büyük* and *Küçük Hendek* streets, literally meaning the "Big" and "Small Moat"). Generating revenue selling these new parcels of land was the main motivating factor at the time.

The walls had surely lost their function and were in a derelict condition in those days. They also posed a threat to the residents due to damages by earthquakes and fires. Perhaps there was no financial source at the time to restore these walls or the way of thinking at the time could not justify preservation. However, it would have certainly been an astounding experience observing the walls of Galata now, passing by a boat.

Below, parallel to the shore, there is the *Bankalar* (banks) Street with a series of neoclassical buildings. Its official name is still *Voyvoda* Street, though this name is not used by many people. Galata was home to numerous banks such as the Ottoman Bank particularly during the last periods of the empire. This tradition is still very much alive. The building of the Ottoman Bank, designed by the Italian architect Alessandro Vallauri, is presently shared and used by the Central Bank and Salt Galata, a noteworthy cultural center.

Ziraat Bank's main door by Sculptor Şadi Çalık

If you look closely towards the shore as soon as we leave the bridge behind, you will see the building of Ziraat Bank, once the Austrian Bank that stands out with statues on both corners of its terrace.

Favorably located in the center of Karaköy, the historical port of Galata (the northern shore of the Golden Horn) and a financial and business center, the building is an epitome of prestige bearing the last vestiges of its era. The lower part of the building is reminiscent of palace architecture, whereas the relatively animated upper part adds a Viennese ambiance to the Bosphorus shore. The building could be defined as one of the most important examples of the "Secession" modernism that flourished in Istanbul at the beginning of the 20th century. It was later extended in the northern direction. We learn from its architects Muhteşem Giray and Nezih Eldem that piles were driven as deep as 37 meters for this northern wing to be built on a land fill. Pile-driving on the shoreline to reclaim land was a noisy, costly affair.

There are only a few buildings with a sculptural program in the city and the Austrian Bank building is particularly important in that sense. We do not know whether out of respect or mere coincidence, the gate of the building that was built at a later point in time is a real artistic piece of sculpture by Şadi Çalık. The artist is mainly known for his 1973 sculpture of "*50. Yıl Heykeli*" ("Statue of the 50th Anniversary") is located at Galatasaray Square in Istanbul.

Just behind there is the other bank building in the square, Yapı Kredi/Halkbank. The visual effect of the building is stunning with its yellowish masonry reflecting the setting sun during the evening hours. The Italian architect Giulio Mongeri (d. 1953) was inspired by the architectural details of Hagia Sophia which were used in the façade of a modern building. Terms like "Neo-Byzantine" have been coined for such buildings. Across the bank in the square, there is an insurance building with its unique pairs of arched windows on each of its two levels. The ground floor of this building was for many years the location of the Baylan Patisserie, which now survives on the Asian neighborhood of Kadıköy.

Ziraat Bank and the Karaköy Mosque before its demolition (1958)

What Karaköy Lost

When we look through old photographs of the square, we immediately notice a significant absence: the Karaköy Mosque (Masjid of Merzifonlu Kara Mustafa Pasha), once adjacent to the Ziraat Bank building, is no longer there. This elegant building by the Italian Architect Raimondo d'Aronco (1857–1932) was dismantled and moved from the square. The plan was to rebuild it in another place, but such a thing did not happen. The idea of rebuilding it is often suggested nowadays, which is certainly possible as it is very well documented and known in minute detail.

It should be noted that we will come across the works of d'Aronco several times during our tour along the Bosphorus. Sometimes his works will not be visible, as they are hidden behind a building or a hill, but still it is important to note that the works of this important architect are there.

We follow the shoreline towards the north as we observe some buildings that are part of the harbor facilities and mostly date back to the Republican era. The Ömer Abed Han, work of the Italian Architect Alessandro Vallauri, stands, unfortunately,

The former Karaköy Pier

behind some less sophisticated buildings on the shoreline and it can only be discerned by looking from particular angles. Its perpendicular roof, which is not in harmony with the local architecture, can also be recognized. In the foreground is the barge of the Karaköy pier for the city's ferries. The constantly relocated barge deserves the adjective "portable". The much larger Karaköy pier sank overnight and the smaller barges that were tied to the shore have been offering the same function for many years, which implies such a larger one was actually not needed. Still, a colossal pier has recently been put into use again.

The following building named as the Quarantine Administration and the *Karantina* Street just behind it remind us that such open waterways and port were once constantly exposed to infectious diseases. We know that some other locations in the Bosphorus, like Anadolu Kavağı, Beykoz, and Kuleli, were also used as quarantine centers.

Next, we can see two office buildings built for the operations of the Maritime Lines. There is a passenger hall between these two buildings. The first one is recognizable with its mainly blue colored tiles and deeper curves on the façade, while the other is called *Çinili* (Tiled) *Deniz Han*. The façade linings of the second are predominantly yellow. While the last floor looks like it has been added later, it does not really offend the eye since its yellow hue matches the rest of the building.

The passenger hall located between the two tiled buildings was in the process of being demolished as these lines were being written. Currently, only a vertical section can be seen. The building was designed by the Architect Rebii Gorbon, who won an international design competition in the 1930s. It was like a living museum. Since even the furniture of the building was designed by the same single designer, we should hope that it can be restored with the very same hight quality details. For many locals, the building is only be remembered as the Port Restaurant ("*Liman Lokantası*"). The number of people who came to this restaurant is definitely higher than the number of people who used the passenger hall during for seafaring. The warehouse with its hard-edged porch was designed by Bedri Uçar during the same years (1939) and the building in this area was aligned with Galata Port Post Office (*Paket Postanesi*).

This port post office, which was once handled large packages and also acted as a sort of customs, was formerly yellow, but was later better known for its pink color. With its monumental dome reminiscent of Sirkeci Railway Station and long façade facing the sea, the building was reminiscent of the coastal representative of the "Main Post Office", "*Büyük Postane*") behind the station across the Golden Horn in the historical peninsula. While the Sirkeci Post Office was the symbol of the 19th century globalization as it was connected to the railway, this post office in Galata was almost like a nautical version connecting the city to the world trade.

The building is currently almost nonexistent, save for its façade along with some ruins of its original structure, which appears like a phantom vaguely outlining its original splendor.

Once you find a space among the Galata Port Post Office and the attached buildings behind, you can quickly glance inland to discern the mosque complex commissioned to Sinan by the famous Ottoman admiral Kılıç Ali Pasha (d. 1587), a.k.a. *Occhiali*, who was originally born as an Italian from Calabria, named Giovanni Dionigi Galeni. This area is a good example of how the geography of the Bosphorus was radically altered, as even these 16th century buildings were erected on a land fill that was once a cove.

The burial area of Kılıç Ali Pasha Mosque makes the building even more remarkable. First of all, it hosts tombs of many sailors, which is a kind of homage to its patron. These tombs, with their references on their headstones, are in harmony with the identities of their owners. The burial area is also rich in terms of headstones without tombs. For example, it is also home for the headstones brought from the Ebulfazl Mosque as it was demolished. The mosque used to be located on the Italian Slope

(*İtalyan yokuşu*), named after the Italian hospital behind the buildings of the Imperial Cannon Foundry, *Tophane-i Amire* (just across the street and easily visible, being on the very slope). The mosque was restored recently, but it might not have been an easy task to match the tombs with their original headstones.

Istanbul Modern Formula as an Answer to Istanbul's Need for Art

The port facilities continue with warehouses built on land reclaimed from the sea. The buildings of the maritime lines, with massive and hard-edged designs, were here for a long period of time. The facilities initially functioned as an entrepôt, but after their cranes were dismantled the buildings were used for passenger liners only. The Warehouse (*Antrepo*) no: 4 was used as Istanbul Museum of

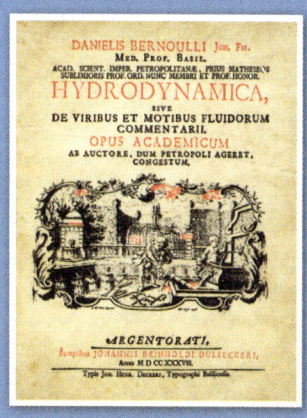

Bernoulli's Hydrondynamica (1758)

Bernoulli's formula on Istanbul Modern's façade

$$P_1 + \tfrac{1}{2}\rho v_1^2 + \rho g h_1 = P_2 + \tfrac{1}{2}\rho v_2^2 + \rho g h_2$$

Modern Art (known as *Istanbul Modern* in Turkish) between 2004 and 2018. It will be here again immediately after the completion of the new building designed by the world-famous Renzo Piano Building Workshop. The institution has been an important initiative to answer one of the most pressing needs of the city. By the way, most probably there is no other institution whose translated name is so much longer than its original. Perhaps this was a measure taken so that the tower on which the name of the museum was written would not be too long to disturb the skyline. The Warehouse number 4 of Istanbul Modern also holds memories of what was until recently one of Istanbul's favorite restaurants. The popularity of the restaurant was such that even the security personnel at the door asked visitors whether they were coming for the exhibition or the restaurant. Istanbul Modern is temporarily open to visitors in the Union Française building on Meşrutiyet Street.

Speaking of signs, the formula on the façade was a work inscribed there by the artist Liam Gillick as part of the 2015 Istanbul Biennial titled "Saltwater". While its use here can seem quite odd at first: the Bernoulli Equation is a fundamental piece of knowledge for those who studied fluid mechanics, and it dates back to almost 300 years ago (Bernoulli wrote his

Tophane in Melling's engraving (early 1800s)

"Hydrodynamica" in 1738). The equation is neither related to the Bosphorus nor to Istanbul (except, perhaps, for the fluidity of the waterway). As far as is known, Daniel Bernoulli was born in Holland and spent most of his life in Switzerland. At the initial installation the artist had made a mistake copying the Bernoulli formula. Quite strikingly, many intercontinental commuters noticed the mistake; and after several complaints the formula was corrected.

The tower carrying Istanbul Modern's sign on it is not the only tower here. The Tophane Sanjak (flag) Tower here is also defying has also stood the test of time. It was undoubtedly a normal and expected practice to build a flag tower here as it was just above here, in the Pera neighborhood, foreign embassies were granted permission to raise their flags during the reign of Mahmut II (r. 1808-1839). The pike of this tower, visible in old photographs, no longer exists. A clock was added to the tower during the reign of Sultan Abdülhamid II (r. 1876-1909) so that the tower would match the fashionable clock towers of the time. The flag tower thus came to be known as a "clock tower" after these changes.

Tophane-i Amire is just behind the Warehouse 4 and it is clearly visible thanks to its elevated position. Next to the Tophane are the Boğazkesen and Yeniçarşı streets and the continuing straight slope going up to Galatasaray was the diplomatic quarter during the Ottoman era. Hence, this area used to be the pier of Pera in the old days.

This remarkable imperial symbolism, which is discernible only in fragments today, first emerges behind the Warehouse 4. The original imperial settings no longer exist. The cannon, which played an essential role in the conquest of Istanbul, was perceived as a symbol of power for hundreds of years. Ambassadors appointed to Istanbul from Western countries landed on the pier at Tophane might have been intimidated, because on their way to their stations they had to pass by the out of commission cannons once used in victorious Ottoman battles, lined up around the square. Most of these cannons and cannonballs are now exhibited at the Military Museum in Harbiye. This pier was also the departure point for those living in Pera (including de the Ambassadors from European countries) when they left for their summer houses along the Bosphorus.

We have a number of images indicating that there was an open market set up in this square. The Tophane Fountain, built by Mahmut II during the years when he also built the Taksim water system, has been one of the symbols of the square since the 1730s.

The square has gone through many misfortunes up to the present day, eventually losing its identity as a square. Even the American Ford Motor Company had a manufacturing facility

Painting and Sculpture Museum will be in Tophane soon.

here between 1930 and 1944. Later for some decades, until recently there used to be a series of stores here, known as the American Bazaar, selling a wide range of goods including imported clothes and electrical household appliances. The area was more recently dominated by nargile (water pipe) cafes.

Beyond the square, we find the Nusretiye Mosque situated at a distance from the pier and close to the street. The mosque was built during Mahmut II. Although elegant in appearance, it was built with materials of cheap and poor quality. Compared with stone, lath and plaster is a material that wears out quite quickly. However, the mosque has recently gone through diligent restoration. Reflecting the Ottoman Baroque-Imperial style, the mosque is also unique for its inscriptions. Yesarizade Mustafa İzzet, the calligrapher for the mosque and its fountain, was a highly productive artist. His work appeared across the city during the reign of Mahmut II. He developed his own original Turkish Ta'liq calligraphy style moving it away from the Persian school where it had originated from.

The *muvakkithane* (workroom of the mosque astronomer) and the fountain of Nusretiye initially was on the corner of Tophane-i Amire (Imperial Cannon Foundery), but they were relocated to their present place when the nearby road was widened. The fountain by the Italian architect Raimondo d'Aronco, which was previously here, was later relocated to Maçka. Next, we have the ongoing construction of the Museum of Painting and Sculpture designed by the Turkish Architect Emre Arolat (b. 1963). The ambitious visuals of the building are quite promising. Once the construction is completed, the state collections of paintings and sculptures, which are on temporary exhibition in the Şehzade Dairesi of the Dolmabahçe Palace, will be permanently exhibited here.

The dark-colored high-rise building behind, on the very top of the hill is the Istanbul Chamber of Industry that emerges incongruously with the silhouette of İstiklal Street. Also known as Odakule, the building was designed by the Turkish Architect

Kaya Tecimen in 1964. We can also discern the St. Antoine Church (1906-1913), designed by the Italian architects Giulio Mongeri and Edoardo de Nari. Although the church building, which manifests itself with its bell tower, is concrete, its façade consists orange brick. The large building on the right-hand side of the church is the *Mekteb-i Sultani*, the famous Galatasaray High School (1868).

Looking downwards again, we see a construction site across the street. The excavation work for the reconstruction of the *Tophane Müşirliği* (Artillery Barracks) at its original location offered rich archeological data. The unearthed sarcophagi prove that there was an ancient necropolis here. The area is not open for visitors at the moment.

Next, on the same side of the street at the beginning of the slope, there is an unusual mosque with a complete glass façade. The recently built mosque was constructed on the very location of the Süheyl Bey Mosque, the work of the Ottoman Architect Sinan (d. 1588) with an octagonal plan; there was also a bookstore on the ground floor.

The building group which starts with the Chamber of Shipping on the coastline was once part of the twin palaces of Cemile and Münire Sultanas. A careful look reveal how these two twin palaces were later connected together in recent times. They were two

Cemile and Münire Sultanas' twin waterfront mansions

separate waterfront mansions when they were first built and were later connected for their new functions. The touches of architect Sedad Hakkı Eldem (1908-1988) on this structure are clearly recognized. If you look closely, you will see that although the northern palace has the same mass and appearance as the southern one, its details are significantly different. It was burnt down completely during a fire in the 1930s. The reconstruction was designed so that the building would closely reflect the original and also display the age difference instead of being a complete imitation. The small building in the south, the Chamber of Shipping, is more or less the same size as the historic building it replaced, but it has a completely different look now. On the ground floor facing the sea, there is a popular seafood restaurant. The other three buildings form the Fındıklı campus of the Mimar Sinan University Faculty of Fine Arts (MSGSÜ). The northernmost small unit was completely reconstructed closely following the original.

Former Akbank headquarters (built 1968)

The street behind is named as *Meclis-i Mebusan* (Chamber of Deputies), as the First Ottoman Parliament was moved to this complex after a fire damaged Çırağan Palace.

With the platform behind the street starts the neighborhood built by the Sultan Suleiman the Magnificent (r. 1520-1566) to immortalize the name of his prince Cihangir who died very young. The Cihangir Mosque, naturally, dominates the landscape in this area.

As soon as we leave behind the MSGSÜ building on the street, we see the former Akbank headquarters at the corner of the *Mebusan Yokuşu* (Mebusan Slope), which extends towards Taksim. The building, which is now vacant, is the work

Molla Çelebi Mosque by Sinan today (top) and once (bottom)

of Sedad Hakkı Eldem (1968). Since it was built over a long period of time (23), its façade looks rather patchy.

Returning back to the shoreline, sculptures by the MSGSÜ students are on exhibition next to their university. The most notable structure at this location is the Fındıklı (Molla Çelebi) Mosque (1584). It is all that is left from the mosque complex (*külliye*) designed by Architect Sinan. Its double bath has suffered the same fate with many other monuments nearby, and it was demolished when during road widening work in 1957. The mosque, which should be at a location where the Bosphorus is closest to the dense urban texture of the city, is presently located in vacant space, standing in stark contrast with its past.

Next, there is the building of the Turkish Industrial Development Bank. The building was constructed with the modern lines of Architect Metin Hepgüler in the 1960s. The higher cost of construction was due to the land arrangement expenses of the rocky soil in the parcel. It has recently been given a red makeup, so it does not show its age.

Now we are at Kabataş, the terminus of the tramline. There are many stories around the name of Kabataş. For some reason, Evliya Çelebi's explanation is usually given precedence. Evliya wrote about flying stones after an explosion in Istanbul during the reign of Sultan Mehmet the Conqueror, he gives the following details: "There lies a piece of stone called Kabataş in the sea in front of the Çizmeciler Tekkesi and to the north of Fındıklı in Tophane".

It is difficult to know whether there could be another source of the name of this area; it could be called "*Kaba Taş*" (Rough Stone) because of the rocky ground, which makes it difficult to excavate (and increases construction costs, as just mentioned). Besides, much earlier than the explosion during the reign of Sultan Mehmet, we know from Dionysius of Byzantium that there used to be rocky formation named Petra Thermastis that extended towards the sea.

As we turn back to the shore side of the road, we come across the Kabataş Hekimoğlu Ali Pasha Fountain (1732). It is wrongly called as "Kabataş Square Fountain" because there are no other buildings around. However, this fountain was not meant for a square. It was initially placed on a higher level across the street,

TSKB by Metin Hepgüler (built 1972)

but it was dismantled for the road-widening work and placed where it stands now. It is also evident that only the façade was meant to be noticed: other than its two surfaces, there are functional elements like inscriptions, decorations, or taps.

Right here there is the ongoing construction of the *Martı* (Seagull) project for the Kabataş transportation and transit center. The project, which is progressing quickly, is coordinated by architect Hakan Kıran, who also designed the metro bridge on the Golden Horn. Piles were driven in the sea for the project, and the Kabataş Square will be enlarged. The area had already lost its characteristics of a square with buses, pier, and traffic. A pedestrian tunnel was planned to reach the Asian shore from here, but its construction was recently suspended.

Conflict Among Embassies

When we look up towards Taksim, we see the former Imperial German Embassy building, which is now used as the Consulate General of the Federal Republic of Germany. Just next to it there is the hotel building whose elevation was brought down by 16 floors to its present height. After several floors were removed, the building was used as a parking lot for a long period, notable

Italian Embassy's former residence (later Park Hotel) and the German Embassy (current Consulate General)

for its bulky, even eerie, appearance. The building was recently redesigned as a hotel with major changes made to its façade.

The building was once the residence of the Italian Ambassador Baron Alberto Blanc (1835-1904). When he returned to Italy, he was appointed as the Minister of Foreign Affairs and sold the property. The Bulgarian Exarchate applied for the ownership of the embassy building, however apparently Russia did not approve of Bulgaria's owning such a imposing, symbolical building and was able to prevent the sale through political means. Besides, neither Germany nor the Ottoman Empire would presumably have wanted to have an embassy of a small and newly independent country just across from the Imperial German Embassy.

On the other hand, the reason why Bulgaria wanted to buy such a splendid edifice in Istanbul was allegedly the need for a building where to establish a "national school" as alleged as there was already one purchased in 1878 (we will come across the Exarchate building on our route soon, in Ortaköy). Princess Clementine thought the main reason why the Bulgarian Principality under the rule of her son Prince Ferdinand was not recognized as a fully independent state was the obstacles set by Russia. Therefore, she planned to spend part of the year in this residence, thinking that having a strategic base close to the Russian Embassy in the capital city Istanbul would help improve relations between Russia and Bulgaria. Apparently, it was more critical for Clementine to be near Beyoğlu where the Russian Embassy was located.

In the end, when the sales were not realized, the building was incorporated into the *Aşiret Mektebi* (Imperial School for Tribes) project. The project aimed at forming loyal generations to the Ottoman state, raising major Arabic and Kurdish families' children (29). As we will later see, the project used some other buildings included in our itinerary but ended in failure. Later, this property was owned by the last grand vizier of the

Ottomans, Tevfik Pasha. His children operated the building as a hotel. Its name was first "Miramare", and later "Park Otel" as it continued up until this day. The Park Otel was enlarged several times, and more rooms were added. The hotel had its heyday between the 1930s and 1970s. A prominent Turkish poet Yahya Kemal (1884-1958), whom we will mention several times on our journey, chose to spend the last six years of his life here. We had earlier stated that the shoreline up to this point had been adorned with the waterfront mansions of the members of the dynasty due to its proximity to the center of Istanbul. Considering their locations, the slopes could not remain vacant either. One of the most splendid mansions belonged to the wealthy Vizier Namık Pasha. The elevated platform in Kabataş was also home to splendid mansions that had great views of the Bosphorus.

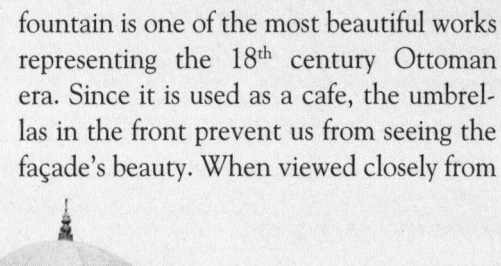

If we look back down at the shore, we will see the park area which currently begins with a gas station. On the shore side of the park there are recreational boats, and on the opposite side of the road is the Koca Yusuf Pasha Public Fountain. The fountain is one of the most beautiful works representing the 18th century Ottoman era. Since it is used as a cafe, the umbrellas in the front prevent us from seeing the façade's beauty. When viewed closely from the sea, it will be seen that the pier is not entirely concrete. A large amount of spolia was used in its construction. The bluish colored and rough-surfaced blocks might have been brought from the ancient city of Knidos in Datça, on the southeastern Aegean coast of Turkey.

Hardships That the Dolmabahçe Mosque Survived

Next, on the shoreline, there is the Bezm-i Alem Valide Sultan Mosque, also known as Dolmabahçe Mosque (1855). The mosque previously was allocated a larger plot of land, but its outer court was "annexed to the road." This is the standard euphemism that minimizes how sad the demolishing monuments for road-widening really was. As clearly seen, the courtyard was completely razed. The *muvakkithane*, currently located by the seaside, was moved here after being dismantled and moved from what is now the opposite side of the road. Dolmabahçe Mosque has survived other difficulties. The Soil Products Office requested to use it as a warehouse in 1941. It was assigned to the Maritime Museum in 1947, and for many years it functioned as a museum with the display cabinets placed inside.

On the opposite side of the road is the Mehmet Emin Ağa Public Fountain (1741). This is another monument which was

Dolmabahçe Mosque and Dolmabahçe Palace

Mehmet Emin Ağa Sebili (built 1740s), historic photo

survived because it was relocated, although some parts of it are integral to the burial place for the benefactor and his family. It is extremely clean and well-kept. However, it has no other function than a burial place, as it no longer functions as a fountain.

As you look towards the land from here, you can immediately notice a deep valley extending towards Maçka. However, the river which created the valley no longer exists. The first building that catches ones' eye on the slope of the valley is the Gümüşsuyu Barracks (1862), which is now the Faculty of Mechanical Engineering of Istanbul Technical University (İTÜ). Just above there is Taşkışla (1852, former barracks again), which again belongs to İTÜ. During the years when it was expected that every historical building would be turned into hotels, many enthusiastic projects were prepared for this building as well. Nevertheless, it maintained its education function and serves as the Faculty of Architecture.

Further inland is the Istanbul Hilton Hotel (1955), which is now called Bosphorus Hilton. The building was designed

Mehmet Emin Ağa Sebili, today, the street level is clearly much higher.

(in collaboration with Sedad Hakkı Eldem) by Gordon Bunshaft (1909-1990), from the American architectural company SOM (Skidmore Owings & Meryll). The name of the SOM design office is currently mentioned frequently in connection to Burj Khalifa in Dubai, the world's tallest building. The Hilton stands out with its horizontal and rectangular mass in line with its international style. A short while after its construction,

Dolmabahçe and its hinterland

the building assumed its present condition when it was enlarged transversely without increasing is elevation. We can see its smaller version in the local films of the 1950s. The details, when looked closely, reveal some added elements which distance it from the modernist style and make you feel that you are really in Turkey. The porch, named the "Flying Carpet," in front of the door is the most famous of these details.

As we move along this slope, there is the Lütfi Kırdar Convention and Exhibition Center, which was built as the Sports and Exhibition Hall (*Spor ve Sergi Sarayı*) in 1949. It was designed by the Italian Architect Paolo Vietti Violi.

On the northern slope, just across Taşkışla, we come across the Maçka Arsenal, which also belongs to Istanbul Technical University (several departments including Management, Conservatoire and Foreign Languages are located here).

A Garden Filled with History

Here in *Dolmabahçe*, (literally "filled garden") it is known that there used to be a cove at the mouth of this valley that was later reclaimed. The Dolmabahçe Stadium (BJK İnönü Stadium) is located mainly on this landfill. It was also designed by the Italian Architect Polo Vietti Violi in 1939, with some annexes added later. Vietti Violi, who has designed many sports facilities in Turkey, collaborated with the Turkish architects Şinasi Şahingiray and Fazıl Aysu. The stadium lost its original looks with the later interventions, in particular after it was recently renovated (and renamed Vodafone Arena). The preservation of the stone towers facing the sea and the minimization of exaggerations that can distort the landscape should be appreciated.

The place chosen for the stadium used to be the palace stables named "İstabl-i Amire." Since the stables were already derelict, they were demolished without any challenges, and a project was rolled out for building a new stadium, which was highly modern for its time. Taksim Stadium (today's Gezi Parkı) was decided to be demolished as well. However, one factor was not taken into consideration: there was a strategically important hospital where animals used for gun carriages were kept and even where animals imported from other countries were admitted and treated. Fortunately, the objections of the Ministry of National Defense were resolved, and the construction was completed successfully.

As we look back to the shore, we see the clock tower at the entrance of Dolmabahçe Palace (1856). The tower was built much later (1895) than the palace, during the reign of Abdülhamit II when clock towers were fashionable. The area between the mosque and the tower is currently used as a car parking area, and the tower is an artistic backdrop to the parking lot. All along the shore of this area, there are shoddy cafes. This construction type is one of the most prominent components of contemporary architecture on the Bosphorus. These are spaces covered with and even surrounded by different types of polymer. We will come across this kind of units all along our route along the Bosphorus.

Dolmabahçe Palace

By walking along the road on the opposite side of the tower, one would move towards the entrance wing of Dolmabahçe Palace, which has a massive neo-baroque plan and a concave

Taşlık by Fausto Zonaro

façade. However, we will continue on our route by boat, viewing the palace from the seaside. Following a square planned garden with a fountain, we first encounter the large mass of palace, which is slightly away from the sea.

However, before examining the palace more closely, we cannot help but notice the garden continuing up the slope, even though it is now separated from the palace quarters. The place has been home to a hotel building which for the last thirty years has jutted out with its glass façades.

The decision to change the function of this area was made much earlier during the reign of the Sultan Abdülaziz (r. 1861-1876). The car park just behind the hotel, where there is a statue of İsmet İnönü (the second President of the Turkish Republic, 1938-1950), was reserved for building a grand mosque. The construction of the mosque, named "*Bayıldım Bahçesi*," started in 1875 in this area. However, the construction could not be completed due to the dethronement of Abdülaziz the following year. We only know that the architect of the mosque whose foundations were laid with marble blocks was Sarkis Balyan. However, we do not have any drawings or illustrations that could give us an idea about its design.

The place is called "*Taşlık*" (Stony Ground) because of the foundation stones that were left there. The name "*taşlık*" lived on, first with the Taşlık Club, which rented the area from the municipality then in the Taşlık Cafe designed by the Architect Sedat Hakkı Eldem until 1990. Later on, the building was demolished as part of a hotel project and was rebuilt on a smaller scale. It is now a restaurant.

If the Aziziye Mosque had been built here, Istanbul would have gained a monument that would overlooked Dolmabahçe Palace and would have had a distinctive impact on the Bosphorus landscape. Most probably no one would have dared to place hotel blocks just in front of such a mosque, but of course, we will never know.

There are a few trees near the palace gate however they are not tall enough to obstruct the façade of the palace. On the southern part of the main mass of Dolmabahçe Palace, is the *Mabeyn-i Hümayun* (public representation rooms).

The façade of Dolmabahçe Palace facing the Bosphorus is the strongest Neoclassical expression of Istanbul's architecture. The columnar façades with triangular roofs, repeated in intervals, add to the shoreline a Classical Greek and Roman

Dolmabahçe Palace's main gate,
view from the garden

Dolmabahçe Palace's Muayede Salonu, Ceremonial Hall

architectural ambiance with some European touches. Palaces and public buildings in the Western world were designed following classical forms since the Renaissance. Dolmabahçe is the most splendid example of this tradition across Turkey. The associations of a temple façade with columns and triangular pediments first became part of the Bosphorus features with Dolmabahçe in a monumental way.

The long, horizontal sections of the palace have two floors. The *Muayede* (Ceremonial) Hall in the middle, however, is actually a single-floor large space that contrasts with these horizontal sections. It reminds us of the heavily decorated 19th century mosques with its columnar arrangement, rich classical details, and overarching dome. Inside, the illusionary features of the dome open it up to the sky, making it appear that the dome connects to the sky. The only grand staircase of the palace complex is located here just in front of the sea.

As you look more closely, it becomes clear that the large, central building block of the Dolmabahçe Palace, known as the *Muayede* Hall, is what brings the whole complex together. The *Muayede* Hall adds splendor to the palace's horizontal composition along the shore that dominates the Bosphorus.

The most splendid of the gates on the waterfront is just across the *Muayede* Hall. Other gates near other sections of the building were also placed on the waterfront. There is a continuous railing all along the waterfront of the palace.

The *Muayede* hall is also known for its magnificent chandelier. It was imported from England, but unlike the long-held belief, it has already been proven that it was not a gift from Queen Victoria.

The chandelier is often mentioned as weighing 4.5 t, but we do not know whether this was because someone had actually weighed it or being the English word "pound" also a monetary unit, the exaggerated expression of a "10,000 pound"

Dolmabahçe Palace's Muayede Salonu, mounting project for the chandelier

chandelier about its cost, led to a misunderstanding as 10,000 pounds (which is equivalent to 4.5 metric tons).

We are talking about such a chandelier that a special mechanism was developed for its installation as the *Muayede* hall was designed. The details of the mechanism are illustrated on a document preserved at the State Ottoman Archives.

It is generally stated that this chandelier had "750 bulbs", but a recently published Ottoman document reveals that it originally had 460 oil lamps.

After the splendid Ceremonial Hall, there is the *harem* (residential quarters mainly for women) which actually covers a much larger area than it appears from the sea. As the long façade of the *Mabeyn* faces the sea, the façade of the harem on the seaside, despite having the same length, forms only the short side of the rectangular plan.

The quarters of the princes, *Şehzadegan Dairesi*, to the north is separate from the other three units. It was planned as in independent edifice with four façades. This positioning preserves the symmetry of the façade of the main structure; however, it also brings to mind the possibility of an attempt in design to separate the princes from the harem.

The last unit of the series of buildings facing the sea was planned for those who are not part of the dynasty. Standing out among the rest with its slightly lower elevation is the *Musahiban* ("Gentlemen-in-Waiting") Quarters. These quarters were used as the Prime Minister's Office until recently (since 2018 there is no Prime Minister in Turkey, anymore).

Next to these units are service areas, including the stables. The structures of this area were rearranged to function as a storehouse type museum. Since it would require a very large area and high costs to exhibit the rich collections of the palace with an equal focus on every piece, many other important pieces were also exhibited in this new installation.

Akaretler and Its Cosmopolitan Residents

As we look at the opposite side of the road, we come by "*Akaretler*" extending inland. More than 130 housing units, creating a commercial ensemble, had been first planned as rental rowhouses (1870s). It was estimated that the income (as the name '*Akaretler*' in Turkish implies) from these houses would finance the construction of the Aziziye Mosque mentioned above.

It was possible to find in this small neighborhood a summary of the history of the Late Ottoman Empire. There was a wide variety of individuals who lived in these houses: in addition to the founder of the Turkish Republic Mustafa Kemal, there were quilt makers, carpenters, colonels, Muslims, Armenians, Greeks, a "Madam" from the Jewish Community, and even the son-in-law of Sheikh Zafir, whose dervish lodge we will discuss soon.

The Ottoman court artist, Italian Fausto Zonaro Efendi, also lived here during the reign of Abdülhamit II. Zonaro's

Bosphorus and Asia from above the Akaretler

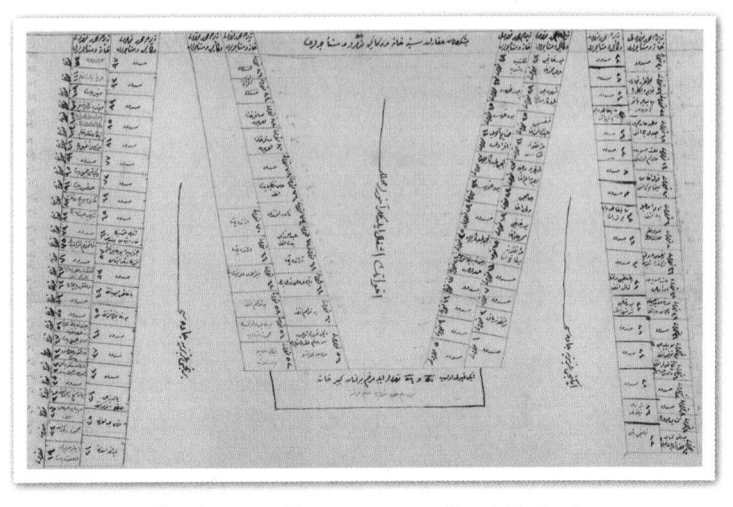

Akaretler, tenants' list: a very cosmopolite neighborhood

Fausto Zonaro's bilingual (Italian and Ottoman Turkish) business card. His gallery was at Akaretler no 50.

residence (number 50) stands out among other residents with its advantageous position at the intersection of both the road and the two rows of houses. As the widest unit in Akaretler, it is much more impressive than the rest of the neighboring row houses. The artist used this place as his residence, workshop and a public art gallery for many years. This building has still a strategic function with its central location and large interior: now it is in use by a local coffee shop chain.

The Aşiret Mektebi, we mentioned above, the predecessor of the Kabataş High School, used some of these houses for education and accommodation the year it was first opened. After its second year, the school was completely moved to Kabataş, then to its present location by the seaside. As we will see later, the

Kabataş Boys High School, which would be established a few years later, did not change its name when it moved to Feriye.

The appearance of the houses assumed their present look with the small unit added later by Architect Vedat Tek (1873-1942) on an unusually shaped plot of land where the end of the rowhouses reaches Dolmabahçe Street.

The rowhouses, more than 100 in number, were built so that they would generate income and also, they would create a protective and almost fire-proof barrier for Dolmabahçe Palace in case of a fire in the Beşiktaş neighborhood, where almost all houses were timber.

As we look along the shore, we can see the pleasant Hayrettin Ferry Pier. There used to be an ordinary, dilapidated run looking building here. It was replaced by this mostly timber structure designed by Hilmi Şenalp (b. 1957) in 2005, with a balanced use of Turkish revivalist features, which had not been fashionable for decades.

The building just behind the pier used to be the Austrian tobacco warehouse built in 1929. The architect and contractor of the warehouse building was Victor Adaman; he was educated in Paris, and started his career working for the Italian architect Alessandro Vallauri.

This warehouse and another on the opposite shore are among the prominent buildings in the Bosphorus. It could be said that these monumental structures are the clear symbols of tobacco as an important luxury item (therefore a tax revenue source) in the newly established Republic.

The historic tobacco warehouse was renovated with the addition of highly spacious units a few floors below the ground level, and it was turned into a hotel. There used to be the aircraft factory of Nuri Demirağ adjacent to the hotel; in other words, aircraft were produced at Beşiktaş Square.

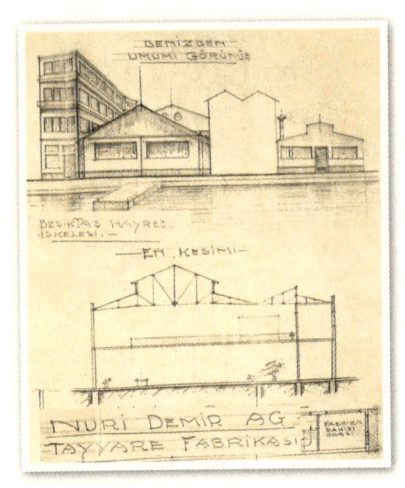

The Beşiktaş aircraft factory founded in 1928

It is estimated that the factory, which was in operation between 1936 and 1949 at Beşiktaş Square, covered an area larger than 4000 m2.

Demirağ, Turkey's first aircraft producer, owned a mansion and a woodlot with a view of the Bosphorus on the Anatolian side. There used to be a uniquely designed petrol station and the Motorist Restaurant at the same location just across the street. Both of them were works of Architect Maruf Önal (1918-2010); even their memories have slowly faded.

Since the 1960s, the plot of land adjacent to the hotel has been occupied, not by the aircraft factory, but by the Naval Museum with its wide coastal façade. The museum was initially only located in the tax office building on the street, and it was later enlarged towards the square with the inclusion of a low-quality concrete building which had been used by the imperial caiques (boats). In 2008 the museum was modernized with the prize-winning project of the architects Mehmet

The Maritime Museum, an interior view

The Maritime Museum from the sea

Kütükçüoğlu and Ertuğ Uçar. The museum is currently the largest cultural facility along the Bosphorus with its indoor space of 15000 m2. The same architects also designed the Yapı Kredi Kültür Sanat building in Galatasaray, which was recently rebuilt and opened to public again in 2017. The renovated exhibition of kitchen quarters in Topkapı Palace is by the same architects, as well.

Relief of a galley (from the Museum's garden)

We should highlight one aspect of the construction of the Naval Museum, which was also expressed by its designers. Throughout the Republican era, no other cultural institution, or for that matter even a public building, was built of this size along the Bosphorus. If we go back earlier in time, the last public building constructed as a museum was the Archaeological Museum designed by the Italian Architect Alessandro Vallauri (1850-1921) during the time of Osman Hamdi Bey. As a matter of fact, even most private museums were developed by repurposing spaces that were built for other functions, as museums. After more than a hundred years, the Naval Museum was fortunate enough to be given an original museum building by design. As a result, the museum exhibits the 40-meter long galley and dozens of imperial caiques under a single roof without any columns dividing the interior space. The museum building, an artwork itself, defines the Beşiktaş coast.

Actually, a special museum could have been designed for the galley alone. The imperial galley has 24 double oars pulled by three men each, requiring a total of 144 oarsmen. The pavilion on this magnificent vessel is a work of art in its own right: the decorations made of tortoiseshell and semi-precious stones, silver plates, geometric and stylized floral compositions all create a density of ornamentation that is difficult to follow. The inscription, completely embossed in mother-of-pearl, is a masterpiece of its kind.

The glass façades on the coast were designed so that these beautiful vessels could directly encounter the Bosphorus, where they once belonged. It can be argued that the building excellently reflects the nautical spirit and the sea, represented by Beşiktaş for centuries, with a modern touch. You can

Sinan Pasha Mosque and its newly reconstructed imperial apartment

now look at the galley and Üsküdar in the background through the window and imagine the Ottoman fleet greeting Istanbul before going on a campaign.

Barbaros Hayreddin Pasha's Neighborhood Beşiktaş

As we talk about Beşiktaş as a symbol of sea and seamen, we should not forget that Barbaros Hayreddin Pasha (c.1475-1546), who once had a waterfront mansion (Turkish *yalı*) here, first gave Beşiktaş this honor. His burial in Beşiktaş has strengthened his ties with the neighborhood even further. Just behind, the Barbaros Hayreddin Pasha tomb is Sinan's first funerary project, a little bit further inland, is the mosque of another admiral, Sinan Pasha.

Here, Architect Sinan (c. 1490-1588) unexpectedly deviated from his constant research for a perfectly centralized plan and made a variation on the theme of the Üç Şerefeli Mosque's plan (built in Edirne in 1447). Perhaps only by coincidence, the next project where Architect Sinan deviated from his line of spatial development was the mosque of an admiral in chief (Piyale Pasha). Today, the most outstanding component of Sinan Pasha Mosque, both from the sea and the street, is its *hünkar mahfili* (Sultan's lodge). Actually, the timber lodge is a recent reconstruction, which had totally disappeared. With the current increased interest in Sultan Abdülhamit II's life

Tombs in Beşiktaş Square

and deeds, Sinan Pasha Mosque has become more noteworthy as it was the mosque used by this sultan two times a year for *eid* prayers away from the Yıldız Palace (rather than the Yıldız Hamidiye Mosque nearby, where he had his Friday prayer).

In the past, the Beşiktaş was an area with many more buildings as old photographs demonstrate. Mostly a land-fill area, even Prost's plan to reorganize Istanbul during the 1930s suggested this place could be turned into a public square. Even though the plan was not immediately implemented, the erection of a statue of Barbaros (done despite the financial difficulties of World War II) was an important step toward this goal and the name of the famous admiral's name was once again commemorated here.

The artists of the sculpture are Hadi Bara (d.1971) and Zühtü Müridoğlu (d.1992), who also sculpted the reliefs that depict the Battle of Dumlupınar (Field Battle of the Commander-in-Chief), and other reliefs in Anıtkabir (Atatürk's mausoleum in Ankara). The monument has inscriptions of the verses by the eminent Bosphorus-poet Yahya Kemal Beyatlı that mention Barbaros Hayrettin Pasha.

Barbaros Monument and Sinan Pasha Mosque

The ferry pier is one of the most elegant structures of the square. The building, which completely reflects the characteristics of the First National Architecture period, is the work of Ali Talat Bey made in 1913. This architect will be mentioned again on the following pages in reference to the Büyükdere and Kuzguncuk piers. While his name is very rarely mentioned nowadays, he had such a high status during his lifetime that he was the only architect to be buried (d. 1922) next to Architect Sinan.

The pier looks like a pavilion by the sea. Its pointed arches and tiles, familiar components of the classical mosque architecture, evoke an Ottoman spirit. Its towers, terraces, and other elements crafted with the art of stone-carving and its symmetrical-horizontal body recall the European-American villa architecture.

Traces from the Remote Past

Barbaros Boulevard, which begins by the shore up the slope towards Yıldız, constitutes one of the symbolic transportation axes of the Menderes (Prime Minister, 1950-1960) era. Before looking any higher, however, on the right-hand side, there is

Beşiktaş Pier

ongoing construction that has changed everything we know about the history of the Bosphorus. Apparently, there was a river bed of a stream (at least one) that emptied into the Bosphorus around the pier.

According to Zeynep Kızıltan, who has recently retired from her post as the director of Istanbul Archeology Museums, burial mounds (*kurgan*) were discovered during excavation work for the metro project. The burial mounds are most probably from the Early Iron Age. Burial goods like stone axes, bronze arrowheads and fragments of earthenware were also discovered. In the light of all this information, it has been suggested that this was a burial ground belonging to a North Black Sea Steppes culture.

These recent archeological findings have shed some great light on the history of Beşiktaş. Even though we had so little information about the pre-Ottoman era, the excavations have revealed something about even earlier period of time.

Actually, we just know about two monumental columns from the Byzantine era in this neighborhood, which was called *Diplokion*: An illustration, which was produced by the Italian priest named Cristoforo Buondelmonti in 1422 for his book *Liber Insularum Archipelagi*, depicts a pair of columns erected in Beşiktaş. The illustration set an example for numerous maps

Recently discovered Iron Age tomb in Beşiktaş Square

of Istanbul in later periods, but we do not know what happened to these columns later on. If the excavations will be continued in different directions, many other details about the ancient world could be obtained. The illustration also depicts a river, which was probably the Ihlamur Stream. This stream no longer exists, and its dry bed now serves as a road called *Ihlamur Deresi*. There are many other rivers (*dere*) that no longer exist, including some which will be discussed later.

Sheikh Zafir's monumental tomb by Raimondo d'Aronco

If we look up the slope of Barbaros Boulevard towards Yıldız, we can see another tobacco warehouse on the right that dates

Ertuğrul Dervish Lodge and Sheikh Zafir's tomb

Fountain by Raimondo d'Aronco nearby Sheikh Zafir's tomb

back to 1950. It is more recent than the other ones in the Bosphorus. Since it was used as the headquarters of a pharmaceutical company until very recently, it does not give many clues about its original function. Nonetheless, the plain modernist lines of the period usually veiled the function of buildings.

Before continuing up the slope, we will see Ertuğrul Sufi Lodge (*Tekke*) at the corner and Sheikh Zafir Tomb, one of the exquisite works of the Italian architect Raimondo d'Aronco. This was built for, Sheikh Hamza Zafir al-Madani by Sultan Abdülhamit II. The sheikh had an eminent name of the Shadhiliyah order from North Africa. It is very often said that Abdülhamid II was very fond of this sheikh and he built this dervish lodge close to Yıldız Palace just for this reason even though it might not be an easy task to find a document to prove this assertion. The library next to the lodge was designed with wide windows to let light in. Currently, it more looks like a storeroom from outside.

The fountain next to the tomb is the work of the same architect, but it is made of a totally different material, white marble, and its design is entirely different, as well. From these points of view, one may easily think that it had initially been designed as part of a different project and was placed here later. After all, fountains are often moved to another location. But a close examination reveals that it is placed on the garden wall and it was designed in a way that it could serve both from the inside of the garden and towards the street. D'Aronco eliminated the problem of the difference in elevation by placing two basins at different heights. All these details make it clear that the fountain was originally designed for this plot of land.

As the street level has been changed more than once, the basin which was placed high is now positioned the fountain remained partially buried for some time; presently looks like it is at the same level as the sidewalk, however, its ornamented outside basin is no longer there causing an odd gap in front of the fountain. Since the size of the fountain is very modest, usually even a single car parked in its front makes the fountain invisible; its lack of a basin becomes not at all noticeable.

Beyond the fountain, we have other beauties by D'Aronco; he is one of those names who left their mark in Yıldız Palace (and on the entire Bosphorus). Both the new wing of the Şale (Chalet) Pavilion and the Yıldız Porcelain Factory are his works. However, the palace is much larger than what is mentioned here; unfortunately, it has been a long time since this unique palace lost its original integrity. Perhaps it was inevitable for such a poetic beauty to be radically altered at the heart of the city center and on such large grounds. Part of it was allotted to Yıldız Technical University. Previously, it had also been used for military purposes. Many sections of the palace have already been diligently restored, and the restoration is continuing on the rest of it. Currently, it is mostly used as the offices of the Presidency on the European side of Istanbul.

We Come by Çırağan

Despite the uniqueness of these works, we will not spend too much time focusing on the buildings on the slopes. As we move along the Bosphorus, we come to Çırağan. Beşiktaş, in summary, is a neighborhood surrounded by three palaces. Very few neighborhoods could enjoy such great honor.

Originally a village, numerous quarters in the neighborhood of Beşiktaş developed here thanks to its advantageous position. One of the few Greek neighborhoods in this area is here and the church bearing the same name (Panagia Cihannüma) can be noticed easily among the buildings of Bahçeşehir University. Once, there was even a court building, for sure, with one of the best views in the world.

From here we could enter the Çırağan Palace area encountring first its annexes. The first group of buildings we see is the Four Seasons Hotel. The building with the wide façade facing the sea is the historical palace. Following its use as a palace, it had some rough days.

Çırağan Palace, currently a hotel

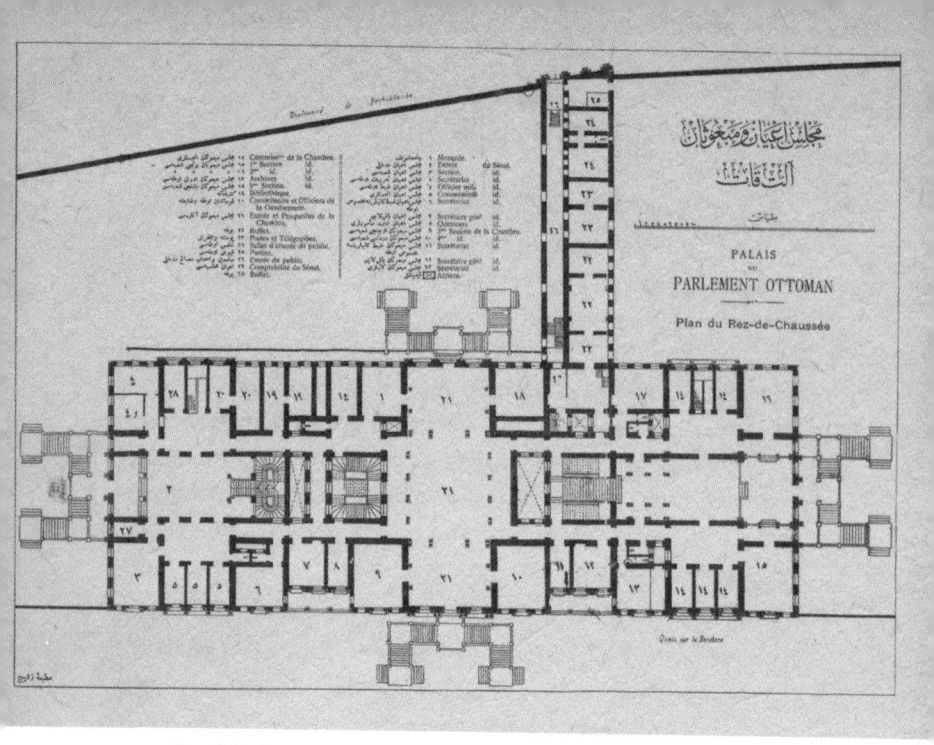

Plan of the Çırağan Palace when it was used as the house of the Parliament
(from the Ottoman Archives)

For example, when the building was used as a warehouse for IETT (Istanbul Electric Tramway and Tunnel Establishments), chipboard panels were nailed on its window. The building was later transferred to the Turkish Electricity Administration. It was planned to be used as a state guesthouse. Eventually, two separate buildings of almost same size were added just a little bit behind the main building on the right and left. Its shoreline was expanded, and some recreational areas were added for its new function.

The next building (the former harem building) is the Beşiktaş Anadolu High School. By the way, when a school bears the adjective *Anadolu* (Anatolian) in its name it simply means that several subjects are taught in English; regardless of whether it is in Anatolia, and in this case it is not. The school building runs perpendicular to the sea; in other words, its long façade faces the hotel, and the short façade faces the Bosphorus. This building, along with other palaces already mentioned as well as other we will see soon, was transferred to the Ministry of National Education. After this building, the main building of Çırağan Palace, whose construction was completed during the last quarter of the 19th century, emerges with all its glory. The interior spaces of the building were designed with a complete Orientalist influence, and its design is primarily imported: its main source was the Wilhelma Palace constructed by the Architect Ludwig von Zanth for Wilhelm I, king of Württemberg.

It is, of course, impossible to discern all these details of the interior as we pass along on a boat. The building lost all its interior components after being devastated by a fire (1910) that broke out when it was used as the Ottoman Parliament. Many suggestions have been made for the use of the building that continued to remain abandoned, but they were rejected because of the high cost such a large building would require.

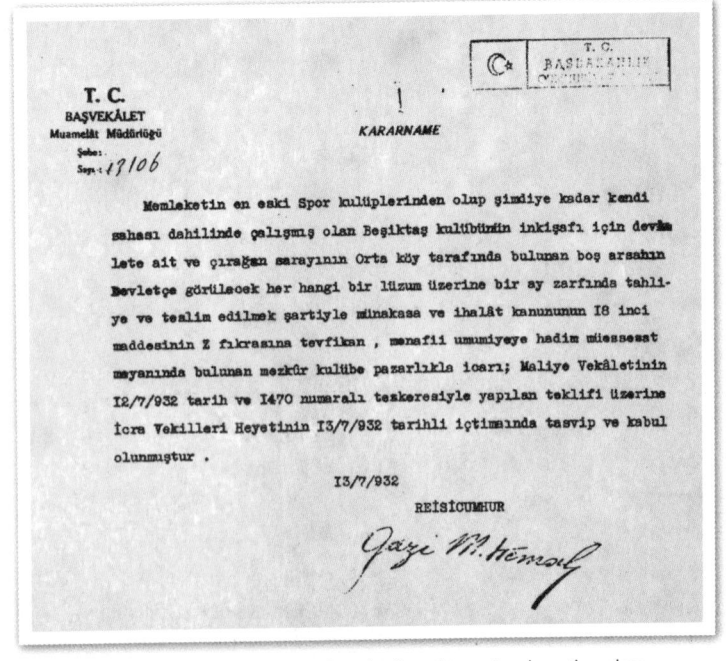

A decree signed by Atatürk: Beşiktaş is allowed to rent and use the palace garden as a soccer field.

We know that as early as 1924, it was proposed that Çırağan could be used as a Museum of Agriculture. In 1928, Francesco Paletto made an application to restore the building and turn it into a hotel and casino. Francesco Paletto was the Italian owner of the famous Grand Hotel de Londres in San Remo in Italy, presently more than 150 years old. The proposal of turning it into a Naval Museum could not be realized due to financial problems. Some of its buildings were put to use as tobacco warehouses. In 1933, a legal decree permitted the selling of one of its gardens to İş Bankası for the installation of a packaging factory. Moreover, in 1945, Lütfi Kırdar, both the Governor and the mayor of Istanbul at the same time, wrote a petition to the Prime Ministry requesting the building in order to operate it as a hotel run by the municipality. However, this attempt failed as well.

The complex continued to look like a haunted mansion for decades until the 1980s. It was turned into a hotel with quite a few modern additions at the beginning of the 1990s, its interior was rebuilt, but the palace most probably did not look as it does now, as mentioned before.

The exterior of the building was preserved to a large extent during the restoration and repurposed. The exterior façades are almost plain compared with the interior ones. There are grids with Gothic details on the upper parts of its windows. These are decorative elements that we could also see in the windows

Çırağan Palace's modern hotel building

of the Yıldız Hamidiye Mosque nearby, and we would see them again at Aksaray Pertevniyal Valide Sultan Mosque.

A contemporary block structure was designed for the adjoining garden. The present swimming pool of the hotel and the modern hotel building behind, which is larger than the main building, are located in this area. The garden was formerly rented to BJK (Beşiktaş Gymnastics Club) with a decree signed by the founder of the Turkish Republic Mustafa Kemal Atatürk. It was functioned as the BJK's main soccer field (Şeref Stadium) until the Dolmabahçe Stadium was built (1947). After that date, until the hotel project began, it was used as the BJK's training ground.

This area on the shore was historically used mainly by the Beşiktaş Mevlevi Lodge until the palace was built there. The Ottoman traveler Evliya Çelebi wrote: "It is a two-storey dervish lodge on the shore with a whirling dervish hall facing the sea. It is unique both in Istanbul and in other countries. Its whirling dervish hall has an artistic ceiling below a red colored dome. Today's masters cannot build such a dome. It is exceedingly high and very popular among people".

The dervish lodge was moved to Maçka by Mahmut II when he decided (1830s) to build the previous Çırağan Palace here.

Çırağan Palace's garden gates

At a later point, the lodge was relocated to Bahariye at the end of the Golden Horn because Sultan Abdülaziz decided to build the Maçka armory.

The planting of palm trees in front of the modern block has nothing to do with the Bosphorus's flora but is an apt choice that follows the sea, pool and palm iconography seen on many touristic brochures. The gates of the palace on the shoreside which welcome those landing on the pier resemble a triumphal arch on the one hand and the monumental portals of the Seljuk-Ottoman architecture on the other. These gates balance the composition with their locations and create unity with the style of the façade. There is an arched opening at the center supported by two elegant columns, and the external columns complement the composition here. The columns follow a classical repertoire, but their details are quite distant from classical motifs. The cubic capitals have motifs of braids and curvilinear branches which could be related to Islamic architecture. The arch opening is limited at the upper section by a series of niches, which is a form generally found in interior spaces in Ottoman architecture. Floral ornaments and capstones on both sides finalize the composition.

Our itinerary mainly consists of what is visible from the sea, but if you happen to be on the road opposite the palace, you should stop and look at the land gates more closely even if you stayed at this hotel and passed by them several times.

The architecture and decorative elements of the gates facing the sea are repeated on the land gates as well, however, in an even more grandiose and intense manner. The composition, in general, again repeats the form of a triumphal arch. However, the decorative elements reflect some local, exotic and even some imaginary Islamic art features. Although the main gate is accentuated by its width and height, the use of thick-bodied columns on the lateral parts creates a feeling of "turreted architecture" on both sides. The fan-shaped components in the

The bridge connecting the Çırağan Palace to its hillside gardens

niches on both of its sides, the pairs of deep-set niches above, the "half-fans" placed in the corners and the bundles of columns in the uppermost section along with many other details are some of the stylistic preferences which herald the decoration of the interior spaces. The way the lace-like decorations and forms on the iron door wings all come together reflect a partially local and partially Alhambra-inspired spirit. As these details make clear, it would not be an exaggeration to argue that the land gates of Çırağan Palace were designed as distinct monuments.

There used to be high walls between the sea and the building. Otherwise, there would be no need for the portals. However, it seems that during the arrangements for a hotel function, wide rectangular openings in the walls were preferred so that the garden would have this view as well.

One famous figure associated with Beşiktaş is the *Muhafız* (Guard) Yedi Sekiz Hasan Pasha, a commander from Beşiktaş who became famous for his suppression of the attempted coup against Abdülhamid II. He is now commemorated by the bakery shop named after him.

This attempted coup, known as the Çırağan Coup, took place on May 20th, 1878 when journalist Ali Suavi raided the Çırağan Palace with a few hundred men he organized. He got the guards out of the way and entered the harem quarter where Murad V was held. As he took him out by grabbing his arms and shouting, "Long live Sultan Murad!", Beşiktaş Chief Police Officer Hasan Pasha came to the place with his soldiers and killed Ali Suavi by bashing his head with a baton. This was one of the most notorious incidents of Late Ottoman history.

There is this ongoing rumor about Hasan Pasha claiming that he signed his name with the Arabic letters for 7 and 8 (٧٨). The rumor has it that this was because he was illiterate (or because he could barely read or write). If an illiterate Pasha was looking for an easy signature made of figures, it could have been easier to introduce himself, for example, as 11 Hasan Pasha, with the Arabic letters "١١."Most probably, some people who were almost illiterate and who perhaps only knew the numerals (it can be easily argued that Pasha dealth with a gang of ignorant people) might have started to refer to the Pasha with these numerals his initials were similar to. A book written about the Pasha states that no such signature as has yet been found.

The palace has a bridge which crosses over the road and connects it to Yıldız Park, which was orginally Çırağan's private garden. It is important to note that almost all waterfront mansions had bridges leading to their gardens, but they were all demolished during the various road widening campaigns. This bridge, which is not really appreciated by drivers, is the only surviving example of the entire Bosphorus, and a particularly elegant one.

Küçük Mecidiye Mosque and Yahya Efendi Lodge

Küçük Mecidiye Mosque, situated just behind the hotel's new unit on the opposite side towards the road, is not easy to see from the sea, but if look closely it can be partially seen from where the hotel ends. What makes this mosque special is the fact that among the three mosques built by Sultan Abdulmejid in this area (the other two mosques being more splendid), only this one named after the sultan. In contrast, Dolmabahçe and Ortaköy Mosques are simply named after their neighborhoods.

We complained because it is out of sight, but if we pay attention to its differences from the other two buildings, one cannot help thinking that perhaps Küçük Mecidiye was not intended to show off, acting virtually like a private mosque.

Küçük Mecidiye, which has almost no ornamentation, has much more simple surfaces than the other two. And although it is an imperial ("*selatin*") mosque, it is quite modest with its single minaret. On the other hand, we should also state that it is part of the palatial mosque tradition despite its plain appearance. Küçük Mecidiye is a mosque directly connected to the Çırağan Palace. There are other mosques with this

Former Feriye palaces (today schools) and the Yahya Efendi Dervish Lodge (above)

Küçük Mecidiye Mosque's dome, inside (top) and outside during restoration (bottom)

characteristic on our route: Hamidiye close to the Yıldız Palace and even the Bezmialem Valide Sultan Mosque just beside the Dolmabahçe Palace. This connection is also implied by the fact that the mosque has a private gate for the Sultan, in addition to its main gate, which was used by Sultan Abdülmecit as he used this mosque for his Friday prayers.

No neighborhoods were formed around since its construction. The relation between the Konya Seljuq Palace and Alâeddin Mosque (1220 c.) and the Sadabad Mosque near the Çağlayan Pavilion from the Abdülaziz era are among those mosques built for the use of the court in earlier periods.

The most recent restoration revealed that the dome was built only with clay pipes. This was not only for acoustic purposes, but also because it is a light building material, and it stands out as a unique example in Turkey (58).

On the opposite side of the road, at the slope just after Küçük Mecidiye Mosque, we see one of the most important complexes of the area: Yahya Efendi Lodge.

The lodge can easily be seen from the sea thanks to its location on the hillside. It could even be more appropriate to say that its view dominates the sea. In the past the grounds of the lodge covered a much larger area. It also had a large 'kayıkhane' (boathouse) on the shore for transport. After the demise of Yahya Efendi, the "milk brother" of Sultan Süleyman the Magnificent, Selim II, who had great respect for Yahya Efendi, commissioned Architect Sinan to build a timber and domed tomb and enlarged the lodge. The lodge assumed its present form, except for the tombs that were later added, with the large-scale restoration by Pertevniyal Valide Sultan, mother of Sultan Abdülaziz in 1873.

Looking at the Bosphorus from Yahya Efendi

The library is the last building added to the lodge complex (*kulliya*) at the beginning of the 20th century. Its books (including more than 4,000 manuscripts) were transferred to the Süleymaniye Library. As it was further developed, it was inevitable that the Yıldız and Çırağan palaces next the lodge would annex a significant part of its land.

The tomb, which can be seen from the sea with its accentuated alternating horizontal brick and masonry lines, is not the tomb of Yahya Efendi, but of Güzelce Ali Pasha. The grave of Yahya Efendi is located on the opposite side of the complex and its façade cannot be seen from the sea. Sultan Süleyman the Magnificent's daughter Raziye Sultana and, Abdülhamit II's daughter Hatice Sultana are buried inside this complex.

The lodge has a vast cemetery: more than one thousand tombstones were recently uncovered and have been catalogued. Yakup Kadri Karaosmanoğlu (novelist, politician d. 1974) and Vasfi Rıza Zobu (actor, d. 1992) are among the locally popular names whose tombs can be found at the lodge's cemetery. The daughter of Vedat Tek, an influential architect of the Bosphorus, is also buried in this cemetery.

On the walls of the buildings, many graffiti were discovered during the restoration work conducted by the General Directorate for Foundations. It seems like the visitors desired to leave some trace of the time they spent here.

Feriye Palaces

From this point onwards, we will be seeing the series of educational institutions which still preserve their waterfront qualities because there are no landfills in front of them. These are

Former Feriye Police Station, now a restaurant

secondary units of the palace, which are named as *Feriye Saray-ları* (meaning "Palace annexes" in Ottoman Turkish). Since the opening of the "Feriye Restaurant" (meaning literally "Annex Restaurant"), this obsolete title has been sounding almost as a proper name. Today they house the Ziya Kalkavan Maritime High School (Yaveran Quarters), Galatasaray University, and Kabataş High School to the north. Since this was where Sultan Abdülaziz died under suspicious circumstances (apparently committing suicide only some days after he was dethroned), it has a special significance in Turkish history.

This series of typical 19th century Ottoman buildings with their rhythmical masses extending along the Bosphorus even if they cannot be directly related to the waterfront mansion architecture, do not contradict the tradition very much. All in all, the public office buildings and the old Istanbul quarter do not differ much from these on the Ortaköy-Beşiktaş-Dolmabahçe line. All these structures are part of the classicist buildings that became popular after the Tanzimat Reform (1839) Era.

One of the buildings of Kabataş High School seems to have been converted to a school just after the Republican Era.

However, documents from the period reveal that the other buildings were used as a tobacco warehouse for a more extended period.

The following building is the monumental Feriye Police Station, at the northernmost point of the Çırağan Palace series. Eight monolithic marble columns are the most distinctive elements of the whole façade. It was largely rebuilt in its present state after a long period of neglect and abandonment.

The waterfront of the police station has a symmetric structure. There is a staircase at the center. On the sides of its façade, there is a two-floor composition, but the uninterrupted pilasters make the building appear like a single-storey structure. The symmetry, columns and the shapes of windows are typical. This composition has gained an almost local expression during the last century of Ottoman architecture, especially during the second half of the 19th century. Palaces, public buildings and especially police stations were built in this style. Feriye *Karakolu* (police station) today mainly is known as a venue for weddings and other celebrations. There was, however, a plan for it to be turned into a museum or a cultural center.

As the Çırağan's estate ends after the police station, we reach Ortaköy where one witnesses how the settlement pattern in the Bosphorus develops: the quite large residences of prominent people cover the shoreline of the Bosphorus almost like a series of interconnected buildings. Here, like many other places to the north, are villages at the mouths of the streams with the houses and agricultural areas of the villagers extending inland.

Mosaic of Cultures: Ortaköy

Although known as a "village" (Turkish *köy*), Ortaköy is a highly populated and multicultural settlement with more than one neighborhood. It is frequently cited as an example where several religious communities live together in harmony and where places of worship are neighbors to one another. It is like a miniature of Istanbul as it is. The entrances of the *Etz Ahayim* (or "Tree of Life") synagogue and a Greek church (*Hagios Phokas*) are better noticed from the street. They are not, however, very noticeable from the sea. The most prominent element of the church from the street is the metal bell tower. The historical synagogue burnt down completely and was rebuilt later.

The Jewish *Akaretler*, the rowhouses known as "*Las dizioço*" in a nearby alley represent part of the Jewish heritage of Ortaköy. There are only a few examples of this typology left in Istanbul; we had talked about another *Akaretler*, which is the most splendid of them. The houses of the Catholic Armenian Foundation' Surp Agop on Elmadağ Street is worth a mention

Jewish rowhouses "Las Dizioço"

as well as a long series of historic rowhouses (they are presently behind scaffolds, which means hope for restoration).

The next structure on the shore that will catch your eye is Büyük Mecidiye Mosque (1850s), as it stands out from all other buildings nearby. The mosque follows the composition of Mihrimah Sultan Mosque in Edirnekapı, a work of Architect Sinan: a cubic mass carrying a hemisphere. It could be defined as an influential variation of the mid-19th century: If you look closely, you will see that a somewhat limited area was spared for worship and the two-storey imperial apartment covers a much larger area than the mosque itself. The mosque looks like a grandiose kickshaw in front of this functional, larger and relatively more uncomplicated structure.

It would not be wrong to define the mosque as a "Baroque jewel" of the Ottomans. Starting from the mid 18th century, the Ottoman art and architecture started to follow European trends. We know about examples with Baroque and Rococo

Ortaköy Mosque and the Beylerbeyi Palace in the foreground (on the Asian side)

lines, comparatively more timid in mosques, and bolder in public fountains, tombstones, and other sepulchral monuments. Western forms became the fundamental components of Ottoman taste after the first wave. Ortaköy Mosque also reflects this taste, and it freely exhibits the Baroque lines and has a vivid sense of motion. The concave walls of the façades with large windows on the seaside and the stonemasonry with wavy lines make the mosque one of the most dynamic and expressive representatives of Baroque, or more appropriately of the Neo-Baroque style.

Ortaköy Büyük Mecidiye Mosque has recently gone through a careful restoration. The old photographs reveal that there was a large boathouse just next to it. It is important to note that there are no other mosques with two minarets in further north in the Bosphorus. They look like they are drawing the boundaries of the symmetrical mosques with the two-minaret mosque in Beylerbeyi on the same line. The minarets ornamented with gold foils are newer than the mosque: as they were severely damaged in the 1894 earthquake posed a great risk to their surroundings, it was decided that they would be demolished and completely rebuilt in 1908. Although they used to be grooved like the minarets of Dolmabahçe, they were rebuilt without any grooves with a smooth surface during the 1909 restoration.

The monumental inscriptions of the mosque belong to the *Hattat* (calligrapher) Ali Haydar Bey. He was Yesarizade Mustafa İzzet's student and made the headstone of his teacher himself. He rests in the burial grounds of Yahya Efendi Dergâhı.

Just behind the mosque, there is an elegant fountain: Nevşehirli Damat İbrahim Pasha (Grand Visier from 1718 to 1730) Fountain, which unfortunately is not visible from the sea is much older than the mosque. It supplied water to the square since the 1720s. Although it is presently situated in an open space to which it was recently moved hence warranting multiple façades, it was originally designed with a single façade.

Only its seaside façade is made of marble, with an inscription and ornaments. The decorations start with palmettes and continue with muqarnas. This series of decorations end with an elegant inscription. An oyster-like motif just below draws all the attention to itself. Two miniature fountains again with oyster motifs above them support the primary composition. As this is one of the oldest monuments in this area, it is quite worth visiting.

Damat İbrahim Pasha Fountain (1720s)

If everything had gone well, there would be an elegant police station by the Italian Architect Raimondo d'Aronco in the square, just close to the pier. The plan of the structure is still preserved at the State Ottoman Archives, but it was never realized.

It is too late to build police stations in the Bosphorus following one hundred year old-projects, so this building will most probably never be constructed. However, one cannot help but hope for such beautiful structures to be rebuilt if destroyed. Feriye Karakolu (police station) was one of the most splendid of these buildings, and one has all reasons to be glad it was restored; though other demolished ones were not nearly this attractive. Still, once we have detailed visual materials of the buildings, it is worth inspecting the drawings carefully and considering reconstructing them.

As we go along the shore, Esma Sultan Yalısı (waterfront mansion) is seen next after the mosque. We cannot really say

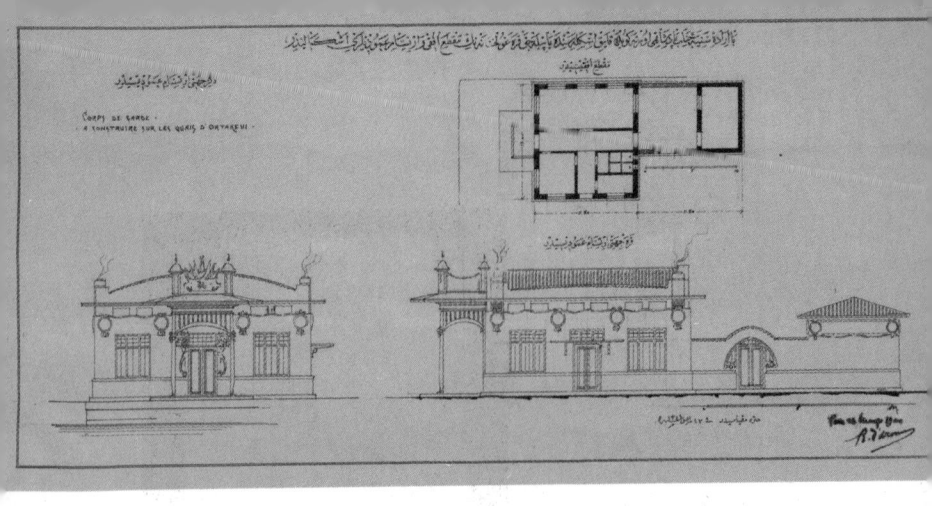

A police station project by Raimondo d'Aronco (early 1900s)

that it is still literally waterfront: facilities, where hundreds of people can have their teas and coffees, have come in between the building and the sea. The Bosphorus shore frequently offers some exquisite examples of shoddy structures of leisure architecture, which is solely a combination of glass and polymer surfaces. Other neighborhoods of the Bosphorus also follow this trend of building forgettable glass cages as coffee shops.

Esma Sultan Mansion's only problem is not the fact that it is now not close to the sea. After changing hands several times, only four walls of the mansion were left erect after a fire in 1975 when it was used as a workshop. The building stayed in that condition for a long time and was apparently liked so much that it was decided to keep the building as it is after the fire and it was not restored. Hence, it assumed the appearance of a historical industrial complex rather than an Ottoman waterfront mansion (Turkish *yalı*). Since it was decided to turn the building into an events venue, an inner shell made of steel and glass was built letting the participants enjoy the view from inside the building. This design isolates the building from all external factors, as well.

This is also where the Ortaköy stream flows into the sea. Although the stream is not discernible today, its memory is preserved in the name of the *Dereboyu* ('along the stream') Street. Now several neighborhoods are located where the stream used

Esma Sultan Waterfront Mansion, burned down in 1975.

to be. The Surp Kirkor Lusavoriç Catholic Armenian Church is also on this street.

Like many other churches of its period, the building lacks a dome and it is very plain. We know that, when its construction started in 1838, the construction yard was flooded by the stream and the work was halted (65). Today, even the idea of a stream which could overflow this location is not plausible, however the fact that the structure was built on an eight-step elevation suggests this risk of flooding rather than creating a monumental effect.

Another Armenian community is represented by the Surp Asdvadzadzin Church. This building is also located quite far from the Bosphorus.

The Bulgarian Exarchate building is on one of the other side streets, which again highlights the multi-cultural nature of Ortaköy. Today it no longer belongs to the Bulgarian Orthodox community, but it is used as a student dormitory.

As we turn back to the shore from where we left, after Esma Sultan, we come across a series of waterfront mansions with narrow façades. The first three of them were extensively

Armenian Catholic church of Surp Kirkor Lusavoriç

restored and put into use as a hotel. Actually, this is not the typology that comes to mind first when we talk about waterfront mansions along the Bosphorus, but there used to be many others like these. One can come across a similar series of narrow waterfront homes in Arnavutköy as well. Although they differ in architectural styles, these series of row mansions, with their locations and ratios, remind us of the canal houses in Amsterdam.

Just a bit further north, though, there are once again the usual residential structures of the Bosphorus. The first two are the Naime and Hatice Sultan mansions, which are very close to one another. The first mansion served for a very long time as a school named after Gazi Osman Pasha, father-in-law

Former Bulgarian Exarchate, today a student dorm

of Sultan Abdülhamit II's daughter Sultana Naime. The building was lost to a fire in 2002 and recently rebuilt. The other mansion is usually referred to as Istanbul *Yüzme İhtisas Kulübü* (a Swimming Club). Both have recently been leased as part of a common restoration and operation project, which includes a car park of thousands of square meters to be built underground that will alleviate the parking problem of Ortaköy.

A Centuries- Old Dream: Bosphorus Bridge

Right after this, we pass under a suspention bridge. Put into service in 1973, the bridge is undoubtedly one of the most iconic structures of Istanbul. It was designed by Sir Gilbert Roberts in cooperation with William Brown who also has his signature on the "Second Bridge" project as well: by the way, this one is called the "First Bridge" (*birinci köprü*, in Turkish), but we have already stated that the first bridge across the Bosphorus was built much earlier. This is the first bridge which was built to be permanent. We are aware of many earlier plans for building a permanent bridge, but none of them had been realized.

Even more than five hundred years ago, even Leonardo (sure, da Vinci) dreamt of building a bridge across the Bosphorus. The architect of the German Embassy on the Bosphorus, Armin Wegner, whom will be mentioned again in reference to Tarabya, also had his own idea of building a bridge. However, we do not know the exact details of what these people had in mind.

From the mid 19th century onwards, on the other hand, we can trace some concrete steps being taken in this direction.

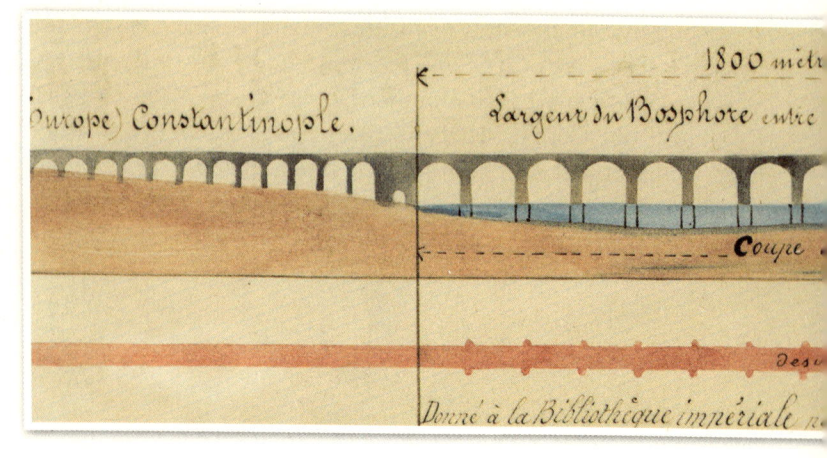

A bridge for the Bosphorus, an unrealized project (1855)

We know that a design, although a very simple one, was exhibited and published for the Exposition Universelle in 1855 in Paris. As frequently seen during the period, the bridge was planned to connect the city center (around Sarayburnu) directly to Üsküdar. 18 arches with a distance of 100 meters to one another were designed connecting the underwater abutments of the bridge. The explanatory information of the design states that its main purpose was to link the European railway lines to Asia. The bridge was proposed during the reign of Abdülmecit when Istanbul had no access to railways. The design assumed a straight railway line leading directly to Beyazıt, unlike the present one, which follows the shoreline. More than one model of the draft project was exhibited during the Paris Expo, including the view of the project on the city map and some other details about its structure.

Coming back to the present day, as we leave the First Bridge behind, we reach what used to be the front of Lido historic swimming pool complex. The land used to be Naima Sultana's property until the Republic. In the 1940s, Architect Halit Femir, who had also worked with Le Corbusier, built a pool there. The initiative was criticized with the argument that there was no need for a pool next to the sea. However, the pool was built with the consideration that the shallow waters of the pool would be used for an additional two months because it would stay warmer than the waters of the Bosphorus by 6 to 7 degrees. The lack of currents in the pool would also allow for swimming competitions. The upper floor, referred to as the club floor, was designed for watching the swimming races and a series of hotel rooms were placed here as well.

The Retired Chief of Staff Ragıp Gümüşpala, whom we mentioned at our point of departure, was elected as the chairperson of the *Adalet* (Justice) Party, founded after the coup of 1960. In 1964, when he was still in office, he was found dead in one of the hotel rooms in Lido just the day before the elections. The event itself has given rise to many conspiracy theories. Süleyman Demirel who became the chairperson after him, began to rise to prominence, eventually becoming the President of the Turkish Republic (1993).

Even after this unsettling death, Lido continued to be one of Istanbul's most favorite clubs. Bedri Rahmi Eyüboğlu (1911-1975) made his first mural paintings for Lido; they are all

The Lido when it was a public pool

unfortunately forgotten because no pieces of the work survived, and no visual documentation was made. If any souvenir photographs show up accidentally, we might perhaps learn more about the work to expand what we know now. For now, not much is known about the future function of the ruins of the Lido.

There are two noticeable structures on the hills above Lido. One of these is the house of Bruno Taut, and the other is the Şifa Yurdu Hospital, which is usually known as a large holding office.

Bruno Taut was a German architect who moved to Istanbul when he was very young. He made drawings for a project for the "Turkish-German Friendship Dorm" (*Türk-Alman Dostluk Yurdu*), planned to be built in Sultanahmet. He came to Istanbul with other entrants in the competition in 1916 and worked on the canvassing of the city in his thirties and was very impressed by Istanbul. He came for a second time after the Republic of Turkey was founded. He is the architect of some noteworthy buildings in Ankara, including the majestic Faculty of Languages, History, and Geography of Ankara University. Trabzon High School is also his work.

Taut designed the residence on the Ortaköy hills for himself. His work harmonized numerous architectural styles in a single structure: it has the characteristics of a waterfront mansion of the Ottoman-Turkish architecture -even though the building is inland- and the turreted temple architecture that he saw during the years he spent in Japan. The back of the house, also including its entrance, is entirely situated on bedrock and its front, which is reminiscent of a pagoda, faces the Bosphorus on two concrete piers creating a flying effect. Originally planned as a rather small residence, the structure was later extended towards the back, but its façade facing the Bosphorus has not been altered (68).

Bruno Taut became ill before he enjoyed his house completed in 1938. He designed a catafalque for Atatürk following his death, and he passed away a month later. He still rests in Edirnekapı Martyrs' Cemetery.

Şifa Yurdu Hospital, in contrast, can be considered a modern building; it stands out with its simple façade and the wide, long balconies surrounding the floors. Despite its considerably large mass, it is not particularly disturbing thanks to its simple design and surrounding trees.

Just after Lido is the Defterdar cape. There is a rather extensive car park next to Lido. In the past there were a large number mansions here that did not survive. This car park was on the plot that belonged to one of those mansions.

The Lido after the demolition, the pagoda-like Bruno Taut villa and the former Şifa Yurdu hospital

Hatice Sultan Waterfront Palace should be mentioned among the most majestic examples of its kind. It is one of the apogees of the waterfront mansion architecture with its rhythmic bow windows creating a sense of movement. One of the artistic details which make it an interesting structure is the repetition of the flower vase motif on its façade closest to the water. This delightful motif was part of decorative arts repertoire all around from India to Iran, from the Ottoman land to central Europe especially during the 18th century. Flowers in this palace, too, reflector the tradition of the Tulip Era and adds a European flavor to traditional Ottoman forms. The neighboring building was completely in a neoclassical style. It is accepted that this was Melling's own waterfront mansion. There are niches on its columnar façade and vases were placed in these niches as one would expect to see in European architecture.

After the car parking area, there is the Defterdar İbrahim Mosque. It is from the 18th century; its minaret was added in the 19th century. Next to it, there is another large vacant lot that belonged to Naile Sultan's waterfront mansion, whose name lives on in the gated community situated on the hillside.

After a short while, we see a very wide park. Since there is no such concept as a "park" per se in the Bosphorus tradition, this land, too, would have belonged to a waterfront mansion which has not survived. The most special example on that line was the waterfront mansion of Sultan Abdülaziz's daughter Nazime Sultana, designed by the Italian Architect Raimondo d'Aronco.

An Art Nouveau Palace: Nazime Sultan Waterfront Mansion

It is best to define Nazime Sultan Waterfront Mansion (Turkish *yalı*) as an "Art Nouveau palace." Its significance in the history of European architecture would undoubtedly have been acknowledged if it had survived to the present day. The architect's Western, and especially Italian background, his ability to discover the potentials of Ottoman architecture and to use them in his new designs, make the waterfront mansion unique. It stands out with its rhythmic eaves and accentuated horizontality. The use of quality material and excellent workmanship

Melling's small but ambitious home together with the Hatice Sultana's waterfront palace (engraving by Melling himself, early 1800's)

certainly greatly contributed to this architectural achievement. The curvilinear and flowing forms of Art Nouveau and the tendency to reconsider the traditional forms with new lines made it into a masterpiece.

Until this land was turned into a park, it was a bit less green; it was in fact almost entirely black, as it was a port facility where cranes loaded and unloaded ships carrying coal. Its name was "*Kömür Tevzii*" (Coal Distribution). Nowadays, the name of the bus stop just in front of the park is all that preserves its memory.

Following this, we see a vacant plot of land of 15,000 m² with a 200m-long façade on the shoreline. It was known as *Kuruçeşme Arena* and used for open air concerts for a time. Today one can see significant construction activity at this site. The company which will be operating the land announced that they made a contract with the Romanian born (1948) Architect Adam D. Tihany, who was named one of the greatest American interior architects by The New York Times in 2001. Since the informative panels on the iron wall around the property do not have any drawings, one has to adopt a "wait and see" approach to discover what this new hotel will look like.

Next, one of the Ottoman works of the Bosphorus, the Fountain of Dürrüaden Kadın Efendi built in 1909), grabs our

Nazime Sultana's waterfront palace: one of the most beautiful Art Nouveau homes in the world, a great loss for the Bosphorus

attention with its asymmetrical structure. Although it cannot be seen from the sea, it is worth viewing if you happen to pass by it when driving on the road.

The fountain has a sleek design, which reflects the artistic and architectural taste of the period in which it was built. We can even define it as "modern." Some classical elements on its façade are abstractions and often there are only small suggestions of the classical forms. On its semi-circular upper section, the structure is crowned with an inscription bearing the sultan's signature (*tuğra*). Thus, the upper part of the façade starts with an almost natural symmetry, and a horizontal rectangle extends towards the asymmetric lower part with a continuous horizontal slant following a shallow relief series of cartouches. Inside what appears to be a brick arch, there is a basin which adds depth to the façade and on the other side there is a bowl which creates a protrusion. The marble keystone is decorated with a relief of a leaf. The fountain has neither a tap nor water. The only consolation is that it was recently cleaned so it is no longer hidden behind the bushes.

By the way, we are now following the shoreline of the district *Kuruçeşme* (meaning "dry fountain"). The slopes above the

Dürrüaden Kadın fountain among the lush vegetation

park in this direction look very different because there are no buildings on them; there are only the buildings of the Turkish national radio and television (TRT) at the very top, and they are not noticeable when looked at from the sea. The whole slope is named as the "TRT Woodlot".

At this very point, we find the opportunity to observe the typical examples of the Bosphorus flora in a continuous line for the first time. Closer to the buildings (where the flag is seen clearly), the forestation becomes more discernible, but the remaining part reflects the Bosphorus's untouched looks which would typically consist of dense shrubs. If visited in the right season, you can come across the first groups of magnificent Judas trees (*Cercis Siliquastrum*) of the Bosphorus. As a matter of fact, the only view of Judas trees within the natural maquis vegetation is in this woodlot.

Locals traditionally tend to complain that all these areas were covered with forests in the good old days but eventually they were all destroyed. The green areas of the Bosphorus, though, should not be compared with rain forests. Most probably there were more trees in some areas. However, other than the areas close to the Black Sea, the preserved and afforested

The MV Savarona was the largest yacht of the world when she served Atatürk. She often sails through the Bosphorus

areas (hence woodlots) and of course cemeteries, , the trees in the residential areas were continuously cut down for construction activities as well as for cooking, heating, and building boats. This kind of activity (hence the lack of woodlands) is consistently visible in the old photographs of the Bosphorus. Interestingly, this unfounded complaint is not a recent one. As early as 1836 the young Helmuth von Moltke (who was later to become chief of staff of the Prussian Army for thirty years) wrote that in Roman era, there used to be many forests and that they were later cut down.

After the TRT Woodlot, we can see housing again, which covers all of the slope. Kuruçeşme used to be a multiethnic village like Beşiktaş and Ortaköy. Although Evliya Çelebi mentions three synagogues, there are no synagogues or Jewish cemeteries anymore; but the Armenian *Surp Haç* (Holy Cross) Church and the Greek *Hagios Demetrios* Church are still visible and are located not far from the very central Tezkireci Osman Efendi Mosque. This mosque has a pleasant greengrocer on the ground floor. The protruded part of the niche above the greengrocer makes it clear that it is a two-storey mosque, with the prayer area is on the second floor.

A series of completely rebuilt wooden mansions

Meanwhile on the shore, just after the area under construction, there are three waterfront mansions, or *yalılar*, which were completely rebuilt where they once used to be, rather than being completely forgotten. The first two of these have assumed a new function as homes (for quite affluent families as one can easily imagine) whereas the third one functions as a hotel. As a comparison of these waterfront mansions would make it clear, the buildings reconstructed as home assume their original better because their need for additional spaces is more limited.

After these waterfront mansions, there are again no surviving buildings directly along the shoreline for quite a long distance. A long and narrow concrete area, with trees planted on it and with motorboats tied to its side, forms the distinctive appearance of Kuruçeşme's shore.

Another unusual aspect of this neighborhood is the fact that just in front of it we have the only bit of land that could be defined as the only island of the Bosphorus (that is, if we do not count the island of Maiden's Tower). The Kuruçeşme Island used to be associated with some eminent names who served for the Ottomans. One of them is the Ottoman Armenian Architect Sarkis Balyan, who once had a house there and another is the Russian artist Ivan Konstantinovich Aivazovsky (1817-1900), born into an Armenian family. Aivazovsky stayed on the island as Balyan's guest and completed many of his paintings there. The island was used as a coaling station by *Şirket-i Hayriye* ferry company for a time. It means that coal has long been part of Kuruçeşme's fate. Later, part of the island was sold to the Galatasaray Sports Club in 1957, and it was later named Galatasaray Island.

Towards the end of the park, we reach the point where the coastal road is split into two. This area was the French headquarters during the occupation of Istanbul after the WWI. In 1919 a fire broke out from here and all the surrounding area was destroyed. Therefore, up to this point, there are no historical timber structures.

Here are two residential plots of land (the former Divan Kuruçeşme restaurant). It can easily be seen how diligently the land of the historic residences (now ruins) was shaped with terraces rising to the slope. The wide niches on each terrace imply that statues or other objects used to be displayed extravagantly alongside the structures by the sea. There are ongoing plans to repurpose the land, to build a four-room hotel on the top two terraces - two rooms on each one - and to use the wide plot near the road as an events venue. These days, a concrete platform is being constructed obscuring this view. We will see the results at some point in the future together.

It is always a problem to reach the upper elevations around the houses on the slopes. Elevators and short funicular lines were established along the Bosphorus to deal with this problem, and they usually have a negative effect on the view.

Here, at the endpoint of Kuruçeşme, we come by an exception to the unseemliness: an apartment building with its external elevator commissioned by Memduh Pasha to the

Historic mansions, when destroyed, expose the terraces, which they were built on.

Italian Architect Raimondo d'Aronco. From a note written on D'Aronco's original sketch, we learn that the building was designed not for its present-day function, but for the Pasha's collections and books.

This building overlooking the Bosphorus from above is one of the most creative designs of the architect. The harmony of the structure of the building and the elevator tower has almost produced a castle in miniature. The leading representative of the Art Nouveau style, the architect, has interpreted a woman's head with ample and tangled hair similar to the well-known depictions of Medusa. The building's geometric mass with sharp turns and the accompanying small touches in horizontal and vertical lines, the balcony parapets and the crowning of the tower all turn transform the small building into an Art Nouveau feast.

New Breath at the Bosphorus

We are now at the cape, Sarrafburnu. Here the coastal road becomes a causeway and is the starting point of the area which was unaffected by the fire. There are eight attached waterfront mansions in a row. The causeway runs along in front of these waterfront mansions and then merges with the land. All the slopes after this line are part of the property of Robert College.

The school was originally established as The American College for Girls. It cost 52,800 dollars the buy the first 13 acres of the property. It was clearly a good deal considering that only a few years later the 5-acre extension cost 60,000 dollars.

Since Sultan Abdülhamit II rejected the idea of an American college here, the construction of the campus and settlement

The former American College for Girls (currently the Robert College)

were somewhat belated. After Abdülhamit II was dethroned, the ban on Turkish girls' being sent to an American school was lifted. Indeed, there was even pressure for the school to admit an increasingly large number of Turkish girls to deal with problems of a teacher shortage the Ottoman Empire was facing at the time. Nevertheless, education in this campus did not start until 1914.

When the construction permit was granted in 1910, the Shepley, Rutan & Coolidge architectural firm assumed the task with the contribution of the Architect Charles Hercules Rutan, who was also a trustee of the school.

The stones for the façade of the buildings were obtained in situ from the rocky soil. The fireproof and robust ferroconcrete

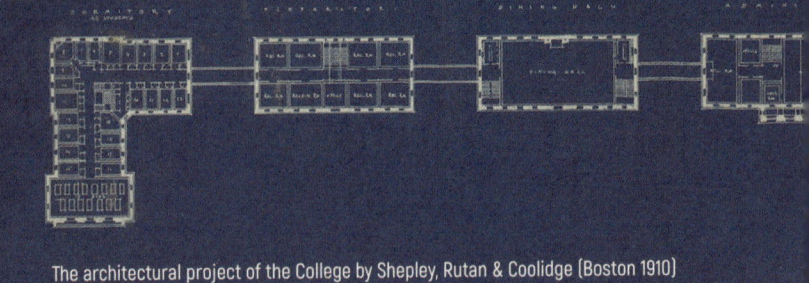

The architectural project of the College by Shepley, Rutan & Coolidge (Boston 1910)

buildings, unlike the timber ones belonging to the Bosphorus tradition, have survived to this day with all their original glory. It is noteworthy that the original symmetric design in the project (preserved in the State Ottoman Archives and hitherto unpublished) could not be completed; only five of the planned buildings were constructed. Although many other structures were added in the last 100 years, there seems to be no effort to complete the main project.

Despite the dense wooden texture, the buildings of the foundation period can be seen on the wide plateau forming the top of the hill when looked from the sea.

As mentioned above, many new structures were added to the earlier ones. The last addition, only a few meters away from the historical buildings, is the social activity building of the Murat Karamancı Student Center designed by the Architect Ahmet Alataş. The building attracted attention on an international scale when it was granted the 2017 Excellence Award, given to Europe's best steel structure projects.

On the coastal side of the school, at its very entrance, there is the Archeologist Halet Çambel's waterfront mansion, which originally had a red ochre color. This Ottoman *yalı* has stood here since the first half of the 19th century, though it has since lost its red ochre. After the death of its owner, the building was granted to Bosphorus University. Diligent preparations to turn it into a research center are still ongoing. The only example in the surroundings where the large garden with its multi-level terraces has survived is this one, but it does not look well-kept for the time being.

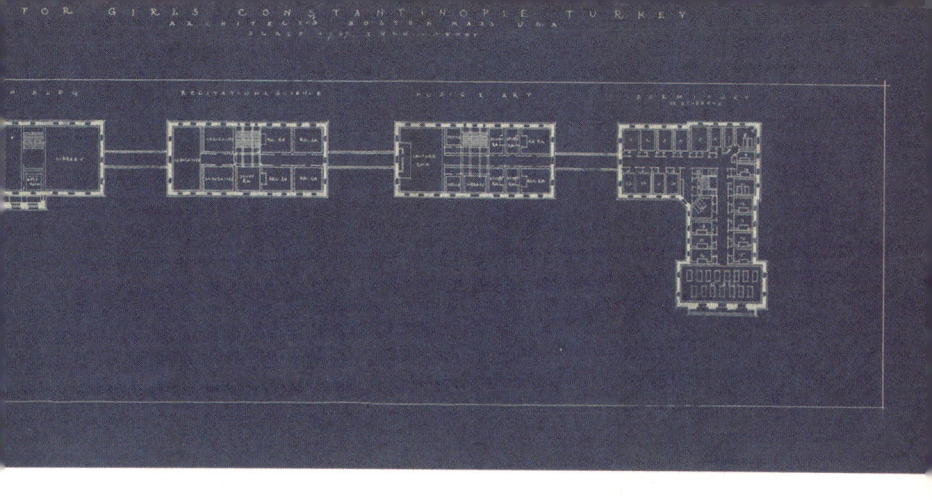

The design and infrastructure of the building, on the other hand, are known to belong to a much earlier date than the 1820s when the foundations were laid.

Although not supported by hard evidence, it is frequently stated that this is the house in Arnavutköy mentioned by the future German Chief of the General Staff, Helmut von Moltke, who is known for the detailed letters he wrote from Turkey when he was still a young captain in 1836.

Granddaughter of a Grand Vizier, Mrs. Halet Çambel inherited the house from her wealthy family. Hence it is known by her name. Her husband, however, is as famous as her: Nail Çakırhan, who won the Aga Khan Award for Architecture

Murat Karamancı Student Center, Robert College, 2016

Çambel-Çakırhan Mansion (early 1800s)

(without any formal education in architecture). Nail Çakırhan fled to the Communist Soviet Union and studied there. He met figures like Stalin, Khrushchev, and Tito and became friends with the poet Nazım Hikmet in prison. Many rich girls fell in love and got married with poor men; this happens not only in movies but also often on the Bosphorus. Halet Çambel and Nail Çakırhan couple is such an example.

When we start to see the causeway separating us use from the land, we have reached Arnavutköy where we will pass by a series of attached multi-storey waterfront mansions with narrow façades. A little further inland is the Greek Orthodox Taksiyarhis Church, which can be spotted by its dome.

As one moves closer to the cape, *Akıntıburnu*, would easily notice a strong current visible on the surface, making it clear why this cape was named "*akıntı*" (Turkish for "current"). Following this, we come across the Arnavutköy Police Station and Tevfikiye Mosque on the opposite side of the coastal road. The police station is a one storey building with a long façade. The mosque is on an elevated platform, which means its courtyard and the prayer area are reached by climbing a flight of stairs. Its façades reflect the Ottoman imperial style with sharp lines and its masonry elements, creating a contrast with the usual timber buildings of the Bosphorus.

The façade of the mosque's ground floor cannot be noticed because of the sunshades of the stores; stopping by one of these one would notice that they are vaulted spaces, most probably former boathouses. Hence, it is more easily perceived that this used to be a mosque on the waterfront before the road was built separating it from the shore. Similar boathouses with different current functions can be found all around the Bosphorus.

As we turn around the cape, we pass by the Beyhan Sultan Fountain (c. 1800) on the side of the road. It had been

Çamlıbel Apartment

dismantled during the expansion of the road, and then remained neglected for decades. Recently its pieces were rediscovered, and the façade panels were reinstalled at its current location, not far from its original spot. However, it seems like many of its pieces are missing. Especially its wide eaves, an indispensable part of the fountains of the period, are no longer in place.

The fountain almost resembles a small version of a marble palace. The Western Baroque-Rococo forms that the Ottoman architecture applied enthusiastically from the middle of the 18th century have been harmonized masterfully. The horizontal and vertical waves alongside the thin stripes and leaf motifs create a Baroque scene on a small scale.

All these characteristics, however, are not sufficient to highlight its beauty, as it often can only be seen as a marble protrusion over the motor vehicles that keep parking in front of it.

Next, we catch sight of a tall Ottoman wall covered with ivy and just behind the wall a series of apartments whose ground floors face this wall. A pair of Ottoman buildings called *Çifte Saraylar* ("Double Palaces") used to be located here. They were built at the beginning of the 1800s and first used by many of the Ottoman sultanas, but after the foundation of the Republic they lost their connection with the Ottoman Dynasty. Like many other similar buildings, they were used as a tobacco warehouse for some time. After 1931 the compound was first used by a school, initially named the Feyziati High School and later as Bosphorus High School. Although the school is now almost forgotten, it was a popular one with its famous teaching staff and numerous graduates who became eminent members of Turkish society. Rauf Denktaş (The Founding President of the Turkish Cypriot Republic), Kadir Has (Businessman and Founder of the homonymous university), and Attila İlhan (a dissident poet) were among the students of Feyziati High School, and its teaching staff included locally important names like Hüseyin

Beyhan Sultan Fountain (early 1800s)

Nihal Atsız (a prominent Turkish nationalist writer, whom the dissident poet Attila İlhan confesses he was quite afraid of) and Nihat Sami Banarlı.

As the name of the street on the slope here recalls, this place is the Pavilion of İzzetabad, also known as *Boyalı Köşk* (Painted Pavillion). Actually, as the case is all around the Bosphorus, the waterfront mansion below and the pavilion above are linked to one another.

Since it was owned by her husband for a period, this house became famous as the residence of the actress Belgin Doruk

Izzetabad Pavillion, formerly an actress's residence, currently a conglomerate's headquarters

and it was used as a movie set for numerous Turkish films. The property was put on sale as a parcel of land after it was demolished by its next owners to build a housing estate instead, but the plan could not be realized. The three-acre property was bought by a holding in 1989. Finally, it assumed its present appearance when the mansion was rebuilt as the company's headquarters.

After Vezirköşkü Street, which borders the parcel of land and refers to the mansion, we see the ruins of a petrol station. This part of the shore is named Çamlıbahçe (hence it was the Çamlıbahçe Petrol Station), but only a few people use this name nowadays. Still, it is worth remembering.

There used to be a restaurant first with the name Süreyya and then S on the upper floor of the petrol station. Apparently, it was too old fashioned elegant for ordinary clientele. It has been closed for many years and it is now dilapidated, but it should be remembered as a unique component of the modern Bosphorus. There was no one during the 2000s who dared to open such an upscale restaurant, be it in the Bosphorus or in any other part of the city. The restaurant's location used to belong to the property of the waterfront mansion Köçeoğlu *Yalı*. Perhaps, it would be wrong to say that it disappeared completely, as; we know that at least the ceilings of some of its rooms were dismantled and remounted in some rooms at the Topkapı Palace. In summary, some of the ceilings we admire thinking that they belonged to sultans actually belonged to one of the cultural assets of the Bosphorus that was aggressively dismantled.

Feyziati Highschool

Before examining the inland areas of Bebek, we see two parcels of land on the shore, which are almost equal in size and once belonged to two palaces. The first of these palaces no longer exists. It belonged to Zeynep Hanım, daughter of Kavalalı Mehmet Ali Pasha. The wealthy and charitable Zeynep Hanım's name is better remembered for the Zeynep Kamil Hospital, which she founded with her husband, Yusuf Kamil Pasha.

Old photographs prove that the waterfront mansion was not smaller than the present shore palace situated on the next parcel of land. The mansion had two bridges which connected it with the woodlot on the hillside behind it. It was common for some large mansions to have one latticed bridge for the harem, the family's residence, and another one reserved for men (*selamlık*) which allowed passage to the woodlot behind. We know that this building was used as a tobacco warehouse for a period before it was demolished in 1930.

The grounds of this palace were now divided into four parcels where we have four modern waterfront villas. The first of these is the work of Architect Kadri Eroğan. We will see another one of his works on the Bosphorus shoreline. There are the Natuk Birkan apartment blocks across the road at the same level.

The last one is one of the few residential designs of Architect Kemali Söylemezoğlu (1951). The façade, characterized by four fine columns, bears both traditional and modern features.

Köçeoğlu Mansion

It could be argued that Söylemezoğlu preferred a kind of modernity for Istanbul which is in harmony with the Bosphorus. The levels between the ground floor and the first floor are reminiscent of the bow windows of the Ottoman waterfront homes. However, there is also an implicit reference to similar country villas in Europe and the United States in the early 20th century.

Bebek: from Egypt to the Soviet Union

The integrity of the next parcel structure has survived together with its building: The Consulate General of Egypt is one of the most significant representations of the Art Nouveau style in Istanbul, and even in Turkey. It could well be compared with European palaces with its symmetrical bulk and steep roofs. In addition, its elegant lines, stonemasonry and woodwork produce one of the most original and refined examples of this style. It is linked to the architectural tradition of waterfront mansions with its monumental, but yet harmonious proportions.

The Egyptian Consulate General, (early 1900s)

There used to be a splendid waterfront mansion of the Kavalalı family where the palace is presently situated. Emine Valide Pasha, daughter of Sultan Abdülmecit and Münire (we mentioned her palace, Mimar Sinan University) and Mother of the last Khedive (Ottoman viceroy) Abbas Hilmi Pasha had the mansion demolished and commissioned the Italian Architect Antonio Lasciac to build the present palace.

Next there is a very wide woodlot with the previously mentioned apartment blocks of Natuk Birkan. Actually, the whole woodlot consists of the gardens of the two waterfront mansions we have seen on the two parcels of land on the shore. However, the property first changed hands via inheritance and then was sold, before construction begun. These two apartments are the most striking of these new buildings. The difference in elevation between the two makes it look like one is situated on top of the other. One of the apartment's entrances is by the shore, whereas the other's entrance is through the woodlot above. They were designed by Haluk Baysal and Melih Birsel in 1955. The name Melih Birsel will come up again in connection to a similar apartment built 20 years later at Rumelihisarı.

The distance between the road and the shore now gets wider, and a lush green woody park dominates the general view of Bebek. This area, which was once the property of a pavilion known as the Bebek Kasrı, that no longer exists, is now the location of the Bebek Pier. There is the statue of the poet Fuzuli (c.1494–1556) in the park made by the sculptor Haluk Tezonar in 1986. Since it is located a bit inland, it is only barely visible among the trees when viewed from the sea. You need to pass through plants, dust or mud if you want to take a photo.

Associating a poet who never travelled far from his hometown in Iraq, Karbala, with Bebek could well be regarded as an experimental approach. Attempts to make analogies with Haluk Tezonar's other statues of great Turkish figures in Istanbul do not help in understanding why it was placed here either.

In contrast, the statues of the admirals Gazi Hasan Pasha and Turgut Reis facing towards the sea in Sarayburnu seem well-matched with their context.

The justification for a statue of Fuzuli on the Bosphorus is found in the words of Bedrettin Dalan, the Mayor of Istanbul at the time: "You may not know it, but there is a much bigger statue of Fuzuli in the Soviet Union. Since Fuzuli wrote in the Azerbaijani language, the Soviets appropriate him. It would be a disgrace on our side if we had not made a monument of a man of whom the Soviets erected a statue and who actually belonged to us. We placed it in the Bebek Park so that the passing Soviet ships would see it".

Bebek Mosque (1913) is right next to the park. It replaced a mosque of the 18th century. Its architecture reflects the choices of the "First nationalist movement": especially towards the end of the 19th century, Ottoman architects occupied themselves with a national style. Discussions of possible ways of representing the national concepts in art and architecture in Europe sparked this interest. Thus, the discussion, which was not national

Fuzuli's statue by Haluk Tezonar

at all, was imported from the West and was given a 'national' context. Blended with some of the early and classical Ottoman characteristics, the mosque assumed an almost modern identity. It became an essential feature of the Bosphorus landscape with its plain and unpretentious bulk.

As the incline of İnşirah Street heads towards Etiler, opposite the mosque, is the Kavafyan Mansion on a narrow street just next to the Orthodox and Catholic churches to the left. The mansion is visible from the sea, but it deserves a special reference as the oldest surviving residence in the Bosphorus. It also stands out among other surviving timber houses in terms of its size.

The Holy Heart catholic church

The Kavafyan Mansion is among the monumental civil examples of the Ottoman architecture's "Western-style" adopted after the 18th century. More precisely, it is one of the oldest surviving mansions among the hundreds of houses lost to fires or decay. The imaginary landscapes painted on the indoor surfaces are among the architectural and decorative details that make the building and its period noteworthy. Examples of such details could frequently be seen during that period, but it is not easy to find original ones which have not been altered by restoration. The trees, sea, rivers and shores, hills, bridges, and buildings of all sizes depicted on the surfaces of domes and niches are all pleasant images that could be seen when visiting the building.

Just adjacent to the mansion on the same street is the Catholic Church of *Sacre Coeur* (Sacred Heart) established by a French Lazarist mission. It is dated back to 1910, and it was built by the Italian contractor Ercole Michelini.

The group of buildings above the mansion functioned as a French orphanage, and it was later inherited by the General Directorate for Foundations (*Vakıflar*). After a series of extensive restorations and reconstruction led by the Architect Sedat Aklan, these buildings function as residences and form an entire neighborhood.

We know that, other than the French church and the orphanage, a French college was opened in May 1840 in Bebek. However, the French and Italian priests could not establish a continuous Catholic education here, and the school lost its function in less than thirty years.

This is certainly not the first missionary school in Bebek. Cyrus Hamlin, the founder of the American school named Robert College, the present Bosphorus (*Boğaziçi*) University, rented a few houses in Bebek for his Protestant seminary before he found property in Hisar. Actually, he was also responsible for some other interesting things as well; for example, he imported a steam engine and established the first mill that did not

Interior of the Kavafyan Mansion

use animals as the power source in Istanbul. He also opened a bakery with the flour he produced there and profited significantly from the privileges granted to religious communities by Sultan Mehmet the Conqueror to produce their own bread independently of the guilds. He even made bread for the British forces during the Crimean War.

The majority of the buildings along the Bebek Bay that face the Bosphorus have been turned into restaurants and cafes, meaning that they are not visible from the street on the other side. They create an impression that they have limbs slowly extending seaward.

There is a small square at the end of this series of buildings. It is not visible from the sea, but the Küçükbebek Street extending uphill is clearly seen in the form of a valley. Some locals in the neighborhood still call it *Dereboyu* (along the stream).

Cevdet Pasha Street becomes visible again as we reach Bebek since it follows the shoreline here. The name of the street refers to the name of the historian, lawyer, and statesman who passed away in his waterfront mansion in Bebek in 1895. However, nothing of his house has survived.

There is a small house on Cevdet Pasha Street which immediately stands out among the rest: the residence of Ragıp Devres which adds a unique flavor to the Bosphorus with its unusual style. The house overturns all traditional expectations with its prominent thin columns and lack of symmetry.

The architect of the building, Ernst Arnold Egli, was born (1893) in Vienna. He was a member of the Faculty of Fine Arts in Vienna as the assistant to Architect Clemens Holzmeister (1886-1883) known as the architect of the Turkish Parliament in Ankara. We remember Egli mostly for his public buildings in Ankara and his work on the Ottoman Architect Sinan. The Ragıp Devres residence is Egli's only work in Istanbul. Architect Egli states that Ragıp Bey's wife, a beautiful and well-educated Turkish woman, made things difficult for him and kept him too occupied in matters related to the details of its interior architecture. Perhaps, this account of the architect reveal why he did not have any other work in the Bosphorus and why he went on his career in Ankara: "Spending so much time and working so intensively for the requests of an elegant, self-assured and polite lady set me back when I thought I was to work for the future of a nation".

As an original representative of German modernism, this house is the manifestation of the international acceptance of principles of modern design. A cubic body, asymmetrically placed windows, and very thin balcony and roof columns are all embodiments of the desire to progress and modernize, and hence integration with the world in the 1930s in Turkey. This house, which can be defined as a road-side mansion and is hardly noticeable from the sea, is still home to the grandchild of the same family.

Ragıp Devres Villa (early 1930s)

Robert College and Beyond

Streets with woodlot names like Ayşe Sultan and Arifi Paşa wind up the hillsides from the Cevdet Paşa street. These names carry a nostalgic value in that they recall the fact that there used to be woodlots where the present apartments are situated. The only remaining woodlot today is the land of the former Robert College, which has been the property of Bosphorus University for almost half a century now.

As stated earlier, this land was bought from Ahmet Vefik Bey. Writing about his memories of establishing of the Robert College, Cyrus Hamlin states that he bought another plot of land in the middle from another person and he was able to get it at a bargain price as he was able to hide his purpose.

Actually, the location was not the first choice of Hamlin who founded the school, but due to various factors, he was not able to acquire land in Kuruçeşme which was his first preference. A pleasant surprise was waiting for him, however. The new location was rocky soil, meaning that there would be no need for extra work and money to bring stones for the construction and the historic buildings of Bosphorus University were made of these grey stones.

This group of education buildings created an American neighborhood on the hillsides above the Rumeli Castle. The

The former Robert College, currently Boğaziçi (Bosphorus) University

buildings are largely hidden behind dense foliage - despite the increased housing.

Fundamentally shaped by British tradition, with bonded brickwork, perpendicular roofs, and expression of classical harmony, the architecture shapes the big block structures and small lodging buildings. Although completely different from Ottoman architecture, the architectural quality and the landscape are in a fortunate harmony.

The nature of the land, actually, is evident in the name of the *Kayalar* (Rocks) neighborhood. The local rock formations can clearly be seen in some areas.

The Kayalar Masjid here is actually a mosque like many other examples named as masjid with its minaret and pulpit. Like the Tezkireci Osman Efendi Mosque we have seen in Kuruçeşme, its niche distinctly extends into the sea and makes itself seen. Its almost completely preserved timber structure adds to its value. The protrusion of the niche on the upper floor indicates that it is a two-storey mosque. The upper floor of the mosque rather than the ground floor was designed as the prayer area. An inscription in its burial area is worth noting: "Al-Fatiha for the soul of his holiness İsmail Maşuki (*Kurban İsmail*) 1508-1529."

The inscription is a memory about the Melami Sheikh İsmail Efendi who came to Istanbul during the reign of Suleiman the Magnificent and gained many followers. He was then executed with a group of disciples by a fatwa decree by the Sheikh al-İslam. It is believed that the beheaded sheikh was thrown into the sea at Sarayburnu (near Topkapı Palace) and he was given a proper burial after his corpse was washed up onto this shore.

Even the Sultan had warned the sheik to go back to his hometown Aksaray in central Turkey before his execution, but the sheikh followed his destiny stating: "I know my doom".

Next, we can see the *Yılanlı Yalı* Apartment and the *Yılanlı Yalı* itself. These houses, separated from the sea by a road in front of them, were actually the portions reserved for the family (*harem*) and men only (*selamlık*). When the timber women's section was completely burnt down, it was turned into a concrete apartment.

Only the stone room of the harem survived the flames; it is still noticeable thanks to an opening left the façade of the apartment. The smaller *selamlık* was covered with timber-looking material. Like in almost all waterfront mansions, it is easily predictable that the plot of land of this splendid mansion was much larger since it included the other buildings behind it.

Yılanlı Yalı

Dead poets'...

Next on our itinerary is Aşiyan Park. A statue of Orhan Veli, which, in this case, is more fitting with its context than the statue of Fuzuli in Bebek, was erected here. The tradition of reaching the statue through foliage, dust or mud has been kept alive here as well, as in the case of Fuzuli. After the park, the Aşiyan Cemetery stretches all the way to Rumeli Castle.

You should, however, look carefully towards the buildings of Bosphorus University in the meantime, and see Aşiyan itself on a slightly lower elevation. This house, named *Aşiyan* ("bird's nest"), was designed and built by the Turkish poet Tevfik Fikret (1867-1915) himself when he was a teacher at the school and when the school was still known as Robert College). It is evident that the house was initially designed as a small, cozy residence thus deserved the bird's nest metaphor and it was later extended into a slightly larger pavilion. However, its name was preserved, and the whole neighborhood was named after it.

The house presently functions as a museum of Istanbul Metropolitan Municipality and is open to the visitors. It still has a direct connection with the campus, but the official entrance is from the road from the direction of the cemetery.

When Tevfik Fikret passed away, he was buried in Eyüp, but his remains were later transferred to Aşiyan. The author now rests in the garden of his house, pretty much against the traditions of Bosphorus.

The house stands out among the rest since it was preserved with its original furniture. There are sketches, drawings, and paintings which remind us that the house was regularly visited by the leading artists of the time. The drawings by Tevfik Fikret himself are still on his desk. There is an inversely proportional wealth in terms of the number of artists' portraits in the house and its size.

Aşiyan Cemetery, after Tevfik Fikret, over time, became a burial place for authors and poets. Attilâ İlhan (1925-2005) among those whose tombs are the most noticeable from the sea. The poet who realized his dream of living in a waterfront mansion during the last year of his life and who died in a waterfront apartment in the Kanlıca Gulf is now in his eternal rest across the Bosphorus.

Other noteworthy tombs included that of Ahmet Hamdi Tanpınar (1901-1962), with "I'm neither in time nor entirely out of it" written on his tombstone, while the tomb of Orhan Veli (1914-1950) looks like a bit like a hotel lobby decoration alongside other famous figures like Özdemir Asaf (1923-1981) and Yahya Kemal Beyatlı (1884-1958). On the other hand, Şemsi Belli (1925-1995), who won many hearts with the most popular Turkish poem mentioning Aşiyan, is not buried here; he rests at Karacaahmet, on the Asian side of Istanbul, much closer to the Haydarpaşa High School where he graduated. Not only with poets, Aşiyan is a cemetery that commemorates many other figures; for example, a former Prime Minister, Ord. Prof. Dr. Sadi Irmak (1904-1990), who was also a poet, rests here too. At least, with his translations of "Faust" from Goethe and "Thus Spoke Zarathustra" from Nietzsche, he made it clear that he felt close to those who rest with him.

Aşiyan Cemetery ends at the edge of the Fortress of Rumelihisarı. At this very location, there used to be one of the most famous dervish lodges of the Bosphorus: the Lodge of Durmuş Dede (from Akkirman, in what is today's Ukraine), who lived during the reign of Sultan Ahmet I in the 17th century. The lodge was actually established by Sheikh Hasan Zarifi Efendi, who lived in the 16th century. Durmuş Dede was a devoted who came and settled here in the 17th century.

Tevfik Fikret's small home on the left and The Boğaziçi University's historic American buildings

The Rev Cyrus Hamlin, D.D. L.L.D.

President of Robert College, Constantinople.

The Farewell letter to the Rev. Hamlin by his colleagues

Durmuş Dede became famous for performing miracles in Istanbul, and the lodge came to be named after him. The Ottoman Archives provide us with an architectural project prepared by a Greek master-builder. The building then had a European touch to it but reflected the traditional design schemes. We have sufficient data which can enable us to rediscover all its details like its façades and detailed drawings of its plan along with some old photographs. The building disappeared without leaving any traces, but most of the tombs in its burial ground are still there. Evliya Çelebi, who mentions Dede, writes that he directed the sailors who in return gave him alms as they came and went. The older residents of the city remember the city line ferries that kept the tradition alive by blowing their horns to salute the lodge. I personally remember the shared taxis honking their horns to pay respects to the departed Durmuş Dede.

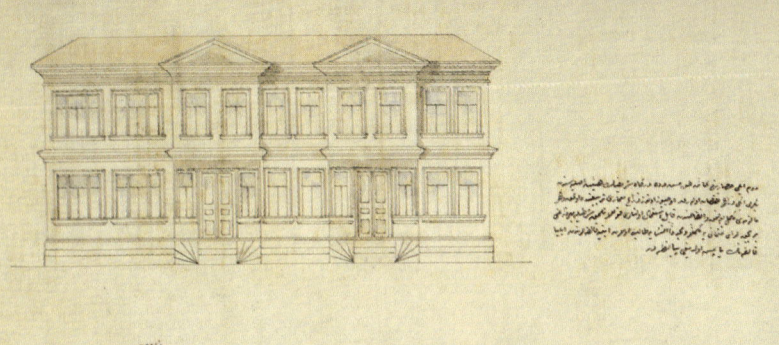

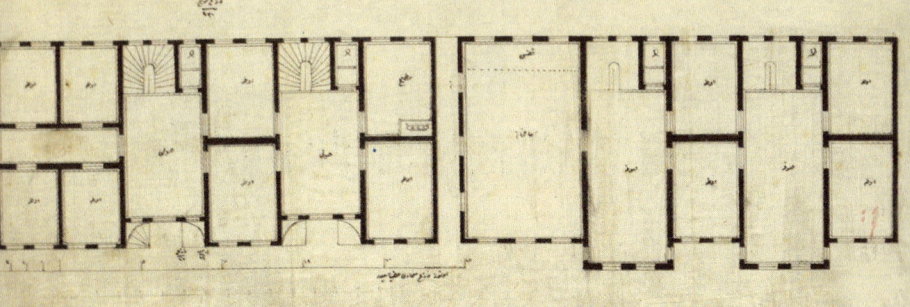

Durmuş Dede Dervish Lodge's architectural project from the Ottoman archives

Fortress of Rumelihisari; to the Second Bridge

The Fortress of Rumelihisarı was built by Sultan Mehmet the Conqueror right across the Anadolu Fortress of his grand-grandfather Bayezid I (*Yıldırım*, the Thunderbolt) at the narrowest location of the Strait. The fortress besides being a building which embodies Sultan Mehmet Conqueror's ambition and vision was also very innovative for its time. The building is focused on the target set by his ancestor when he was building the Fortress of Anadolu half a century earlier, and it acts as a quick bridge to accomplish this goal.

This site was undoubtedly a common place to cross the Bosphorus in earlier periods as well since it is where the two continents are closest to one another. We also know the existence of different structures like temples which are believed to protect or serve passersby in line with the religions, dominant at the time. As a matter of fact, a large amount of spolia from Byzantine buildings can be found on the walls of the Fortress of Rumelihisarı. The fortress, however, has fared much better than what came before.

Cyrus Hamlin, writing about the land he bought for his school, explained his confidence in the campus he built by giving the Fortress of Rumelihisarı as an example of a 400-year-old monument.

Researches on a doctoral level were carried out about the Fortress of Rumelihisarı, thus, we should no longer take Evliya Çelebi's account about this monument as truth: it was penned when a bird's eye view was not available. He says that the fortress was planned in the shape of the sultan's name in Arabic script to add value to his construction achievement. However, in reality, there is no part of the construction that can resembles a script inscribing the name Mehmet. Indeed, it is simply a legend and it is not hard to imagine that Sultan Mehmet had no time for wordplay or decorative schemes in the Bosphorus when even the smallest incremental detail meant additional cost during a speedy period of construction focused on the Conquest.

Of course, the fortress is not less worthy because it does not involve wordplay in its design. The structure is remembered for its construction process which was completed in a few months. Its unprecedented round towers keep the names of Halil, Saruca and Zağanos Pashas alive on the Bosphorus. The many marble spolia of Byzantine structures which have been used as

An early Byzantine capital from Rumelihisarı

A 19th century painting of Rumelihsarı, mistakenly defined as a Genoese castle by the anonymous Florentine painter

construction material on the walls of the fortress can be taken as harbingers of the demise of Byzantium.

The other two names might be made-up, but the inscription on the Zağanos Pasha tower bears the date 1452 together with the name of the vizier deployed by the sultan and the date of the structure. It is also the oldest Ottoman inscription in Istanbul. The Arabic inscription, published by Halil Ethem (Eldem) in 1911, very clearly states the role of Zağanos Pasha: "The constructor of this steep and high building was ordered by the Greatest and Grand Sultan Mehmet bin Murat Khan. Let his grace for his subject and reverend vizier Zağanos Pasha bin Abdullah be eternal. It was completed in the month of Recep in the year 856 (July-August 1452)".

The passive defense tactics, which lasted from the Antiquity to the 15th century, changed drastically during the Renaissance with artillery. Fortress architecture was an indispensable component of this shift. Built in 1452, the Fortress of Rumelihisarı is one of the first examples of such fortresses in Europe, in fact it might even be the first example.

It would not be misleading to state that the fortress almost totally lost its function just after the conquest. Hence, the inner and surrounding areas of the fortress were opened for development in the following years. It is known that there used to be a neighborhood of numerous timber houses within the fortress until the mid 20th century. In 1953, the 500th anniversary of the conquest Istanbul (or fall of Constantinople, depending on the point of view), it was decided that the fortress should be restored. Three female master architects were assigned for the restoration: Selma Emler, Cahide Tamer and Mualla Eyüboğlu. The internal arrangement was realized by Doğan Tekeli,

A reconstruction drawing of Rumelihısarı by A. Gabriel (early 1940s)

Sami Sisa and Metin Hepgüler after they won a competition; but subsequently the Fortress was turned into a venue where high-decibel concerts are organized even though the area is largely residential. The most recent restoration work was for the rebuilding of a masjid whose minaret partially survived.

This project (1958-59) was one of the first contributions of Doğan Tekeli and Sami Sisa to Istanbul. Just one year later they designed the Istanbul Drapery Market (İMÇ). Some other milestones of their work are: the Halkbank building next to Galatasaray High School on İstiklal Street (end of the 1960s), the Vakıf high rise apartments (beginning of the 1970s) in Nişantaşı which were recently renovated entirely with the name VK 108 and in more recent years the towers of İş Bankası and Metrocity.

Coming back to the fortress, since there is no one left who remembers the times of the masjid, which was demolished at the end of the 19th century, all Istanbulites knew the place as a theatre. Many people remember the place with touching concerts of their youth and of their later years. The interruption of the functionality of such an iconic venue of summer concerts, for many, meant a major tear in the fabric of local community. However, one of the architects of the present venue, Doğan Tekeli states that his own interventions on the interior of the fortress have been much lighter and limited. He argues that a more severe intervention was made as Muhsin Ertuğrul (Turkish actor and director, 1892-1979) started his theatre and a great mistake was made by allocating the venue for concerts. His personal suggestion is to get rid of the seating area, considering that the newly restored mosque cannot be allowed to be destroyed again.

We learn from Ms. Cahide Tamer, who restored the Fortress of Rumelihisarı, that Muhsin Ertuğrul was the person who decided the location and stage of the theatre. Muhsin Ertuğrul had even decided to build a theatre at the Fortress of Yedikule in the light of his experience in Rumelihisarı.

There is an often disregarded issue when discussing or criticizing the restoration of the Castle: in any of the interventions, including the ones in the 20th century, the towers were not covered with conic roofs, which were almost certainly there when the fortress was first built. Refitting the towers once more with these cones would be the most determining factor for a new reconstruction project. We know that the towers were covered with these cones up to the 1830s and they protected the timber parts between the floors both from climatic factors and from potential fires inside.

From this point on we will follow the shoreline of the residential area of Rumelihisarı. We first will see the Hacı Kemalettin Mosque, and then we pass by the Ali Pertek Mosque. There is a large residential area behind these mosques. These residential areas, which most probably developed along with the neighborhood in the fortress, constituted the biggest Muslim neighborhood of the Bosphorus.

One of the oldest buildings of the Bosphorus, the Nafi Baba Lodge is also part of this texture. The burial ground, known as Şehitlik ("Martyrs") Cemetery, preserves an impressive collection of tombstones around it.

There were no traces left of the building. A few years ago, it was reconstructed in the southern campus of Bosphorus University. It functioned as the Byzantine Research Center for a period, and then its function was changed. It was announced that the building would be used as a museum, but it has not been repurposed as such yet and continues to be used as an education facility.

A tombstone from Nafi Baba Dervish Lodge's graveyard

We also know that the leader of the sect, Nafi Baba, who lived in the 19th century and who played an essential role in the revival of the lodge was very friendly to foreigners. He even provided the lands needed for the enlargement of Robert College.

If we look back at the shore, undoubtedly the most striking building in the neighborhood comes just after the pier: the Yusuf Ziya Pasha Mansion. By the way, the pier's name still remains "İskele" ("Pier") but its function has changed, and it now serves as an upscale restaurant.

The ambitious mansion project of Yusuf Ziya Pasha, the aide-de-camp of Abbas Hilmi Pasha, the last Khedive of Egypt, is completely different than all the other buildings of the Bosphorus including its disproportional look. It could not be completed because of the abolition of the institution of the khedive and the outbreak of World War I. The unfinished project was called as *Perili Köşk* (Haunted Mansion), which, today, is used more commonly than its original name. It was entirely rebuilt by Architect Hakan Kıran a few years ago and is now used as an office building by a holding company, therefore it can only be visited on the weekends. Visitors can also go up to the terrace and enjoy the view from there.

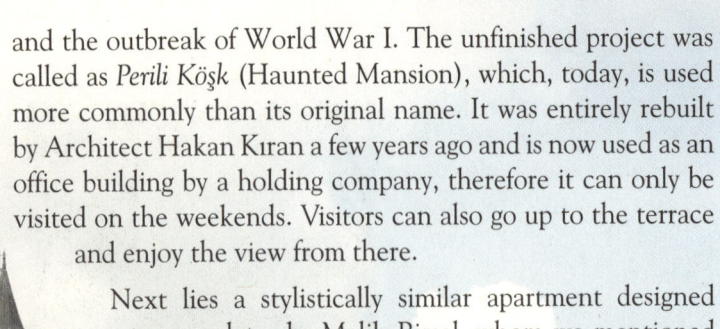

Next lies a stylistically similar apartment designed twenty years later by Melih Birsel, whom we mentioned in relation to the Natuk Birkan apartments in Bebek. The

An unusual construction for the Bosphorus: The Haunted Pavilion

owner of the property, Industrialist Jak Kamhi, states that he himself contributed to the production of steel construction components and this apartment was the first of its kind in Turkey.

The Mansion of Zeki Pasha, Grand Master of Artillery, has somehow an unlucky location. It is just below the Second Bridge and is completely (and literally)

An apartment from the 70s

Zeki Paşa Mansion by the Italian Architect Alessandro Vallauri

overshadowed by the bridge. The building primarily stands out with its height. It does not have any of the traits like the other mansions in the Bosphorus, which are defined by their light and horizontal stance, and it does not reach out towards the Bosphorus like some others, which can even appear as if they are hanging over the sea. On the other hand, because it is made of stone, it has survived all the fires which destroyed many other mansions. It is one of the most splendid examples of the mansions along the shores of Bosphorus.

The relatively fragmented design of its façade and the different window styles on each floor add movement to the heavy-looking building and break a possible monotony. The mansion has some architectural details that highlight its classical value. The corners are highlighted with a series of stones, and it has low and wide arches, the window openings are interrupted with tiny columns, the last floor is crowned with a series of horseshoe arches, which creates the impression of a "loggia" and the whole composition is surrounded with parapets. In all cases, its architectural impression could be perceived as being more in relation to the 19th century Ottoman public buildings, of which, as stated earlier, the Italian architect Alessandro Vallauri was an expert.

We cannot know for sure whether Zeki Pasha built this mansion by scrimping and saving. We know from a recently published archival document that he wrote a petition to the

Another unrealized bridge project (Karl von Rupert, 1867)

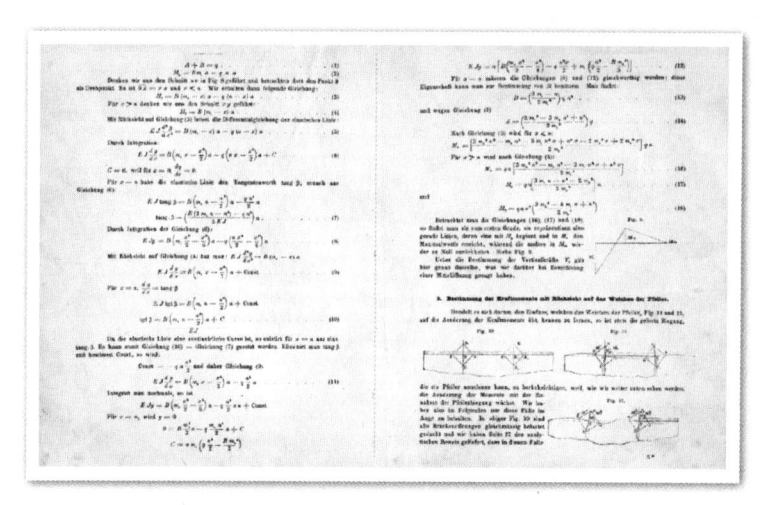

Ruppert's book about how to build a bridge

Sultan underlining that he "was very much disheartened by hearing that the Grand Vizier was granted 16,000 liras" and he requested "to be granted 5000 liras, to be paid in weekly installments of 100 liras".

By the way, we have just passed under the Second Bridge. It was opened for service in 1988, 15 years later than the first bridge on the Bosphorus and besides a few small differences, it could be observed that it was built with the same concept of the first bridge, at least from a visual point of view.

We earlier mentioned the bridge project proposed in 1855. The design of another Bosphorus Bridge exhibited at the Paris Exposition Universelle 12 years later is worth remembering here.

Only a few years had passed when this project was rolled out. This new project was much more developed in terms of engineering. Having only two bridge piers in the sea, the openings between the piers were much larger. If, instead, the monument designed by the Austrian Karl von Ruppert in 1867 had been realized, the Bosphorus today would have a very different look.

Moreover, this bridge was going to be built between the fortresses of Anadolu and Rumeli, more or less where the present second bridge is located. The calculated cost for the completion of the project was almost 3 million US dollars. The primary purpose of this project was to build a railway on the bridge, but it was also aimed to create a strong impression in the Bosphorus with its monumental style and statues that would adorn it.

The American Engineer John Augusts Roebling, of German origin who designed the famous Brooklyn Bridge in New York, also had plans for a Bosphorus bridge but he passed away before the completion of his Brooklyn Bridge; hence his plans for a Bosphorus bridge could not be not realized.

James Eads, who built the world's longest arched bridge on the Mississippi River in the United States in 1874, also had a plan for a 1800 meter-long bridge for the Bosphorus. The planned cost for this structure, which would have had both a railway and a land road, was about 25 million US dollars. The building time was estimated to be at least six years. It is not surprising that this costly building project was not approved when even the previous one was could not be realized. Furthermore, since this bridge would have had a height of 35 meters only, many large ships passing through the Bosphorus today would not be able to reach the Black Sea. Most probably, the bridge would have been demolished due to international pressure.

Other than these, French Préault in 1891 and American Fredrik E. Strom in 1902 suggested building a railway in a tunnel designed as a viaduct, but these proposals were not realized either. The Bosphorus waited for a railway tunnel (Marmaray) until 2013 and for a tunnel for cars (*Avrasya* - Eurasia) until 2016.

Putting these non-existent bridges aside and looking beyond the present bridge, we will first move towards the Zeki Pasha Mansion first and then towards Baltalimanı. The buildings we are passing by are ordinary apartments without any unique features. Since the regulations do not allow building activities, the existing edifices cannot be renovated. The renovation of an apartment from the 1970s in this area by the architects Kerem Erginoğlu & Hasan Çalışlar could be shown as an exceptional example.

We have now arrived at *Baltalimanı*, "Axe Harbor": the name again includes a geographical definition. It is stated that the neighborhood was named after Baltaoğlu Süleyman, the admiral-in-chief of Sultan Mehmet the Conqueror, who kept the navy here during the preparations for the conquest. However, the present looks of the area does not give any clues about its former use as a port. When looked closely, it could be observed that the slopes are rather recessed into the land and the neighborhood is largely situated at the mouth of a valley. The Baltalimanı Stream, which forms the alluvial deposits of the

An apartment in Baltalimanı before (1970s) and after (2010s)

area, is still flowing. It is rather difficult to estimate original the size of this cove 565 years after the Conquest; but the fact that the Admiral-in-Chief Baltaoğlu Süleyman kept his 400 ships here suggests that it has significantly silted up since.

Baltalimanı *Sahilhanesi* (Waterside Mansion of Baltalimanı) is one of the most splendid palace examples of the Northern Bosphorus. Masonry construction was preferred instead of timber, the building material of traditional mansion architecture. The structure with its columnar entrances is an expression of Neoclassicism. The deep interest in Western culture which was felt strongly in the Ottoman society during the *Tanzimat* (1839 Reforms) Era enabled a more consistent transformation of art and architecture following Western traditions. The building's extraverted Neoclassical style is also reflected in the interior as well. The classical decoration of the main hall, also including figurative ornaments, and its high quality implementation is worth noting.

In 1857, Mustafa Reşit Pasha commissioned the Italian architect Luigi Storari to plan a settlement for his land extending towards Emirgan, and he also offered him a possibility to realize the project. The planned settlement, with a pattern of a checkerboard and distinguished with right-angled streets, is still discernible.

Mustafa Reşit Pasha's waterfront mansion by the Italian Architect Fossati

The name of this intermediary location is almost forgotten, but it lives in the name of the bus stop: Boyacıköy. It is believed that the name Boyacıköy comes from the profession of the families brought here from Thrace by Sultan Selim III. Someone who just started learning Turkish might get confused, because "*boya*" means both "paint" and "dye"; these people did not paint walls, however. They were the artisans who produced the red fabric dye, which we are familiar with through the fezzes. Today the new residential buildings, stylistically different from the Bosphorus tradition, seem dominate the view, but actually, the area offers surprises when examined closely: one of the Byzantine cisterns, almost all of which are found inside the walls of the historical peninsula, is located here.

In addition, there is a noteworthy former Greek school next to a church on the slope. The school, built in 1905, was designed by the architects Yenidünya & Kyriakides, whom are best remembered from the Ravouna Hotel, one of the most elegant edifices of İstiklal Street, and the Frej Apartments dominating the Şişhane Square. The building was deemed too elegant for an educational function with its temple-like façade shaped by triangular pediments and acroteria at the corners. It is currently used as a residence.

A former Greek school, currently used as a single-family home

Emirgan: a Centre of Attraction in the Bosphorus

Shortly after the almost forgotten Boyacıköy comes Emirgan, a much more famous neighborhood. Emirgan, as one of the leading centers of attraction of the Bosphorus, is known to even those who do not know much about the Bosphorus. Its woodlot has always been famous, and its memory was revived

Şerifler Mansion, one of the best-preserved Ottoman homes of the Bosphorus

Şerifler Mansion is not a waterfront home anymore because of the new costal road

even more when tulips became fashionable in recent years. The neighborhood's popularity increased even further with the exhibitions at Sabancı Museum and the advertisements of these exhibitions. However, there are other monuments worth seeing before we reach those.

The Şerifler Waterfront Mansion, for example, is almost a summary of the *yalı* (waterfront mansion) architecture of the 18th and 19th centuries. Among the examples of tall and short, cubic or prism-like, simple or grandiose mansions, the Şerifler Mansion seems to have found the "middle way." Its bow window protrudes from the center of the façade, balanced sizes of eaves and its elegant proportions make this structure special. Despite its exterior plainness, the interior sports passionate colors and fine details of Rococo decorations. These compositions exhibit all the tastes and experiences of Ottoman architecture during the Westernization period. The mansion's spectacular, high quality decoration is comparable with Topkapı Palace and the palaces of the Golden Horn.

Moreover, an author who tried to describe the ideal, perfect waterfront mansion, Prof. Dr. Haluk Dursun, shows the Şerifler Mansion as the best example (when its waterfront was not blocked by the road).

Next comes the Hamid-i Evvel Mosque. The name gives reference to Sultan Abdülhamit I, however its many imperial

Interior details from the Emirgan mosque

stylistic hints, make us think that it should belong to the period of Sultan Mahmut II. The main building material of the mosque is stone. The sultan's pavilion next, giving the impression of a different structure, easily creates the same spectacular effect even though it is made of timber. The area in front of the door of this part is defined by four monolithic columns. These columns have been used as the bearings of an extension, enlarging the upper floor of the mansion. Its outer door with an inscription grabs one's attention when looking towards this direction from the sea.

Next, we notice the slightly secluded fountain and the *muvakkithane* (a mosque astronomer's workroom) which are not easy to spot anymore. The name of the latter structure lives on with "*Doğru Muvakkithane* Street" that extends inland through the mosque and the fountain. We should also state that although it is rather difficult to imagine it today, the *muvakkithane* was perfectly waterfront before the coastal road was built. It is known that the mosque complex (*külliye*) had more elements, but no traces of the mill, bakery, and hammam are left.

Following this, we reach the Prince Mehmet Ali Hasan Mansion, now known as the Sabancı Museum or *Atlı Köşk* (the Horse Pavilion).

The horse statues of this mansion have become landmarks: the first horse is a copy of a horse in Italy, ordered and brought to Turkey by the Sabancı family. The location of this horse

The Italian horse statue of the Sabancı Museum

looks like a spacious coastal garden, but before it was placed here, the coastal area was probably more densely housed in line with the tradition.

Once there used to be the waterfront residence of the Embassy of Montenegro here. The Ottoman Archives have even the drawings of a new proposal for this building: the design belongs to the Italian Architect Raimondo d'Aronco, whom we have already mentioned several times before.

Coming across such projects do more than just reminding us of what has been lost in the Bosphorus. If no major troubles had occurred (a series of wars is no small trouble), the Bosphorus would have been adorned with many other gems.

The Montenegro Embassy project is proof of this lost chance of observing additional beauties: many inspirations can be discerned among this relatively complex architecture. The columns placed between the windows, along with atmosphere in general, create a classical appearance. The details, on the other hand, have some Baroque-Empire elements and the dome gives it a monumental "turn of the century" look. Its stone texture is reminiscent of Renaissance architecture, the colossal key blocks in Mannerist style and the flat Baroque window arches assume meaning in the diversity of this composition. If they could have been preserved, all these would be in Emirgan, on the shores of the Bosphorus today.

Soon after the WWI, the estate of the King of Montenegro was expropriated by the Ottoman government. However, the Ottoman Empire came to an end before the committed payment could be made, and regardless, the Kingdom of Montenegro did not survive either. The young Republic of Turkey stayed loyal to its debt and remembered that Jelena (Elena), daughter of King Nicola of Montenegro became the Queen of Italy through marriage. The new Turkish government thus decided that the price of expropriation was to be paid to her. The plot of land, which used to be the property of the Egyptian

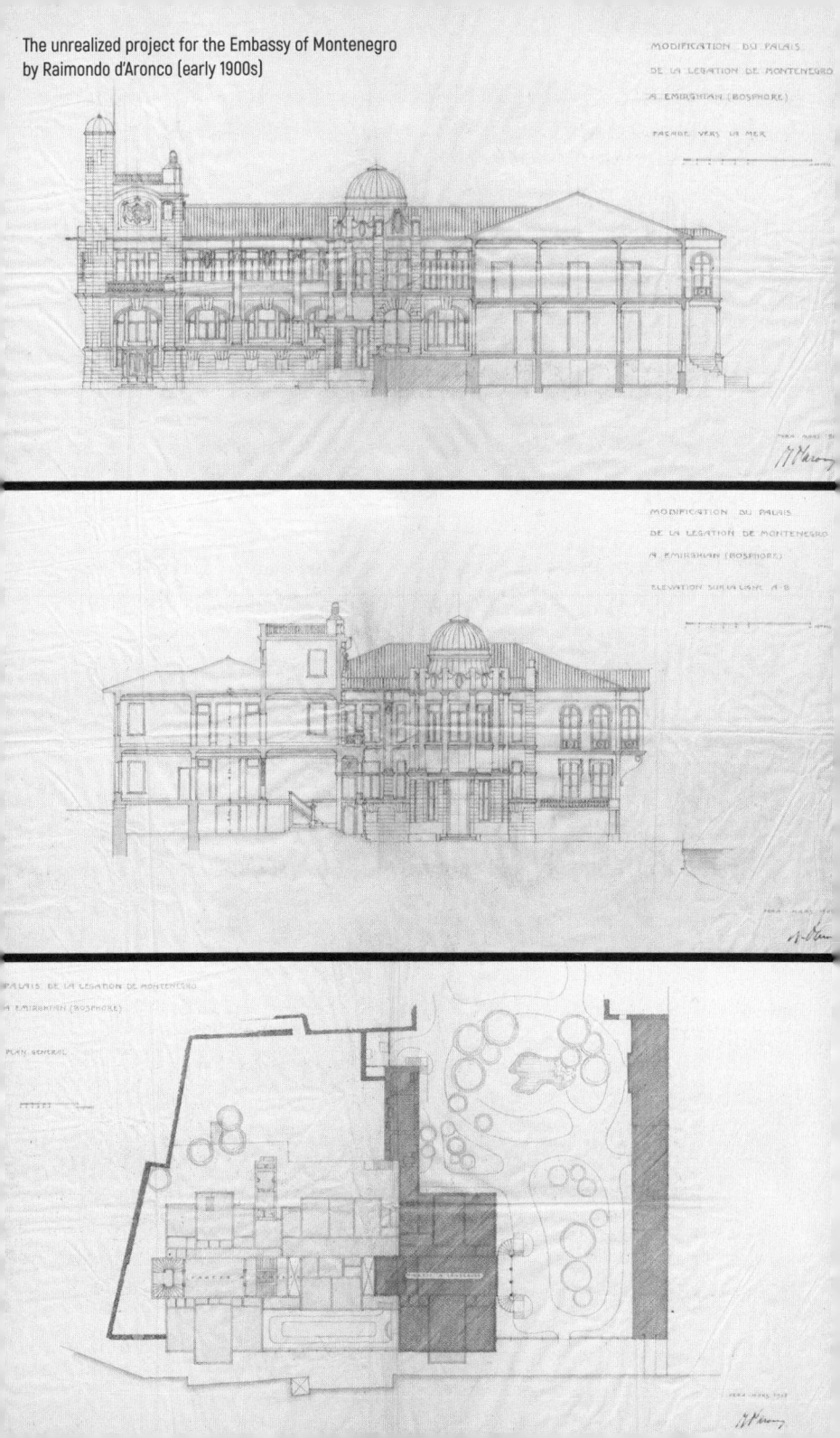

The unrealized project for the Embassy of Montenegro by Raimondo d'Aronco (early 1900s)

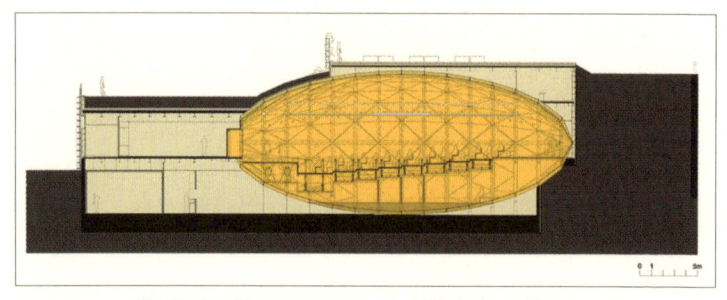

The Seed multipurpose event space of the Sabancı Museum

dynasty, was sold back to Prince Mehmet Ali Hasan from the same family (dynasty of Muhammad Ali).

Almost a hundred years later after the failure of Raimondo d'Aronco's project, a modern building was built on the same land. This is one of those modern structures which are still considered unusual on the Bosphorus. For some unclear reason, the name of this modern building is in English: The Seed. We could still entertain the idea that it was an acronym starting with the "S" of Sabancı had it not been for the article "the" in the beginning. The design belongs to Architect Nevzat Sayın and his team.

The French horse statue and the gardens of the Sabancı Museum

The interior of the Seed

It cannot be said that the structure is in direct harmony to the spirit of the Bosphorus. However, it took a considerable effort to build and it achieved the remarkable success of not violating the legally "untouchable" view of the Bosphorus. Hence, its highly ambitious interior cannot be perceived from the sea. It does not reveal any hints about its interior even from a close distance.

The main building of the Sabancı Museum

The shell of the newly built volume, seen from the exterior, reminds us of terraced walls. And when looked more carefully, it is clearly seen that they are actually stones in metal cages. These stones are from the excavation work for the building. A 21st century version of what we have seen in the building of the American edifices of Bosphorus University: a significant amount of the building's material was obtained from the foundation excavation.

The result was so natural that there are some people who state that these walls had been there much earlier and that they had been built there to terrace the hill. Anyway, the architect says almost the same thing: "The exterior wall is the rebuilt version of the wall which had been there before. As we were rebuilding it, we wanted to have a new wall in memory of the older version."

As we move higher in the garden, we reach the much older rampant horse statue of *Atlı Köşk*, which was made in the 19th century in France, and which had been owned by other people and displayed at other locations before it was brought here.

As we come along the road, we observe that the landscape of the slope is very much "cornered" due to interventions like the one we mentioned.

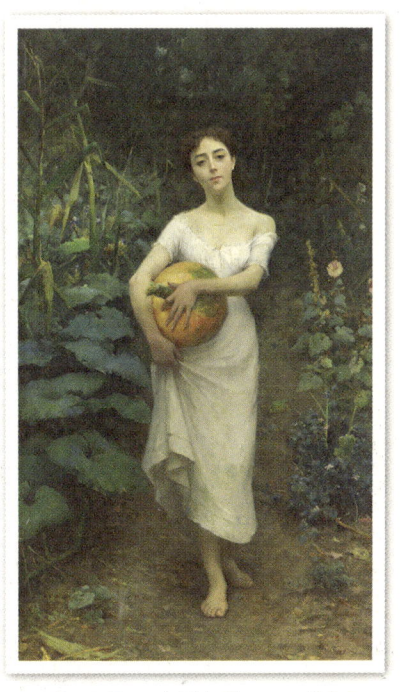

Fausto Zonaro's "girl with a pumpkin"

"Tughra"s from the Sabancı calligraphy collection

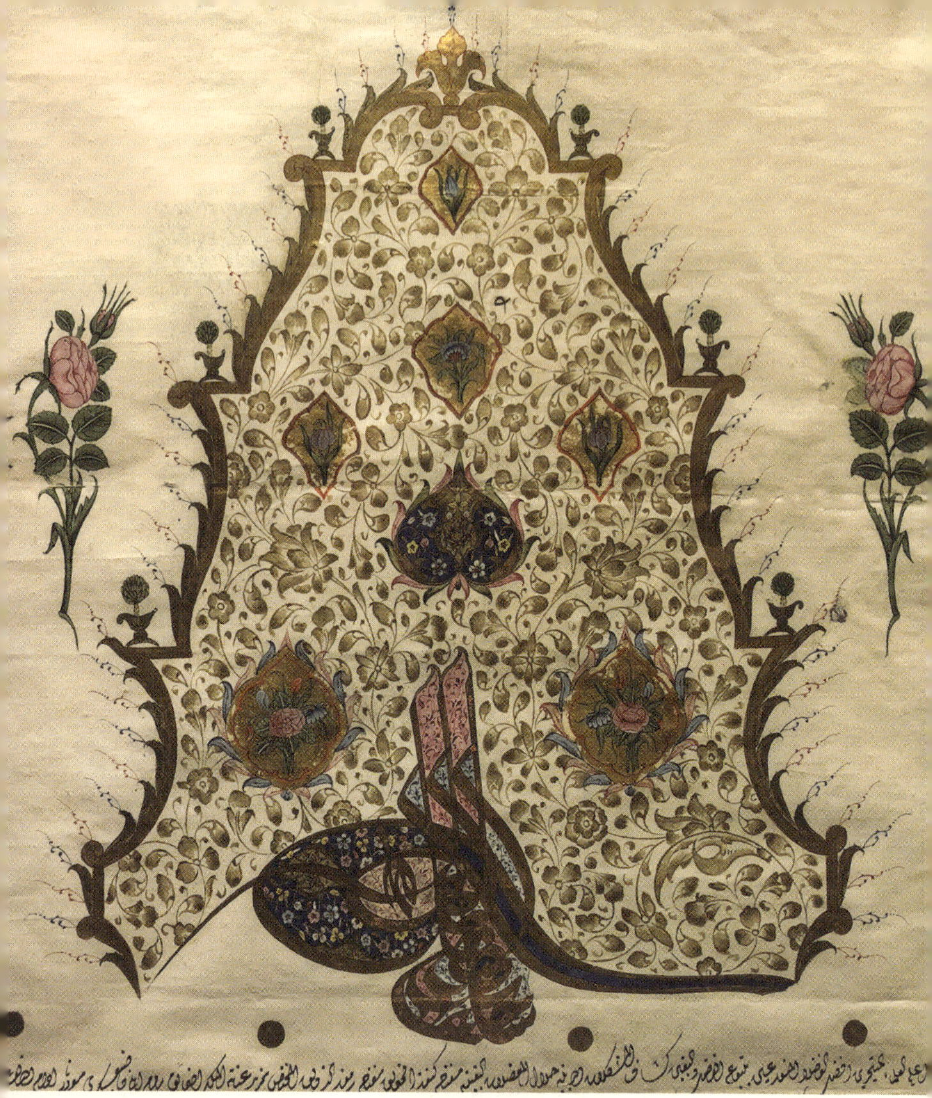

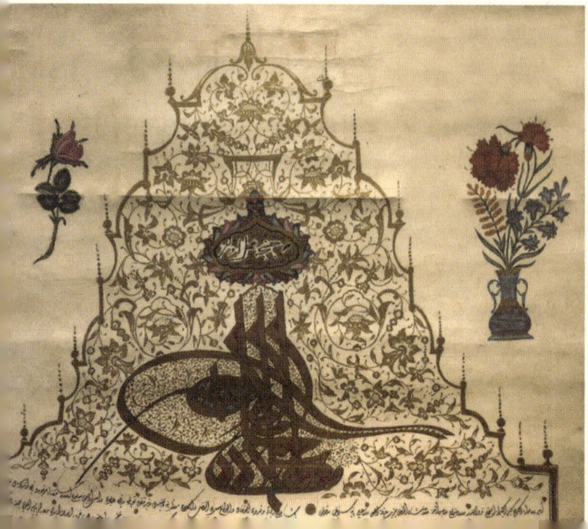

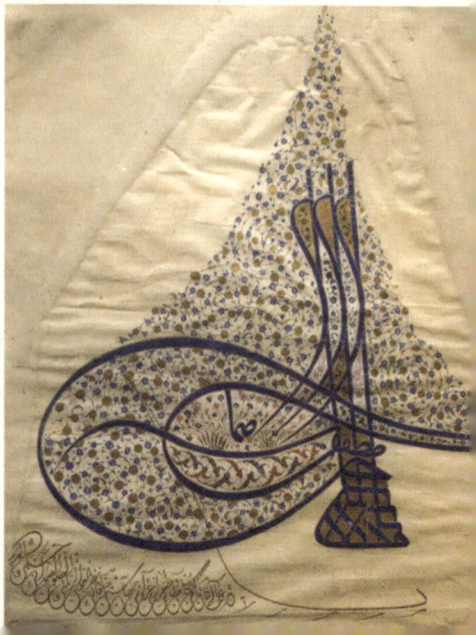

It is worth climbing up the slope to reach the mansion.

By the way, the Egyptian Prince Mehmet Ali Hasan Pasha, the owner of the mansion, never had a chance to live here in the mansion that was designed in the 1920s by the Italian Architect Edoardo de Nari. Initially, it was assigned for other members of his family, and the land was later sold by his heirs to Hacı Ömer Sabancı. It was thus moved to its present function: the Sakıp Sabancı Museum of Sabancı University.

We already stated that its name is frequently mentioned in connection with exhibitions, but the museum is well worth visiting frequently for the mansion together with its items of furniture and the permanent collections of calligraphy and art even when there is no exhibition.

The Emirgan woodlot is located behind the mansion. Its owners, Khedive Ismail Pasha's heirs, sold the land to Satvet Lütfi Tozan, an arms dealer of the period. The extraordinarily beautiful woodlot later became the public property of the Municipality of Istanbul. Nowadays it is particularly famous for its tulips.

The area from Emirgan to the cape, Tokmak Burnu, is the land of İsmail Pasha Mansions and Woodlot. These mansions

Tulips, Emirgan Woodlot

A villa (1930s) by Orhan Adaş, respecting the plane tree

have been demolished and their lands were subdivided. There are a small number of villa-like houses spread over a wide area around the cape. Since housing is not dense, the name of the location is not mentioned very often and is usually quickly forgotten. The ones we see first as we arrive are the three villas on an elevation of one floor a little bit set back from the road. The first is the Muhlis Erdener villa built by Seyfi Arkan between 1939 and 1940; the second is the Uşaklıgil Mansion by Sedad Hakkı Eldem from the 1960s, and the third is a mansion by Orhan Adaş from 1939.

The architect of the last mansion designed a smaller volume behind the plane tree on the land and a larger volume where the plane tree does not reach. Apparently, he thus prevented people from making possible plans for cutting down the tree to have a better view. This noble plane tree is known to be older than 250 years. Most of the trees spotted relatively recently at the Uşaklıgil Mansion have unfortunately since died. It is still evident that there used to be a narrow passageway in front of these houses and no coastal road as wide as the current one was planned.

After leaving the cape (*Tokmak Burnu*), we can come across the 'Halas' vessel if it is not on a journey. 'Halas' is presently used as a flybridge, but actually, it is a Bosphorus ferry. The production of the ferry for the '*Şirket-i Hayriye*' in Britain was commissioned just before the World War I broke out. Two events mark its story: First, the ferry, which was going to be part of the company's fleet with the name 'Reşit Pasha', was seized by the British at the shipyard. Then, after being used even to lay mines, it came to Istanbul in 1918 but stayed at the service of the British occupation forces for four years. Only after the Armistice of Mudania, it was entrusted to its real owner and it assumed its present name meaning "Salvation."

The next place we will notice is Müşir Fuat Pasha Waterfront Mansion. The only surviving structure is its *selamlık* (men's section). There used to be a harem a bit further towards the cove and a hill pavillion on the slope further behind, but they no longer survive. The manager of İstinye Shipyard used to live in the mansion for a period, prior to which it was used as a workshop. It was also previously used as the summer residence of the Iranian Embassy. The building is presently used

Halas ferry and the Fuat Pasha mansion

as the International Permanent Secretariat of the Black Sea Economic Cooperation by the Ministry of Foreign Affairs.

In order not to confuse the two Fuat Pashas, let us state from the beginning that the one here is not the Keçecizade that we remember from the Kanlıca Agreements. Müşir Fuat Pasha was associated more with the Fenerbahçe district.

There is a steel and glass building of the Vessel Traffic Management Information System headquarters where the harem section of the Fuat Pasha Mansion once was located: seeing this building reminds us of the great effort and cutting-edge technology used for managing the sea traffic of the Bosphorus. Without such efforts and investments, we might have to face more unimaginable accidents. The system is operated with the most advanced technology. It was established 15 years ago by the Lockheed Martin Company, which is known for their ambitious warplanes like F16 and F35.

Beyond this point, we begin to lose sight of the coastal road for a time. When the coastal road reemerges at the cove, something unique can be witnessed: this is one of those rare areas of the Bosphorus with access to the view and where daily life continues among shops. We cannot know whether it can stay like this. Soon we will see that the inner gulf area in Tarabya was gradually turned into entertainment venues.

Vessel Traffic Management Information System headquarters

Yeniköy: Place of Mansions and Cavafy

Once the cove ends, the road disappears again, and we can see a series of Yeniköy waterfront mansions.

"*Yeni*" means "new" in Turkish. It is a tradition in Istanbul to designate residential areas and buildings as "old" and "new." This is valid both for the Byzantine and Ottoman eras. *Nea Ecclessia* ("New Church") or *Yeni Cami* ("New Mosque") along with the old and new hammams in Eyüp are a few examples. It is clear that *Yeniköy* ("New Village") was founded during the Ottoman era, most probably in the 17th century. After the end of the 18th century, it evolved from a small, old fishing village into a neighborhood preferred by the prominent Greek and Armenian families serving the Ottoman State. The patriarchs of Jerusalem also preferred spending the summer months in this small neighborhood. It is known that there was at least three Greek districts named after their churches (*Aya Nikola, Aya Yorgi and Panagia*).

In the back, there is the Osman Reis Mosque which is not readily noticeable if one does not look carefully. There is another pleasant surprise here: as the niche of the mosque opens up into the garden between the mansions, we will come across a surprising relief as it has quite an unobstructed view of the Bosphorus.

The small mosque is the product of the architect's attempt to revive the Ottoman forms and motifs. The colorful decorations adorning the interior serve this ambition, and they create the effect of tiled surfaces.

The mansion which partially obscures this mosque and makes it difficult to notice its dazzling dynamism, is also the work of the same architect Alessandro Vallauri who was mentioned earlier in reference to his other works along the Bosphorus and in Istanbul. He designed both the mosque and the mansion for the same

Two works by Alessandro Vallauri together: Ahmet Afif Pasha Mansion and Osman Reis Mosque (partial view)

person (Ahmet Afif Pasha). However, the unexpected variety of styles produces different stylistic effects.

It is certain that Vallauri is an architect who diligently studied some fundamental aspects of Ottoman residential architecture. The sequence of windows, sizes and proportions, mass movements, the role and aesthetics of protrusions and finally the place of the eaves (beyond its function) were of great concern for Vallauri during the design process. From the perspective of Bosphorus buildings and his studies of the same, we can define him as the "Sedad Hakkı Eldem of the 19th century"; indeed, Sedad Hakkı did in the 20th what Vallauri had done

Yeniköy has a big variety of waterfront mansions.

in the 19th. Both mixed research, creativity and productivity following their contemporaries, leaving a lot of original works on the shores of the Bosphorus.

The Afif Pasha Mansion and the enormous wooden Greek Orphanage in Büyükada and the Yanyalı Mustafa Pasha Mansion, which has not survived, are some original examples of Vallauri's stylistic attempts.

It could be highlighted that Vallauri made use of the Ottoman "Baroque" style in the Afif Pasha Mansion. The elegant towers offer specially designed lightness to the recreational atmosphere of the Bosphorus.

The following waterfront mansion, the Ebu Ratip Efendi Yalı attracts attention with its still, but proportional body. The Ottoman residential architecture was reproduced with the harmony of the ratios of floor and windows. It stands out with the features of a "pavilion-mansion."

The Selahattin Adil Pasha Residence is distinguished with both its modern style and as an example of the characteristics of an American/European summer resort. We can find similar ones with timber and cast-iron details, as well. The buildings are very different from the traditional waterfront architecture of the Bosphorus. An asymmetrical mass, balconies embracing the waters of the Bosphorus along some classical decorative elements add movement to the building.

In his memoirs, Selahattin Adil Pasha, who, after his military career remained in the defense industry as a commission agent, states that he had health problems due to the difficulties he had during the construction of this building. He states that he went to a sanatorium 1939 because of these health issues. However, he does not tell us when the mansion was completed. The pasha passed away here, at home in 1961.

The Tahsin Yücel Mansion from the year 1938 is one of the earlier projects of Sedad Hakkı Eldem. In a way evoking the Hasip Pasha Mansion, which we will see in Beylerbeyi, the mansion stands out with its curvilinear and convex midsection. Eldem also found an opportunity to revise and extend the building around 40 years later. The present condition of the mansion mostly reflects this second phase.

The next *yalı* is distinctive with its continuing series of balconies in its façade on both floors. It is currently used as a restaurant. There are large spaces in front of it and along its

A Minister and a Prime Minister owned two of the houses in this row.

sides which are covered with mainly plastic canopies that have no distinct design features.

After these mansions, which are located on wide plots of flat land and which are more in line with the Bosphorus tradition, we again come by a group of adjacent mansions on narrow plots.

First is another work by Sedad Hakkı Eldem that was completed in 1967. Soon after, it was praised as "an architectural masterpiece with national characteristics that contribute to the surrounding buildings. The mansion, although located in a historical environment, does not distort the texture, it even contributes to it with harmony". It was built for a former minister, Mr. Reşat Şemsettin Sirer.

By the way Sirer is the person who dismissed İsmail Hakkı Tonguç from the General Directorate of Primary Education during his ministry of National Education as he considered Tonguç a leader of purported communist activities at *the Köy Enstitüleri* ("Village Institutes"), founded to train teachers for rural regions of Anatolia. Mr. Sirer also held the office as the Minister of Labor, and he is remembered for his experimental approach to

Şehzade (Prince) Burhaneddin Efendi mansion and its hill pavilion

strikes and democracy: "If they say they don't want any squabble with strikes and lockouts ... which do no good to anybody, it would mean that a democracy without any strikes and lockouts emerged. This would be what the majority demands."

Next, there is a mansion, which kept Dr. Rasim Ferit Talay's (a close friend of Atatürk's, b. 1888) name alive for a long time and which later became famous with the name of Prof. Tansu Çiller, the only female Prime Minister of Turkey (1993-1996). The round dormer window, which did not exist in the original design, is now the distinct feature of the mansion.

Further on we have one of the most splendid coastal residences of the Bosphorus which have survived to this day: *Şehzade* (Prince) Burhaneddin Efendi Mansion. It is remarkable not only for its splendor, but also for the fact that it still reflects some traditional features. Although its bridge was demolished during the expansion of the Köybaşı Street behind it, the terraced gardens in the back still belong to the mansion. The mansion was connected with the other buildings of the complex including the pink one on the side of the hill, which has timber panels over a concrete surface, but at least has the same color as the mansion. The pavilion is used as an apartment with its flats being rented.

If you walk behind it, there is the beginning of an arch which slightly protrudes from the wall on the pavement on the opposite side towards the road. This is a trace of the bridge which enabled passage to the woodlot and, which had been demolished during the road expansion.

This mansion is followed by a series of three adjacent mansions: the one on the left has the features of chalet architecture, but it also showcases some elements of the Victorian style summer houses, mostly seen on the Asian side which are known as "Erenköy Pavilions". The Cemil Topuzlu Pavilion in Caddebostan is an example that comes close to some aspects of the

Three mansions in a row; different styles seem to stay together unwillingly.

"national architecture" seen at the beginning of the 20th century. The one in the middle could be stylistically defined as Victorian with its general characteristics and especially with its festooned eaves. Its eaves and balconies accentuate its lightness.

The Kara Todori Mansion on the far left is somehow an unusual example of architecture of Istanbul and even more so for the Bosphorus. This one has an air of a European urban palace. Within the context of Ottoman architecture, its first impression is that of a public building rather than part of the residential architecture. It almost brings in a solemn spirit to the lighter air of the Bosphorus with its simple neoclassical composition.

There was once the trendy Carlton Hotel where the present car parking area is located. It was the only large hotel of the Bosphorus other than the Tarabya Hotel. It was discovered that it was unstable during the renovation work in 1986 and was demolished to avoid any risk. Actually, a ship had crashed into this waterfront hotel, but the building had survived the crash.

Sait Halim Pasha Mansion

It could have been an important touristic center of attraction with its more than a hundred rooms and the possibility of using it together with the Sait Halim Pasha Mansion next to it. However, the project could not be realized despite the attempts to rebuild it for more than a decade.

Thanks to the open space here, we can see the Aya Nikola Orthodox Church and the old Greek School (today part of the Tarabya British Schools) just above it. Although it has a small mass, its completely brick surface greatly adds to the attraction of the building.

Once we look towards the shore, we come across the Sait Halim Pasha Mansion. The present mansion actually constitutes only a limited part of the property. The woodlot covering most of the hill behind it is actually the mansion's garden. Its small and elegant pavilion, restored by Architect Dr. Sinan Genim, is still in the woodlot. We know that there once used to be more than one bridge from the mansion to the woodlot. A truss bridge of the harem section and an open bridge near the *selamlık* is a tradition that can be seen in many large mansions. The mansion was demolished during the road expansion work in 1958. It burned down almost entirely in 1995, and it was rebuilt under the guidance of Architect Acar Avunduk.

The first owners of this property were the Düzyan/Düzoğlu family, a Catholic Armenian family who managed the palace mint and later fell from grace. The mansion then became the property of the Aristarkhis family , and the existing building was completely rebuilt in its present form. Its architect was Petraki Adamandisis from Çanakkale. He was the father of Architect Victor Adaman who built the Beşiktaş Tobacco Warehouse. The father of Sait Halim Pasha bought it from the Greek family, and when the father passed away, the Pasha has acquired their shares of the inheritance and became the sole owner of the mansion.

Sait Halim Pasha, who held the office as the Grand Vizier for four years during the most challenging times of the Ottoman state, resigned from his post in 1917 and he was assassinated in 1921 in Rome. After his death, his funeral was held at his mansion and then was buried in the burial grounds near

Sait Halim Pasha's tomb

the tomb of Mahmut II. Following the demise of Sait Halim Pasha, the property lost its integrity as the mansion and the large surrounding land was divided into smaller parcels. It is frequently told that the secret agreement which brought the Ottoman Empire into World War I with Germany was signed at this mansion.

This edifice was for a period of time home to a casino whose majority partner was a foreign company. Those who complain about bureaucracy today might find consolation in the fact that those who made money out of gambling in those days had to write the amount of money they won on their passports if they wanted to spend their foreign currency.

Sait Halim Pasha made changes in the mansion in line with his eclectic personal taste: for example, he added an "Egyptian" room to the mansion. The mansion used to have spaces where the Ottoman atmosphere was accentuated with tiles from Kütahya, Louis XIV style furniture, Japanese influences, Orientalist paintings and Italian touch. Today, the mansion has

An Italian style waterfront home

lost much of its former splendor because of the fire of 1995 and its new function as an events venue.

Has any building ever benefited from a fire? Perhaps it is some cold comfort, but the rebuilding process after the fire has cleared some of earlier restorations that altered some of its original features. So, it could be argued that the mansion somehow benefited from the fire. Of course, locals had become accustomed to its appearance as it was restored by Sedad Hakkı Eldem before the fire. The harsh restoration lacked its lantern, which was, for Eldem, against the features of Ottoman architecture. Now it has assumed back its original form. The two lion statues facing the sea are the most well-known components of the complex. They are presently in glass showcases.

A residence built by the Italian Architect Paolo Vietti Violi, better known for his sports facilities, is the next structure we come across. This small palace combines 20th century modernism with traditional elements. It is not a typical Bosphorus structure; its location by the waterfront brings to mind the image of canal, river, and lake structures of the architectural works of Venetian canals and elsewhere in Europe. The splendid composition of buildings on the shore and the columnar entrance of the main building are signs of palace-villa architecture. Its "Palladian" windows, symmetrical arrangement and balanced

A twin waterfront mansion by Raimondo d'Aronco with traditional Ottoman motives

The Armenian Catholic Church of Saint John the Baptist's interior

composition bring it closer to the architecture of Palladio and the urban and rural architecture of 16th century Northern Italy.

The twin mansions of Faik Bey and Bekir Bey is one of d'Aronco's original designs which he realized with a consideration of the traditional Bosphorus style and using traditional Ottoman forms. He adapted the small niches of traditional architecture into a façade by enlarging them to gigantic proportions. He accentuated the curvilinear eaves in the middle which gives it a Baroque impression. Finally, the shape of the windows with small openings and the miniature lodges in the middle together with the whole composition has created a Neo-Ottoman scene facing the Bosphorus.

The same church, view from the sea

After a while, the coastal road on the northern side of the İstinye Gulf meets the sea again. At this very point, we can look towards the slope and see the Surp Hovhannes Mıgırdıç (St. John the Baptist) Armenian Church on the very first terrace. Since it was built with an eastern orientation, its apse, instead of its façade, faces the Bosphorus. Since it is on a slope, its buttresses enjoy a majestic dominance over the view. Its interior, on the other hand, is exceedingly plain and humble. The entrance is on the opposite side towards the road. There is a recently renovated mansion in front of it. Its boathouse was covered with glass and looks like it has been turned into a living room.

Once we pass the boathouse, we come to the Cezaryirliyan Mansion which is separated from the sea only by the coastal road. The mansion was built for Mıgırdıç Cezaryirliyan (1805-1861). He was both a silk producer and a merchant, who was also remembered for his philanthropy on the one hand, and with the vast amounts of credits he extended to some of the prominent names of the period on the other. Mustafa Reşit Pasha and the Egyptian Khedive Abbas Hilmi Pasha were among

Cezayirliyan Mansion; currently owned by the Austrian Consulate General

his clients. It is also known that he was the owner of Istanbul customs when he was at the peak of his power.

The architect of the building is Hagop Mèlik (or Mèlikian), one of the first Ottoman students at the Ecole de Beaux-Arts in Paris. The construction began in 1849. Dozens of workers from France were brought for the job. However, Cezayirliyan was unable enjoy his mansion even for a minute, because he was defamed and all his property was seized before he could even pay for the construction. The funeral of Cezayirliyan was a grand one thanks to the great number of people who felt thankful to him due to his philanthropy. Documents reveal that the building was used as a hospital for Italian soldiers during the Crimean War which broke out shortly after the dramatic downfall of Cezayirliyan. When it was used as the summer residence of the Embassy of the Austro-Hungarian Empire, it was not in good condition as it can be observed on the photographs of the period.

The building, which hosts the Austrian Consulate and the Austrian Culture Office today, reveals a clear and distinct union of masses in a solid symmetry when viewed from the sea. The middle of its three sections that extend to the front is highlighted, which is an expected move of architectural design. A triangular pediment, a familiar element of the temple

The Mansion when it was being restored by the Austrians (late 19th century)

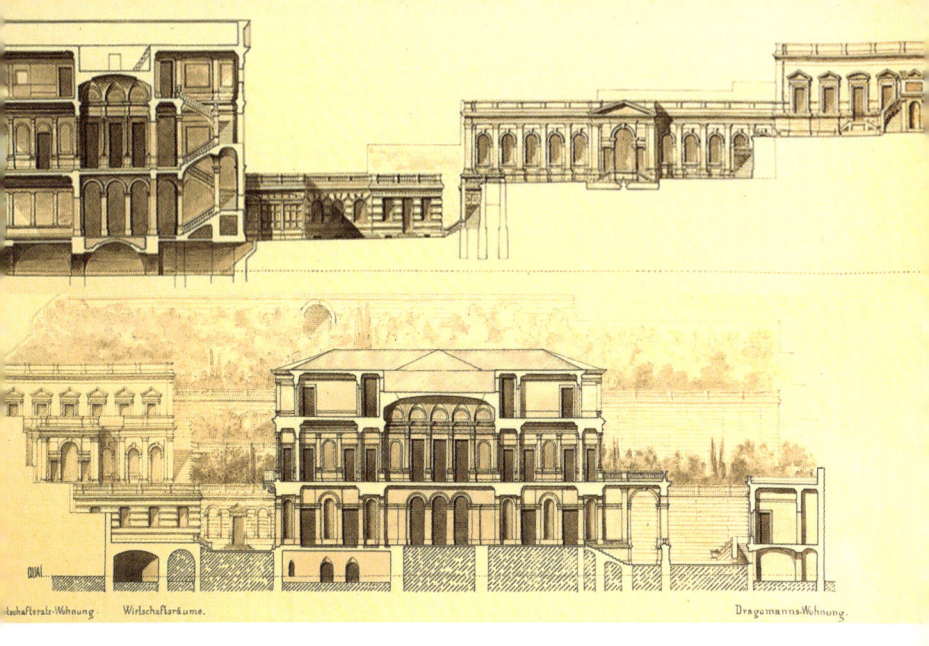

Architectural drawings of the mansion showing part of its terraces

architecture, completes the composition. The top and the two corners again are highlighted with components of the architecture of the antiquity. A double-headed eagle on the inner surface of the pediment has opened its wings majestically. The building is essentially a continuation of Renaissance architecture in the 19th century with its arrangement of windows, railings and repeated column-like components on its entire façade.

The land rises up in terraces, and its depth towards the slope is much more than its width. This is a tradition of Bosphorus mansions. A drawing and photographs kept at the Austrian States Archives show how the building looked when it was transferred to the Austro-Hungarian Empire during the reign of Sultan Abdülhamit II. The goals of the restoration are also revealed in these documents in detail.

When the Austro-Hungarian Empire was divided into two different states, Austria emerged as the lucky party following the division of their shared international properties: The mansion is still owned by Austria. Although the building is not open to visitors, it is possible to enter on days when there are events. Keeping an eye on the Austrian Cultural Office's events program is ideal for planning such a visit.

Before leaving Yeniköy, we can remember that the poet Constantine P. Cavafy (1863-1933), whose many poems were translated into English and several other languages., spent time here between the ages of 19 and 22 and even wrote poems about Yeniköy in his later years.

Huber: an Arms Dealer in the Bosphorus

One solitary structure on the shore shares a garden with an anonymous concrete building behind it, is the Kalender Pavilion. One can observe that there is a deep valley in the back with alluvial land. These fields were a popular recreational area during the Ottoman period. It is named after Kalender Çavuş, the construction official of the Sultanahmet Mosque (1616). The sultans used the pavilion here during daily excursions. It presently has the same appearance as it did after it was built during the reign of Sultan Abdülaziz. We know from old photographs that it was surrounded by high walls, but the walls

Arms dealer Mr. Huber's home, now the President's summer residence

were demolished when the road was widened, and it started to look like a roadside building. It was used as a school for a time. Afghanistan requested to use it as the summer residence of their embassy in 1938, but the project could not be realized, because even if it was officially assigned as such, soldiers were stationed in it. The process of its being transferred to the Ministry of National Defence continued in the 1940s and 1950s. The building was called as "*Yanık Kalender Köşkü*" (Burnt Kalender Mansion) during this period. It is still part of the Officers' Club. Its restoration will soon be completed.

The next building is the Huber Mansion. Its owner, the rich arms dealer Mr. Huber was connected to an ever-increasing arms trade during the last periods of the Ottoman Empire as it moved closer to Germany. "*Mösyö Huber Biraderler*" (Monsieur Huber Brothers) as the Ottomans called them, were the '*Dersaadet* Agency', the Istanbul representatives of the Krupp and Mauser companies. Krupp produced cannons and the Mauser company was known for its rifles in Anatolia (the name of the company '*mavzer*,' is still a common Turkish name for riffles). Considering the fact that the number of Mauser rifles in the army during the reign of Abdülhamit II approached one million, one should not be surprised by August Huber's owning a mansion with a woodlot of tens of thousands square meters.

Similarly, with the Ottomans and Germans losing World War I, the Huber family's leaving this mansion was quite normal. After changing hands several times after it was bought from its beneficiaries (it was used as a school run by French nuns for a period of time then another owner decided to transform it into a hotel), it was expropriated in 1985 to repurpose it as the Presidential Summer Residence. Two modern buildings were added up on the hill in the direction of Kalender for the new function of the building. These two new additions are not easily discernible because they are located above the eye level and partially hidden among trees. These are the main office spaces.

The historical units of the mansion are on a 5-meter-high terrace by the sea. These were recently restored. The architect of the historical buildings is not known, but the latest expansion and adaptation were realized by the Italian architect Raimondo d'Aronco - whose name as we have already seen is frequently mentioned in connection to the Bosphorus.

Next to the Huber Mansion are the summer residences of the German Embassy. The unity of these buildings, their view, and being located in a large forest area almost recall the German countryside. All of this is accompanied by a diligently arranged garden. The main building, its tower, and the arched middle part with a perpendicular roof are partially influenced by Victorian architecture. We come across such buildings in American and European summer resorts. The same style, as might be accepted, dominated the summer houses of Istanbul during the Ottoman era, especially on the Asian side around the Bosphorus as well as Yeşilköy.

The young architect Armin Wegner, the executor of the project, states that he actually pursued an opposite approach: He preferred an *"alaturka"* (Turkish style) timber building, instead of an *"alafranga"* (European style) stone building. It is also stated that the Ottoman structures in the garden, like the hammam, were kept in respect for the sultan (127).

There is a restaurant nearby which is located on piles in the sea. Its architect is likely Kadri Eroğan, who also designed the Tarabya Hotel. The restaurant was covered with a brick-like (possible polymer) material. There used to be friezes of exposed concrete on the cloakroom/reception counter of the building.

The Summer Palace, a summer hotel just across, was closed down in 1950 and the area was subdivided into residential parcels. It is presently named as the *Sümer* Woodlot (with an incorrect reference to the Sumerians simply because the English word "summer" was not understood by locals). Of all the

Sometimes pieces of contemporary architecture are hidden in the woodlots.

luxurious and large buildings, one of the most recently built ones is the work of architect Ahmet Alataş, an example of a modern residence.

While these buildings were only used as summer houses in the past, they are now used throughout the year. There was a tradition of spending the winters in more central neighborhoods of Istanbul and taking refuge on the breezy shores of the Bosphorus during summer. On even hotter days, people moved to the mansions up on the hills. There are many reasons that this tradition no longer exists. Nowadays, when the summer comes, people tend to escape Istanbul's heat and prefer even hotter places like the Mediterranean with its hellish heat.

Tarabya Stream is also an example of a deep estuary. The stream, which once formed the gulf, is no longer visible, but its name lives on in the Dereiçi Street that goes inland. Once, it was largely a Greek neighborhood; the main mansions are still named after the names of the Greek families, former owners of the mansions. It might be called an irony of fate: the ones used as restaurants still carry their former owners' names and their names are thus still remembered.

The northern end of the gulf is dominated by the Grand Tarabya Hotel which extends outwards and covers the corner completely. Previously, the owners of the famous Tokatlıyan Hotel of the İstiklal Street in Pera kept this place as their summer business. However, it shared the same tragic fate of many timber buildings. At its place, Tarabya Hotel, designed by architect Kadri Eroğan, was built as a block building in stark contrast with the architectural traditions of the Bosphorus. The new project needed a larger space than the former timber hotel, and some adjacent lands were expropriated for a larger touristic area. The hotel was operated for many years as the property of the government retirement fund. After a long restoration and a significant amount of investment, it was later completely renovated.

The summer residence of the Italian Embassy (early 20th century)

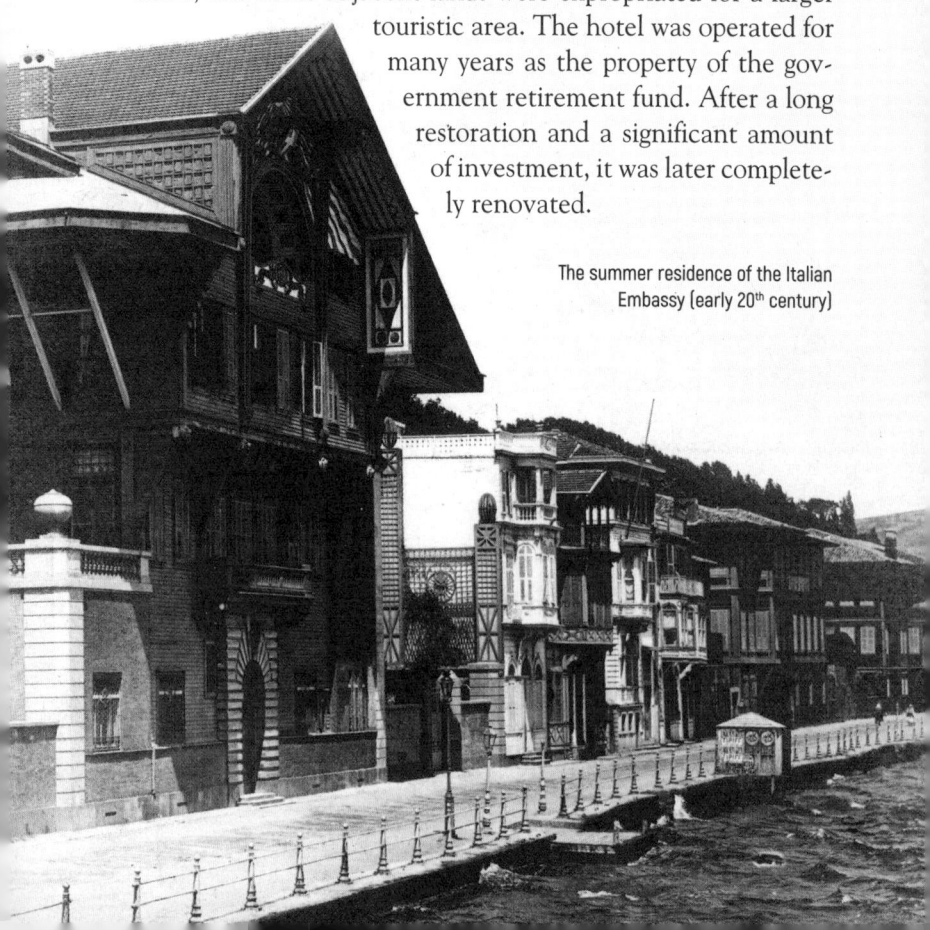

The next structure we see is a sad sight, as it looks like it is waiting for its sad end behind the scaffolds. It used to be the summer residence of the Italian embassy in the Bosphorus. Once again, its architect was Raimondo d'Aronco.

As seen clearly in old photographs, there used to be a timber building with a narrower façade along the coast. Later, the architect from Udine was commissioned for the construction of this new one. It has a small woodlot behind it, which has a typical Bosphorus garden with several terraces.

The unique architecture of the building is unfortunately not discernible today. Yet when looked closely, however, we see all the defining characteristics of Raimondo d'Aronco: his unpredictability, his harmonizing the extremes and opposites, his ability to blend different cultures together seamlessly. D'Aronco achieved all these intensively and naturally. The agreement of stone and timber is also another example of the same harmony of balance and oppositions.

A door with a stone frame on the seaside mainly manifests itself with its material. On the axis of this door, higher up towards the tip of the pediment, lies a series of architectural elements protruding into the sea. The load of the balcony is on two cantilevers on each corners of the door and with three arched windows, a bay window above this balcony is carried by more protruded cantilevers and at the top another balcony bordered with a single arch that covers the three arches below.

A triangular pediment, as wide as the building itself, has very deep eaves and hangs over the whole façade facing the sea. The eaves are cut abruptly on the southern direction in an asymmetric manner and turns into a wide composition in which the eaves dominate the garden. The entrance below is located on a timber mezzanine terrace one floor above the ground. Despite all this emphasis on the seaside façade, the real entrance to the building is on the side façade which is reached through the garden. The

A well-disguised contemporary office

wide eaves which cover the terrace here completely are at present so derelict that they cannot be discerned.

Restorations plans have been made for a very long time with a sort of build operate transfer model, but no final decision has been made yet. The hope of passersby is that the necessary steps can be taken before it will be too late. The building is also significant in the sense that it is the only housing project of Raimondo d'Aronco that has survived to this day in its original form (129).

Next, we come across a grey-colored narrow building just next to the mansion. One could complain about the fact that there are only very few examples of modern architecture in the Bosphorus. A pleasantly executed exception welcomes us here. The timber residence of the past was long ago destroyed and turned into an ugly mass of concrete and the Architect Ahmet Alataş has transformed the building into an office space in harmony with the materials and expectations of our century in the same mass and again in a timber shell.

Next is the İpsilanti Mansion complex; a small unit of it was fortunately able to survive to this day. The mansion was used as a summer residence by the French embassy. It has a woodlot which covers a large part of the slope. The property has long been used for educational purposes. The Ipsilanti Mansion was actually a much larger building. The section which is seen today was only the "*dragoman*" (translator) quarters of the embassy. As seen in old photographs, it was a neoclassical building with a triangular pediment, but when the main building, which was closer to Ottoman style, disappeared, this stucture was reshaped to to look like the long-gone building. It was allocated to Marmara University for a time, for the department of public

Memduh Pasha's mansion by Raimondo d'Aronco

administration, where courses were given in French. Apparently, the agreement did not last long. Today, it is difficult to understand why instead of rebuilding the Ipsilanti Mansion on it, the property houses container-type units for educational purposes.

As we pass by the cape Kireçburnu, the most noteworthy building we will see is without any doubt the Memduh Pasha Mansion. This is again the work of Raimondo d'Aronco. Presently, it is not used as a residence, but as an office. It looks quite clean and well-kept after the restoration. Even if it faces the see, the word "waterfront" should be used very carefully for this building (and for many other mansions) when there is the road in front of it. The drawings of the architect reveal that he designed some components (especially the metal parts) to have different colors to enhance the visual effect. It is difficult to discern these nuances in the building because all the components were painted white during the restoration.

The Third Bridge

Seeing the Black Sea

As we pass by this part, we reach the last fold of the Bosphorus. Hence, we see the entrance to the Bosphorus from the Black Sea and the Third Bosphorus Bridge which is an attraction in itself.

The Third Bridge, designed by the French Engineer Michel Virlogeux and built as a Turkish-Italian joint venture, was opened to traffic in 2016. It broke some world records: besides, there is no need to mention that all bridges uniting two continents are unique - and possible only in Turkey. This is also the world's widest suspension bridge, and it has the longest span as a bridge with a railway (not active yet) system.

Since we have just seen the most splendid bridge of the Bosphorus built so far, it could be useful to go back in time and have a look at a number of examples of plans that were never used:

The first of these belongs to Ferdinand Arnodin, and it is dated 1900. Instead of a bridge that directly crossed the Bosphorus, it was designed as a transport bridge, which was popular during those years. Passengers would be transported between Sarayburnu and Üsküdar in cabins suspended beneath

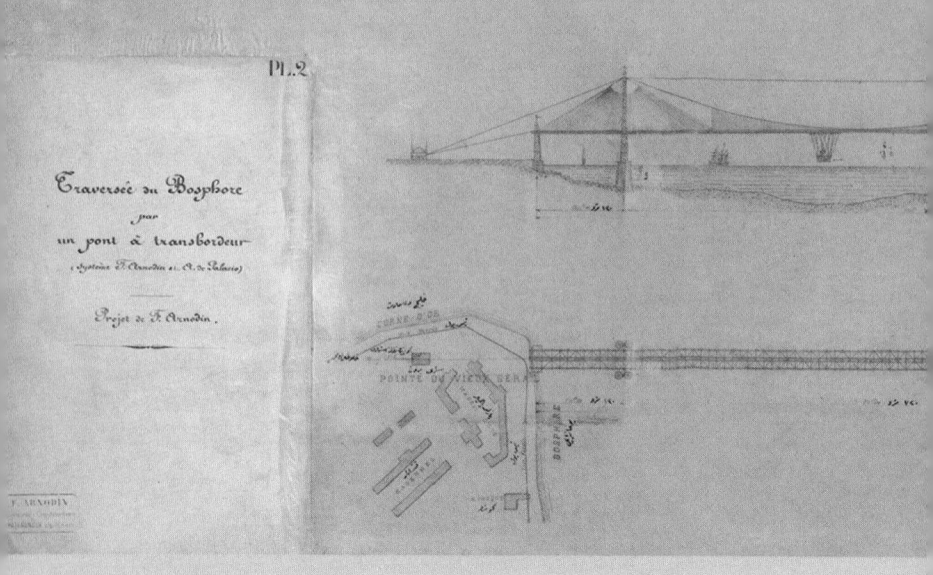

Two unbuilt bridge projects for the Bosphorus (1900)

a mechanism 50 meters above sea level. The anchorage points of the bridge on the opposite side of both continents were designed as miniature mosques with two minarets, which would have added a special Istanbulite flavor to the project. Other than this, it was a completely industrial design.

The second would have had a completely opposite appearance: obviously even its designers knew that it could not be fulfilled, and they were openly inspired by something which could not be imagined and presented an image of the East which was already imaginary. Although it is not much different from the European concept of "transition from one building to another" of its time, the idea of "transition from one mosque to another" added originality to the design.

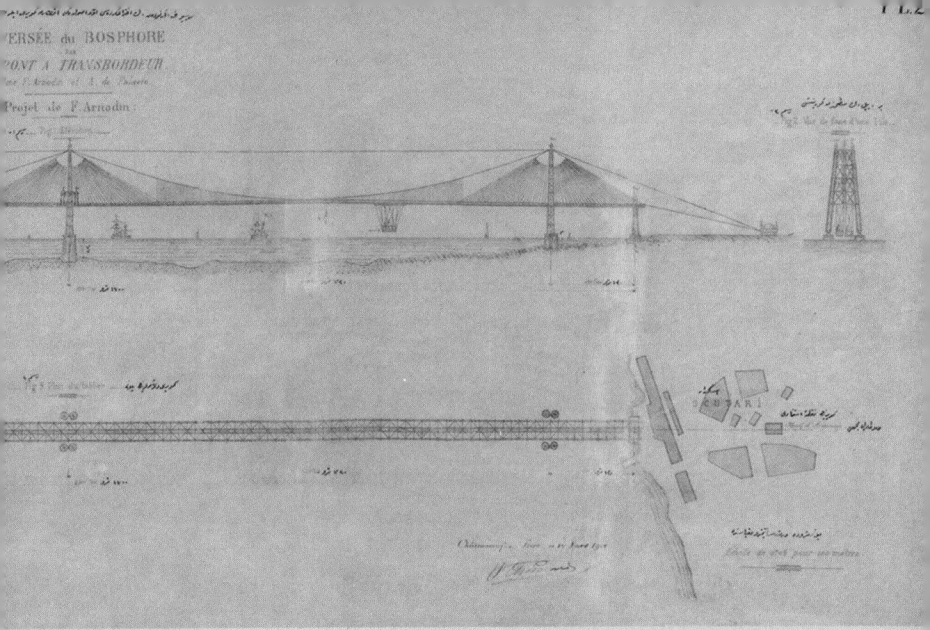

These mosques had no place in the architectural tradition of Istanbul, and they reiterated the characteristics of mosque architecture of Islamic Egypt. These foreign elements made it impossible for them to be a dialogue with Istanbul, especially with the Bosphorus. This project cannot find a place in architecture or engineering, but only in Orientalist art.

Being able to see the Black Sea means we are now able to see the end of the Bosphorus. From now on, there not so many pieces of architectural heritage on the way and reaching the bridge would increase the amount of time of our tour, we will move towards the cape Selvi Burnu on the Asian side and begin to explore the shores of Asia on our way back to the Golden Horn.

Still there are a few things we would miss as we head towards the Asian side of the Bosphorus; it will be good to mention them. If we were to look towards the coast through the cove ahead, we could admire the green texture of the Belgrad Forest just after Büyükdere.

The neighborhood of Büyükdere ("Big Stream"), as its name suggests, refers to a stream which created quite a large alluvial deposit. Without any surprise, there is a football pitch now using a part of the large flat meadow area.

When a nursery garden was decided to be built in Istanbul in 1926, the "Büyükdere Imperial Meadow" was chosen to be the most suitable location. In 1930, Leopoldo Bologna, from Italy, and İbrahim Fuat Tezcan established the Fruit Breeding Institute on an almost 80-decares of land. The institute was established with a vision of international collaboration and the relations with Italy were expected to be long-lasting. The Prime Minister's Archive reveals that collaboration on breeding with Italy lasted until 1960 and there were Italian members of the staff during that time. The area, where we still have similar activities, is not far away from the mosque named after the great sailor Cezayirli Gazi Hasan Pasha.

Shortly after, we come across a building that reflects the characteristics of the First National Architectural Movement:

The Coast Guard Command, formerly Aero Espresso terminal

the sincere proportions, pointed arches and the blue tiles coloring the front façade. Here was born the first airport terminal of Istanbul. The meadow in the back was used for some additional functions like fuel tanks and hangars. Italy's first aircraft company Aero Espresso, a few months after its establishment, rented the entire property in 1924. The company had regular flights from here to Athens (Greece) and Brindisi (Italy) for more than ten years. Later on, with Italy's establishing its national airline company, Aero Espresso stopped its operations. Turkish Airlines' establishment followed not much later.

This area, Büyükdere, was also the major site of industrial brick production that began at the end of the 19th century. We know that the bricks used in most of the buildings in Beyoğlu were produced here. During the dismantling of brick walls, which are the most striking elements of the (haunted) Yusuf Ziya Mansion, it was noticed that some of the materials were from Marseille and others produced in Büyükdere. These bricks were preserved as much as possible and used again in the totally reconstructed current building.

In 1955, one of the most severe landslides of Istanbul took place here. The main causes were the excessive earthmoving for brick production and heavy rain.

The Aero Espresso terminal in 1920s

At the moment, almost all the waterfront mansions, it can be said even the whole Büyükdere neighborhood, are cut off from the sea because of the causeway. The Old Büyükdere Pier is among these structures no longer by the sea. There are some nice shops in it and the shoreside of the pier is operated as a cafe. The pier attracts attention with a group of statues erected on the seaside (their style and aim are difficult to determine).

There is the Surp Boğos Armenian Catholic Church where the causeway meets the coastal land. It is the work of architect Krikor Hürmüzyan, whose name is known only through this building.

Just before that, we have the summer residence of the Spanish Embassy, which is a little bit set back from the sea. Despite all its imported forms, the building is not so far away from the Bosphorus architectural tradition with its symmetrical and balanced body and timber façade, however, when this first impression fades, one notices that the building was designed in the Western tradition enlivened with openings, that is to say mainly with a "loggia" which became part of the architectural repertoire during the Renaissance. The symmetrical and relatively massive components on both sides are crowned with two triangular pediments. The acroteria of these pediments are completely in the neo-Greek style. The inner surface of the pediment is filled with floral motifs creating an Empire style spirit.

On the same row, we next have the Sadberk Hanım Museum, open to the public since 1980. The museum is in the

Aero Espresso hangars

The Armenian Catholic
Saint Paul's Church

mansion named after its former owner, the Catholic Armenian Azaryan family. This mansion preserves its original looks to a great extent. Its residential characteristics are visible in the very suitable arrangement of the museum. It keeps the tradition

The Spanish Embassy's summer residence

alive with its plan including a middle long room. On the façade, its cross bearings highlighting a construction with a timber frame system, its accentuated roof and the arrow-shaped stop element at the top bear are traces of chalet architecture. The mansion is the work of architect Andon Kazazyan, whose name is known only in connection to this building.

After the museum, on this line, which is called Piyasa Street, there are not many noteworthy buildings other than some edifices which are again cut off from the water by the road, though they still have a view of the Bosphorus. One building among these is worth mentioning: a residence by Seyfi Arkan, whose villa we saw earlier.

The summer residence of the Russian Federation is an exception in this dense series of buildings.

Furthermore, the building at the end of Piyasa Street is partially preserved. However, it is only one of the many properties of its owner, and they do not live in it. It has recently become famous as the set of several TV series. It is open to public as an annex of the Sadberk Hanım Museum and houses a permanent exhibit

Sadberk Hanım Museum

Modern architecture on the Bosphorus, a house by Seyfi Arkan

of historic Anatolian carpets. A visit to this museum is also an opportunity to have a look at its terrace gardens behind.

At the end of the road, there is a police station built during the reign of Sultan Reşad (1911). It resembles many other examples of the period and like others, it is decorated with a flamboyant Ottoman coat of arms.

Detail from the Russian Embassy's summer residence

In the meantime, we realize that we have reached the rural settlement of Sarıyer, which extends deeply in land. This area is also an alluvial deposit which indicates the existence of a river. As usual, whenever there is a football pitch close to the sea, one can guess there is an alluvial field in the area. Otherwise, it is not that easy to find a flat lot of land along the hilly Bosphorus where one could play football. Hence, it is certainly not a coincidence that the road from the Yusuf Ziya Öniş Stadium to the Sarıyer Tunnel is called Çırçır *Deresi* (Stream).

Next, we reach Telli Baba in the area of Rumeli Kavağı. There is a tendency to relate the world "*kavak*" (poplar tree in Turkish) to a real poplar tree. There are even some narrators who believe their own story that there are or were "two poplar trees on either side of the Bosphorus." Actually, poplar tree could be of some use, but generally, it is not a favorite tree. It is not a tree planted on its own. Besides, the trees that stand out in Kavaklar are not the poplars but the century-old monumental plane trees.

It seems more probable that the word "*kavak*" was used as "*kovuk*" (hollow), a "well-protected shelter." The name is also

Sarıyer's former police station, now an officers' club

An unused recreational facility on the shore

used for two areas in Istanbul, chosen for shore palaces, with easy access to the sea: Üsküdar Kavak Palace and the Aynalıkavak Pavilion on the Golden Horn. The latter is a museum well worth of a visit. As a result, it would not be wrong to state that this expression actually referred to places where ships coming from the Black Sea first found shelter.

Just after Kavak, there lies one of the few beaches of the Bosphorus where you can swim in the sea. A little bit further on, as we pass under the Third Bridge, is Garipçe. The settlement and the fortress have been famous as a sunday breakfast venue for a long time. As the place was chosen to be where the piers of the bridge on the European side would be built, it became even more popular.

Above, there is the Hasan Pasha Tower which is a vigorous defense structure. A little bit further on, we reach the Rumeli Feneri Lighthouse, which is the last point of the Bosphorus. As its name speaks for itself, this spectacular lighthouse, is the main landmark of the area. There is a rather large fishing port in front of it. The "*öreke*" stones are witnesses to a long history. There is a long tradition of identifying these as the mythical Clashing Rocks in the travels of Jason and the Argonauts. The stones have been situated a little bit outside the mainland since the Antiquity and now they are almost totally integrated with the port. As the remains of a monument known as the Column of Pompey, they continuously have assumed mythological significance. The first lighthouse for securing the entrance to the Bosphorus was also built here.

There were most probably no great expectations in the architecture of lighthouses other than their functionality and a little bit of splendor. A 16th century document at Cambridge University has a detailed illustration of the lighthouse. The illustration, most presumably in a realistic way, reveals that the lighthouse met all these expectations.

As one of the original examples of lighthouse architecture, based in the function of guiding sailors, the Rumeli Feneri Lighthouse is depicted with its massive architecture with a few stories. Its polygonal body rises on a wide base. The lower parts of the lighthouse were

A 16th century depiction of the Rumelifeneri

built with stone, and the upper parts with brick. On its upper section, which is reminiscent of medieval architecture, there is another part which is narrower and shorter, but with the same geometry. Finally, the tower of the lighthouse is completed with the last small part and its cone which is the source of light. As mentioned before, we can define the northern end of the Bosphorus with a virtual line between the Rumeli and Anadolu lighthouses. This means it is now time to change directions and head towards the Asian shore.

The Asian Shore

As might be easily guessed, just the opposite shore is the Anadolu Feneri (lighthouse) village. This place, too, has a lighthouse, restaurants, and a beach. A mosque was built here during the reign of Abdülhamid I.

As we start following the Bosphorus on our return, we reach Poyrazköy, which has been becoming more popular following the completion of the Third Bridge. As soon as we pass under the bridge, we enter into the precinct of the Yoros Castle just the opposite of the Rumeli Kavağı Fortress. Yoros Castle is the most attractive historical monument of this area. Part of military structures might have distinctive aesthetics, but we cannot say the same thing for the military

The Yoros Castle

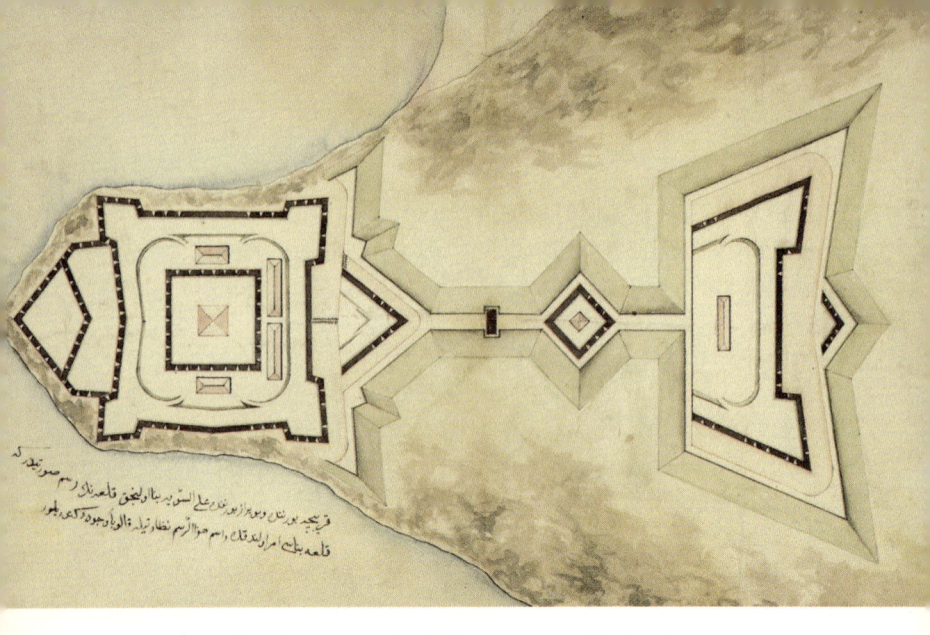

An unbuilt castle project for the upper parts of the Bosphorus

lodgings that interfere with the view of the castle. They were built in the early 80'ies, just after the coup d'état.

As we move further south, we will be moving along the Macar Tabya Street on the shore for some time. The hill where the so-called tomb of Yuşa Hazretleri (Saint Joshua) is located is named after him. His holy precinct can be reached only by going inland.

Since we have crossed to the Anatolian side, we are in the Beykoz municipality. The majority of Beykoz surface consist of forests, therefore protected areas with a significant portion on the Bosphorus coastline. Hence again it is under protection. This amount of protection made Beykoz the administrative unit with the largest natural reserve areas on the Bosphorus. It should certainly be difficult to manage a neighborhood with so many restrictions where people also have to live and work.

On top of all these, the still existent petroleum-derivatives station in Beykoz stands out as a combination of awkward green cylindrical tanks. The Law on The Bosphorus, dated 1983 and numbered 2960, does not allow such facilities, but it did not outlaw existing ones. Hence, some facilities which are absolutely not allowed to be built along the Bosphorus now, are still functioning thanks to their acquired rights. We will see a similar facility just next to the Çubuklu Ferry Pier. Also, that one is quite eco-friendly with its green color.

The Russians are coming

We are now once again aligned with the return route of our vessel. We are close to the cape Selvi Burnu. We have now arrived at the location of the Treaty of *Hünkar İskelesi* (meaning "an imperial pier"), which was mentioned at the start of our voyage. During the Revolt of Muhammad Ali of Egypt, the Russians came here, to today's *Beykoz Kundura* with thousands of soldiers to support Mahmut II, where they stayed for months.

We know that the camp built for the Russians was located on the slopes of Yuşa Tepesi (hill). This location meant that there

Eco-friendly, green petroleum derivatives

was a significant Russian existence on both shores of the Bosphorus together with the summer residence of the Russian Embassy on the opposite shore. It is even told that the area used to be an important tourist attraction for travelers visiting Istanbul at the time. As the Russian troops were leaving the place after the treaty, they left a monument in remembrance of the solidarity between the two states. The monument, consisting of a solid rock of 25 tons, was intended to be seen easily from the sea. The monument stayed there for a long time, but when World War I broke out, it was blown up by a group of Ottoman students.

There used to be inscriptions in both Russian and Ottoman Turkish on the monument: "*Bu sâhraya misâfir geldi gitdi asker-i Rusî*" ("The Russian soldiers came to this field as guests, and they have gone") was the opening line of the inscription in Ottoman Turkish. Although they were guests, it was obvious that the Russians benefited from this visit. They collected the sensitive information that could assist in a possible attack on the Bosphorus. They studied the physical geography of the Bosphorus and especially its roads, waters, and currents. They also recorded where the Turkish soldiers were positioned. Presumably, they assumed that they would be fighting against the Ottomans after a short while. As a matter of fact, the Crimean War, which had significant outcomes for this geography, was to break out only twenty years after this date.

The imperial pier in an engraving by Melling shortly before the agreement of the 1833 with Russians

Industrialisation and The Hills of Beykoz

After the cape Selviburnu, we reach an industrial plant spread on a very wide area: the *Beykoz Kundura*, the former Beykoz Shoe Factory which has recently started being part of the popular culture. Most of the coastal area consists of large fields which are likely reclaimed land from the gulf extending deep into the land. What we have said about reclaimed land from the Dolmabahçe Stadium to Sarıyer, applies to this place as well. There are several football pitches in this area, too. Beykoz/Hünkar Çayırı (meadow), is a very large recreational area, and again alluvial land.

The mouth of the river here is easier to notice when compared to others along the Bosphorus. This probably played an important role in industrialization. We know that, although it later failed, at the beginning of the 19th century there was a paper industry here marking the beginning of the creation of an industrial zone.

The Beykoz Shoe Factory was opened as a military production facility at the beginning of the 19th century. It became part

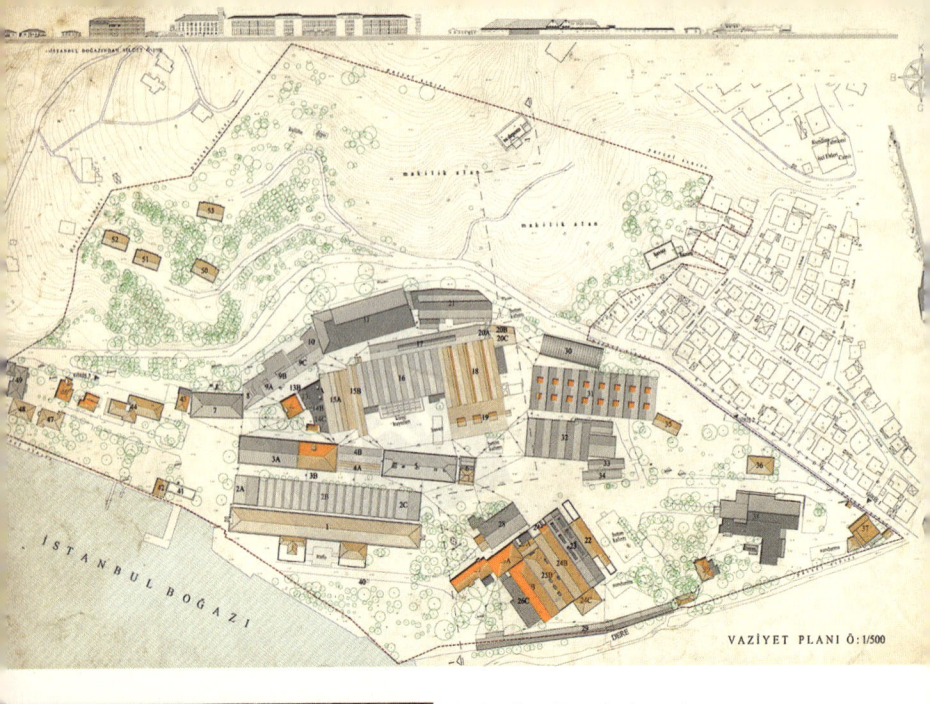

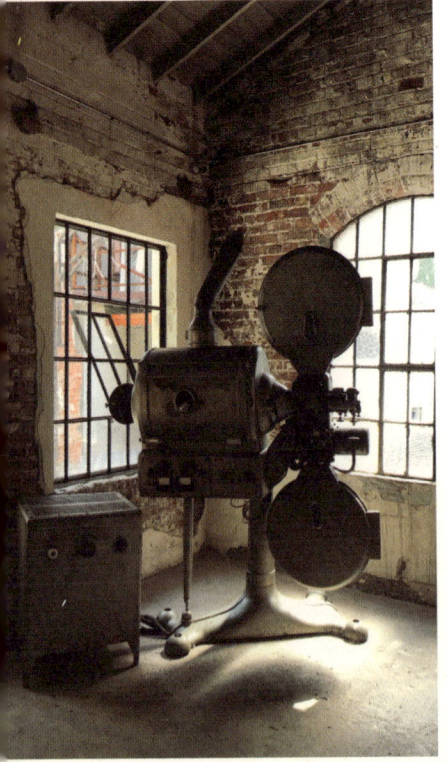

Beykoz Shoe factory's plan and a memory from the days when workers watched movies together

of Sümerbank in 1933. When it closed down in 1999, the production stopped. It was then sold to its present owners with the privatization decision in 2004. The family has a difficult responsibility of researching and preserving the cultural heritage of this facility. Both registry work for historic buildings and many initiatives like studies of oral history were undertaken. The aim is to record as many details to keep its memories alive. It is planned that the old boiler room, which is currently being restored, will function as a cinema and a theater hall in the near future.

On the hill about this area is the Beykoz Hünkar Pavilion. After the aforementioned revolt and the ensuing series of tensions, Muhammad Ali of Egypt, just before his death in 1848, decided to build this pavilion for Sultan Abdülmecit as a token of his loyalty to him. The construction of the building lasted more than ten years, and it was completed at the time of Muhammad Ali's son Said Pasha. In the meantime, Sultan Abdülaziz acceded to the throne. The stones for the façade were brought from Italy. The ceilings are quite high, and this adds a monumental effect to the building. Like many other imperial buildings along the Bosphorus, it is not intended for staying the night. Hence it has no kitchens or baths.

Hünkar Pavilion was used as the Pediatric Hospital of Chest Diseases during the 1990s. It stayed derelict for a time. It was opened to visitors as a unit of the Department of National Palaces. Its internal furnishings were apparently enriched with pieces of furniture listed in the Department's inventory and a successful impression of a habited palace was created. In the square we are now approaching is the İshak Ağa Fountain, which cannot be seen from the sea as it is in a depression. Named as *Onçeşme* (ten fountains), this structure has a special place in Ottoman fountain architecture as it represents a miniature "*Sadabad*" (the monumental 18th century Ottoman waterside recreational complex near the Golden Horn) arrangement with its tresses and ditch.

Looking towards the slope, we can see the Beykoz Woodlot; it is first narrow and then widens at the top; it was known earlier as the Abraham Pasha Woodlot. Although what we know about the pasha is based on hearsay, it is known that he was very wealthy. He had vast properties on both sides of the Bosphorus, including this one. The area was expropriated during the reign of Abdülhamit II and was opened as a public park.

The running of the park was privatized in 1914, an unlucky date when World War I broke out. This was the beginning of an important investment. The group of buildings was extended by the Italian architect Edoardo de Nari to serve as a major entertainment center. Although it went through some serious difficulties during the years of war and occupation, it survived until the 1930s. However, like many other buildings along the Bosphorus, it was unable to survive fire, and was completely destroyed. There is a public facility at the woodlot today, but it does not evoke anything about its previous condition.

Some public buildings like a cultural center and a wedding hall attract our attention just across the coastal road. These are new buildings; as such it is extremely difficult to assert whether they represent modern architecture or any historical heritage of the Bosphorus with their design and chromatic approaches.

Next, we can see almost in ruins, the Paşabahçe ferry (built in Italy in 1952) at the pier. It is one of those large passenger ferries of the city line which are called "*bahçe*" (garden) type ferries, not because of a certain typology or origin (the others were built in Scotland) but because all their names ended in "*bahçe*".

After this, we will see a long series of the abandoned buildings of Türkiye Şişecam A.Ş. Paşabahçe factory, which made

The Hünkar Kasrı, imperial pavilion of Beykoz

Paşabahçe famous as a brand through Turkey and even in the world.

The Beykoz region was already the center of glass production much before the foundation of this factory. There is a popular story about a Mevlevi (Rumi) dervish named Mehmet, who went to Italy during the reign of Selim III (r. 1789-1807) and started glass production after his return to Istanbul. However, we may be wiser not believe this story without confirming it.

While the legend remains unconfirmed, in fact, there used to be a public glass factory in Beykoz during the Ottoman period. The State Archives has a rich body of documents about this establishment revealing that glass masters were employed for the "*Billur ve Cam Fabrika-i Hümayunu*" (the Imperial Glass and Cut-Glass Factory) as early as 1846. The documents also contain a significant amount of information about the construction of the buildings needed, sending an official to Europe to visit the glass factories there and buy machines.

It is noteworthy that only foreign workers were employed at the newly established factory. Similarly, the private glass factory Levi-Modiano which was also established here, prioritized foreigners. This was against the concession agreement which made the establishment of the factory possible, which angered the Ottoman workers. That's why during the workers' movement that started in 1908 after the declaration of the second Constitutional Monarchy the first workers to go on a strike in Istanbul were in this factory.

The Modiano glass factory had further problems later, and it was closed down in 1922. After about ten years, Şişecam was opened. The factory, whose foundations were laid by İsmet İnönü and Celal Bayar, stopped production at the beginning of the 2000s.

Beykoz Public Hospital dominates a wide area a little bit inland towards the shore after the remnants of the factory. We then begin to approach Paşabahçe Square. As we approach the pier, we see the twin Andonaki mansions. They have been built together but are now separately owned like many other similar houses. Next, a bit in the background, is one of the new mosques that follows the plan of Şehzadebaşı Mosque, which Architect Sinan discredited as a work of his early career.

This mosque is known, not for its architecture, but for another reason in popular culture: It was next to the Tekel (State Monoply) Alcoholic Beverages Factory, which was established during the 1930s. Even though only consumption of alcohol is considered a sin by Muslims, locals still asked the religious authority whether the usage of heat generated through alcohol was allowed. A fatwa issued by the Beykoz Muftiate allowed the heating of the mosque to be done by the steam coming from the alcohol factory. But when the factory stopped production, the mosque was no longer heated for some time.

The shoreline below the woodland that comes after the factory is accessed through a narrow street from the coastal road. Just before the series of warehouse structures, we come across a building with a mysterious style that functions as a municipality-owned restaurant.

This is followed by two more social activity venues operated by private companies: one is more for the upper middle class, whereas the one in further south is set up for class A clients. When we talk about social events along the Bosphorus, people generally think of weddings. This place is no exception. Between these two venues there is a pool which is not intended for swimming. In other words, here we find an opportunity to celebrate poolside weddings.

Next, there is a hospital building at the top of the hill which is reached via a winding road. The former hospital of the SSK (Social Insurance Institution) dated 1966 is one of the first hospitals for workers in Istanbul. The existence of this hospital here is the result of the long-lasting industrialization attempts and the ensuing labor struggle in the area. In other words, we just mentioned that this is a neighborhood where workers went on strike as early as the beginning of the 1900s. Let us remind that this strike was one of the crucial turning points of the history of labor movements.

The tradition of industrialization in the region - except for the Kazlıçeşme area - resulted in the emergence of the first illegal housing zones in the city. It is clear that as the Beykoz Shoe Factory was including its own systematic and planned lodging buildings in its vicinity, the workers who came to the area to work from other factories tried to settle there. Hence, they built houses along the slopes and this has a noticeable visual effect on the surrounding area.

Çubuklu

When we look back towards the shore, following the wedding venues we previously mentioned, we again see green tanks containing petroleum products. At the beginning of the cove that follows, on one side there is the Çubuklu Ferry Pier: this is the only place on the Bosphorus where cars can travel by ferry to and from Europe (İstinye). Sazlıdere, flowing into the Bosphorus next to the pier, contributed to the formation of a very wide alluvial field for centuries. This bottomland, known as Çubuklu, used to be a vegetable garden for the Ottoman palace. Poles for beans, tomatoes and pepper, which are essential for a vegetable garden, were extensively used for producing for

The Khedive's pavilion in the Çubuklu woodlot

the palace here, giving rise to the name of the neighborhood "Çubuklu" (with poles).

On the opposite side of the bay, a wide woodlot starts at the slopes: the Çubuklu Woodlot which was given to the Egyptian Khedive İsmail Pasha was later expanded by the Khedive himself through acquisition of more land. On top of the hill shrouded by the woodlot is the Khedive Palace.

When observed from the sea, only the top of its tower can be seen. Largely because of the unchecked forestation, this woodlot, which is essentially part of a palace precinct, has been turned into a forest area. The trees block the view that spans from the pavilion to the sea, and the building is hardly visible from the outside.

When Abbas Hilmi Pasha, the last of the Egyptian Khedives who was connected to many places along the Bosphorus, decided to settle in Switzerland after the declaration of the Republic, he tried to sell his land in Çubuklu. However, those were the days when the capital Ankara received more attention, and Istanbul was not popular. The Bosphorus was becoming deserted. During summer months, *Şirket-i Hayriye* (Şehir Hatları Ferries Corporation) carried the belongings of families moving to the Bosphorus for free. It was not possible to sell this property to anyone at the time, so the Municipality of Istanbul bought the land for a modest price. During the following years, it was restored by Turing and the Otomobil Kurumu (Automobile Club) as a luxury restaurant. But the agreement between the two entities recently ended and the place is used again by the municipality and currently run as a mid-tier restaurant.

Looking back at the shore, we see the terraces of the roadside mansion which trail into to woodlot where the Hıdiv Pavilion

A completely reconstructed Bosphorus-view mansion

is located. These terraces represent a modern interpretation of the Bosphorus tradition. It also sets a beautiful example of topiary which is rare along the Bosphorus. An almost unnoticeable elevator was installed for easier access to upper terraces.

The rocky platform on which the mansion rests was arranged as an additional lower floor that encompasses the lower part of the garden with wide windows overlooking the view. This is not a feature of the usual Bosphorus architecture either. This building, like many other similar examples, is a reconstruction. The building used to be owned by Erzurumlu Şeyhülislam (Shaykh al-Islâm) Çelebizade Hüseyin Hüsnü Efendi, but no remnants of this period have survived.

There are blocks of apartments built adjacently and trailing unto the slopes of the woodlot from the shore. These flats, with different colors that resemble a sort of public housing architecture, now cover the whole area by which we are passing.

A densely built housing project between two woodlots

From Keçecizade Fuat Pasha to Modern Architecture

The large land and the mansion of Keçecizade Fuat Pasha, the famous vizier of the Abdülaziz period, bear no traces of their past. Earlier we mentioned the physician Prime Minister Sadi Irmak at the Aşiyan Cemetery. Vizier Fuat Pasha was also a physician. He graduated from *Mekteb-i Tıbbiye* (the Ottoman Medical School) with highest scores.

Fuat Pasha crossed paths with many prominent names along the Bosphorus: After his graduation, he worked as a doctor for a period, as a protégé of the Grand Master of Artillery, Fethi Ahmet Pasha.

Following this, because he spoke very good French, Mustafa Reşit Pasha, the Minister of Foreign Affairs at the time, appointed him to the membership of *Bab-ı Ali* Chamber of Translation. He continued to climb up in bureaucracy and when the new sultan Abdülaziz ascended to the throne, he was still in the limelight. He also won the favor of the new sultan to be given the titles of Seraskier and Vizier. You may have noticed that the fate of many elements along the Bosphorus from the 19th century was directly related to Egypt. During his visit to Egypt, Sultan Abdülaziz kept Fuat Pasha by his side at all times, and he granted him the title '*Yaver-i Ekrem*' (Honorable Assistant). When Fuat Pasha voiced his opinion against the Egyptian Khedive's marrying his daughter, Sultan Abdülaziz dismissed him from the prime ministry.

Fuat Pasha was one of the founders of *Şirket-i Hayriye* Corporation, which played a crucial role along the Bosphorus. While his mansion no longer exists, the mosque complex he founded, which is one of the important examples of the Ottoman Orientalist architecture, stands in Sultanahmet in all its glory.

During the time when Fuat Pasha was working as the Minister of Foreign Affairs, there were some agreements and treaties negotiated and signed here. These agreements are called the Kanlıca Agreements. These agreements, signed with many western countries starting with France in 1861, regulated the Ottoman trade with more than ten countries from the US to Mexico.

Just after this, in an area where the green spaces are more protected, we see a relatively short apartment known as *Kartal Yuvası* (Eagle's Nest) Apartment. The architect of the building is Kaya Tecimen, who was mentioned early in connection to the offices of Istanbul Chamber of Industry on Istiklal Street. The structure here is much lower than Odakule. While Odakule distinguishes itself with its glass façades, this building's façade is shaped by the distinctive forms created by expressions of the ferroconcrete technique. Looked from this perspective, we notice the same approach in Galatasaray Han, adjacent to Tecimen's Odakule. When looked closely from the sea, it is noticed that the top floor of the Kartal Yuvası Apartment is slightly recessed in line with the slope of the hill.

Actually, all the floors of the building were intended to recess back with the same rhythm, but it could not be done because that design was not compatible with the regulations. If this design could have been implemented, most probably we

Architecture from the 70s. a well disguised apartment

would have a residence in much more harmony with its surroundings than the present one we currently have, painted in green. Still, we can say that a much less intrusive result was achieved compared to many other Bosphorus apartments. Unfortunately, only one of the two-century-old pine trees in front of the building is still alive. They were both diligently protected during the construction. The second one reminds us of its once presence with only with the lower part of its trunk. The other one still presents itself in full glory.

Mansions Laid Together

After this apartment, the road moves away from the shore once again and leaves us with a series of waterfront mansions. First emerges the Ahmet Rasim Pasha Mansion, which is often quite animated with wedding and graduation ceremonies, especially in the summer months. The present mansion is relatively large even in its present condition, but it looks much bigger in

A former mansion, later a school and finally a small hotel

old photographs. A large section of it was demolished when the road behind it was being built, and it assumed its present form.

The building is owned by the Municipality of Istanbul, and it was used as a school for some time. It was later completely rebuilt and opened as a small hotel with 17 rooms. The series of balconies that cut through the roof transversely on the top floor have no relation with the Bosphorus' architectural tradition.

Just above is a mansion reached via terraced gardens that recalls the terrace tradition of the Bosphorus. It was originally the hill-side pavilion of the next mansion, but it is currently a separate property. Not too long ago it was reported that one of the richest businessmen of Turkey lost his life here when he fainted during his workout. We again see some diligent examples of topiary on its terraces.

On the shore, at the very tip of the cape, there is the dark red Asaf Pasha Mansion. The mansion's *mehtabiye*, or *gurub köşkü* (pavilion for watching the moon or the sunset), which was relocated in the garden as a protrusion into the sea, and its modern sculpture collection showcased by the property owner for the admiration of passersby add flavor to the Bosphorus. Its *kayıkhane* (boathouse), which was deserted then uncovered a few years ago, has been repurposed as a gym room with a glass façade.

This was the traditional red color for the Ottoman waterfront mansions.

The following buildings are generally the ordinary concrete buildings of the 1970s. Some others are made of concrete with timber covers, which make a reference to older forms. Around the Kanlıca Pier, such two mansions were combined into a single structure by installing an elevator in between. The incident was talked about much in the media not because people were particularly sensitive against cultural assets but mainly because the houses belonged to a famous singer.

The most striking structure at Kanlıca Square is Iskender Pasha Mosque, but when viewed from the sea, not much can be seen other than its minaret. Since it was originally a *'tekke'* (dervish lodge), it has an authentic characteristic. There is a radar tower next to the mosque.

Vegetable Gardens and Mansions in Çubuklu

The name 'Kanlıca' is mostly famous for its yogurt. Just as there were vegetable gardens in Çubuklu, this area was allocated for dairy farms. Hence, the fact that this area's dairy production is more famous than the others is quite understandable.

The yogurt of Kanlıca should actually remind us of the distribution of productive functions along the Bosphorus. Even though many of them are no longer there or even forgotten, many neighborhoods along the Bosphorus focused on products specific to them and the distribution of production was not arbitrary. Çengelköy's cucumbers and Arnavutköy's strawberries are quite famous locally and should be thought of in the same context.

Just after the Kanlıca Pier, we see an unusual mansion with its small tower on the opposite side of the road. The arch of the boathouse is rather large in proportion to the main building. Actually, when the lands of big mansions were divided into plots, the boathouses which lost their function were transformed into separate mansions. This is an example we see in more than one place along the Bosphorus. Hence, this disproportionality could be explained with the much older history of the building. On the other hand, it is difficult to understand why the building is covered with timber-looking material, because there was no timber in the original construction of the building. In addition, the boathouse looks like the window of a basement floor because a dock was added in its front. The garret window, which reaches full length with its French window, is also something unusual for the Bosphorus architecture.

Soon, one of the most spectacular mansions of this area will be seen: Saffet Pasha Waterfront Mansion. This mansion was

The Saffet Pasha Mansion was rebuilt from scratch, like many others.

once completely demolished, and it was recently completely rebuilt based on its old photographs.

As the series of concrete buildings continue along the shore, the slope on the other side of the road is the location of the Kanlıca Cemetery. There are many famous figures who rest here: first comes to mind Barış Manço, who gave his name to the road behind the mansions. Kayahan, another name from the world of music, also rests here. Sedat Simavi, founder of the national Hürriyet Newspaper and the grandson of Saffet Pasha, whose mansion we mentioned earlier, are also buried here. He hd demolished the mansion and had it rebuilt in concrete.

If we turn our attention back to the mansions, leaving behind the cape, we can see a couple of buildings. One of them is Hacı Ahmet Arif Bey Mansion. The size of its windows is smaller than the usual windows of timber mansions of the Bosphorus. It might have gone through such a transformation as it was adapting to its new concrete structure. The curled eaves, which is a common feature of the period of Abdülhamid II, gave way to more solid forms.

Another mansion in this series is Ali Mazhar Bey Mansion, whose structure was completely transformed into steel.

Formerly an Ottoman mansion, now it has only the looks of it.

Another one is Ethem Pertev Mansion, which stands out with its decorative balcony, another unusual element in Ottoman architecture. The façade of this mansion, which was completely rebuilt by its owners, was severely damaged when a ship recently crashed into it. We observe that the two-unit boathouse under the mansion was enclosed with walls during construction. Mica Ertegün the widow of Ahmet Ertegün, founder of the Atlantic Recordings company was the interior designer of this mansion.

A little bit further on, the shore slightly coils inland. Under normal circumstances, this recess would be defined as a "bay" or even a "cove", but it is known as a "gulf" ("*Körfez*"). It is this place that comes to mind when people just say "*Körfez*" instead of "Kanlıca Gulf." As mentioned earlier, the shore on the Asian side is almost completely flat. Hence, only this example is used as a proper noun. The gulf is now like a parking area for the boats of the mansions. As might be remembered, Bebek Cove had a similar function.

On the shore of the gulf, the mansion named after Princess Rukiye is strikingly large. It has a vertical arrangement which is unusual in mansions covering a large area. The balcony in the middle has a distinctive façade. Next to it is the apartment where poet Atilla İlhan spent the last year of his life, just next door to his sister, actress Çolpan İlhan. The next building is the one which hosted Körfez Restaurant for long years. It now changed hands, and after a pompous arrangement of the façade, it is currently used as a single-family home.

On the slope behind this series of mansions is Mihrabat Woodlot, which used to be the garden of Rukiye Hanım Mansion. Currently it is a recreational area operated by the Directorate General of Forestry.

Further inland from Körfez is the neighborhood of Kavacık. The name of this neighborhood was not mentioned frequently in our urban life. When the Asian pier of the Second Bosphorus

Bridge was erected there, it became a central location. The stream with the same name seems to have formed this cove over the years.

At the innermost part of Körfez, a plot of land which has been vacant for a long time now hosts a historical looking mansion which was rebuilt entirely. After Körfez, there are a few mansion apartments along the shore until the bridge, which all look neglected. These buildings do not have any special feature in relation to their periods, so redesigning their looks with a modern approach would certainly add aesthetic value to this coastline.

The Kanlıca "Gulf" is actually a small cove.

Hekimbaşı Mansion and the Balance in Architecture

There are some units which are used as restaurants below the bridge. These are followed by the red mansion named Hekimbaşı Salih Efendi Mansion. The mansion is seated on three levels going down from north to south. The existing part of the mansion rested on three levels to the north which created perfect symmetry. One of these fish restaurants is located where the *selamlık* (the portion of a house reserved for men) used to be.

When Hekimbaşı Mansion closed its shutters, its "closed box" appearance made it one of the elegant designs of Ottoman architecture which sought harmony in the unity of proportions. Finding this balance is surely not easy, one can feel the experience of centuries in the background. The "loggia" on the first floor contributes to the balance created between the introversion and embracing the Bosphorus. The main characteristic of the group of buildings lies in the measured composition of the masses sized in accordance with their functions.

Only the Harem section of the Hekimbaşı mansion had survived and days after this photo was taken an oil tanker heavily damaged the remaining portion.

We are next welcomed by a façade arranged in a repertoire of imported motifs uncommon to the Bosphorus. By this point, we come across a façade with unusual elements from an imported repertory. Behind the waterfront unit a much bigger one was recently added transforming the gracious home into a large residence.

On the seafront façade there is a large glass window that point to the entrance of a former boathouse. It is undoubtedly fine to protect historical monuments as they once were but there is actually no harm in putting boathouses to new uses instead of merely preserving them for boats. We noticed a good example of this in Şerifler Mansion. There the quite splendid structure, formerly a boathouse, is now being used as a classroom.

Behind the road, on the upper elevation of this mansion, there was once a residence known as *Pervaneli* (with a wind rose) Mansion. Instead of a timber mansion with a small tower currently, we see glorious concrete terraces on the plot of land. As the mansion is being rebuilt, it looks like a concrete

Slightly invasive interventions for substructures

Nuri Pasha Mansion at sunset

monolith. The timber that will be attached on the façade will perhaps remind us of the past.

The next historic waterfront home is named after Nuri Pasha. The façade of this mansion also frequently sports the flag of a sports club of which the owner of the property is a member.

Amcazade Mansion

We are now passing in front of a Bosphorus mansion which had one of the longest façades. It would not be wrong to think that the whole slope beyond the coastline behind the mansion and the once quite narrow road used to be the land of the property. This mansion is Amcazade Hüseyin Pasha Mansion, also known as Meşruta Mansion. Hüseyin Pasha Amcazade is known for the madrasah he built in Saraçhane. He was the nephew of Köprülü Mehmet Pasha, the most famous person of the Köprülü family. His tomb is just next to the madrasah. But the pasha is mostly remembered for his use of the oldest mansion (during summer months) which is now derelict on the Bosphorus. Only the *divanhane* (the hall of audience) of its *selamlık* has survived. We can come across many foundations of timber houses on the property. The existing structure is hidden behind wooden scaffolding: we can deduce, from what is painted on it that there is an intention of rebuilding all the structures that used to be here (although from different periods) in an adjacent manner.

Although its beauty and historical value cannot be noticed today, Amcazade Mansion was a center of attraction during the time it was standing. Photographers like Sabah and Abdullah Brothers were able to find very good photographic material here during the 19th century. The Italian architect Fossati whom we know with his restoration of Hagia Sophia is also among those who visited here and produced documents about the mansion. It is told that during the Ottoman-Russian War of 1877-78 refugees were placed in the vacant harem quarters of the mansion accelerating its destruction.

Just after the end of the property, there is the *mehtabiye* (moonlight corner) of Zarif Mustafa Pasha Mansion. Until a couple of years ago, it used to be an ordinary structure located a little bit inland and covering half of the land starting from the road. It was rebuilt, and it now dominates the sea view.

The real Zarif Mustafa Pasha Mansion, whose *selamlık* has survived, belongs to a different family. It is an impressive mansion with its bay window in the middle and the consoles that support and characterize it. It was heavily damaged when a Romanian cargo vessel crashed into it in the early 1990s. It later changed hands and was restored.

Amcazade mansion's interior details in a book published in 1915

Zarif Mustafa Pasha's mansion

The next waterfront mansion, Yasinci Yalısı, was not there until very recently. It was just a plot of land, but it was rebuilt as a striking red mass. As far as can be observed from the outside, it is built diligently and without any exaggeration.

Further on there is another series of coastal residences until the Anadolu Hisarı Pier. Two of them are detached, and the other three are adjacent buildings. All these mansions were reconstructed. In the same series, there is another group of mansions known as Manastırlı İbrahim Hakkı, Köseleciler, Talat Efendi and İlyas Bey. These mansions add a beautiful texture to their surroundings.

Building "historic" mansions today

"Hisar Peçesi" (Veil of Fortress)

As we move, pass the unique series of the mansions, we begin to approach what is beyond any doubt the most important building here: the *Anadolu Hisarı* ("Anatolian Fortress"), which is also the name of the neighborhood. This place is also sometimes called as "*Güzelce*" (beautiful). This first fortress was most probably built not for the hope and aim of preventing the passage of ships from the Bosphorus completely, but to protect the nearby, navigable Göksü Stream. It was built at the mouth of this stream so that a permanent fleet could be kept there to perpetuate the Turkish existence along the Bosphorus, which the fortress was successful in doing.

During the reign of Sultan Mehmet the Conqueror, it was covered (1450s) with an external wall which was called "*Hisar Peçesi*" (Veil of Fortress) and it covered a much larger area compared with the Yıldırım Beyazıt's period (1390s). It was built on the coast, but as time passed, residences, mostly mansions, were built around it as alluvial land at the mouth of the Göksü stream extended, eventually surrounding the fortress.

Just outside the veil (the outer part of the fortress), there is one of the rare surviving examples of a *namazgah* (outdoor

Anadoluhisarı and its open-air prayer area

prayer place) in Istanbul (another example on the Bosphorus is in Küçüksu). It cannot be seen from the sea, but it adds a special flavor to this area.

Today there is a road passing through the "Veil of Fortress" open for motor vehicles. This road should certainly not be there.

The Göksü Stream (guarded by the Fortress) and Küçüksu Stream (just to the south) created a wide alluvial plain. When it was still covered with grass, until the 1970s, the area used to be called as Küçüksu Meadow. It was a well-known recreational area during the Ottoman Era and also attracted attention from the Western world. It was called as the "sweet waters of Asia," and was presented as the Asian equivalent of the recreational area in Kağıthane / Sadabad on the European side.

As the First Bridge was being built, the area, being the closest large vacant area on the shores of the Bosphorus, was used as a construction site, which brought an end to the recreational function. The plans were to end its function as a construction site, but it was utilized in the same way for the Second Bridge as well. The park was thus damaged greatly, and afterward, it was left partially vacant. Part of it was enclosed, and part of it was opened for construction to be turned into a university campus.

Mihrişah Sultana Fountain and Küçüksu Pavilion

As usual, there are cafes and restaurants on the coast between the two streams. Although it is now difficult to see, one of the most attractive fountains of the Bosphorus is still here. Mihrişah Sultana Fountain was built when there was a timber pavilion nearby, fifty years before the present pavilion. The fountain is on a low terrace reached with some steps. The *mihrab* stones placed on its sides recently made it more evident that it was originally a *namazgah* (outdoor prayer place).

The fountain, which was built at the very beginning of the 19th century, is named after the mother of Selim III and reflects a type of fountain in Ottoman architecture that was developed during the Tulip Period (1718-1730); a relatively peaceful period in the Ottoman Empire, during which the first westernization tendencies started. Many of the fountains built during the Tulip Period were designed as independent structures. Some of the most well-known monumental examples are the Fountain of Ahmet III in front of the Topkapı Palace, the Tophane Fountain that we passed by at the beginning of our voyage, and the fountain of Sultan Ahmet III in Üsküdar that we will pass by, towards the end of this journey.

The Mihrişah Sultana Fountain was added to this series of fountains at a relatively later date with its cubic body, symmetrical façades, its inscription, and wide eaves. It is reminiscent of the Fountain of Ahmet III in front of the Topkapı Palace with its dome in the middle and the miniature domes at the corners.

Küçüksu Meadow; the Second Bridge and the Küçüksu Pavilion in the background

Mihrişah Queen Mother's fountain (early 1800's)

All of the surfaces of the structure and the part under the eaves are fully adorned with rich decorative elements. Foliage scrolls and the oyster shell motif complementing the composition are part of the repertoire of Rococo styles incorporated into Ottoman art.

Just nearby, the most important building in this neighborhood is definitely the Küçüksu Pavilion: it is indeed one of the most dynamic and attractive structures of the Bosphorus. It is an example of 19th century Ottoman architecture that directly reflects the influences of Western European palace architecture. The delicate yet impressive structure is best understood within the context of the French-German Rococo art. The façade is completely covered with stone ornaments in relief. An all-embracing wide Baroque stairway, twisted columns, garlands, vases in niches, masses of other decorative elements placed in a balanced harmony, all show the artistic quality of this structure; in other words, they announce the imperial diligence.

The Küçüksu Kasrı also marks the end of a tradition: from the early years of the empire, the sultans used to have their meals alone. When Grand Duke Konstantin Nikolaevich, brother of Tsar Alexander II, stopped by Istanbul after his return from his visit to Jerusalem, Sultan Abdülmecit ate with him at the same table.

It is (not) possible to walk across a modern bow bridge from the garden of the pavilion to a park area which stands idle. Once there used to be the public beach of Küçüksu, but currently, it is kept vacant and partially planted. Its shore was once a public beach, now it remains inaccessible.

Despite all these unfavorable conditions, an initiative was taken for the reclamation of the Küçüksu Meadow, and the first step was to rebuild the Mihrişah Valide Sultan Mosque which was in ruins just behind the pavilion. Instead of being restored by the authorities of the period, which was how derelict buildings were treated in the 1950s, it had been demolished. Its reconstruction was recently completed.

After the point where the old beach ends and the shore sharply changes direction, we come across the very long façade

Küçüksu Pavilion

of the Kıbrıslı Waterfront Mansion. Most probably, until the end of the Ottoman period, the residents of the Bosphorus were more used to such flat and low mansions. It seems only later there was a trend for more floors. In the inner part of the garden, close to the road, quite withdrawn from the sea, we notice a residence designed by Sedad Hakkı Eldem. The hill behind is known as *Sevda Tepesi* ("Love Hill"), and it is preserved as a woodlot. In the past, it used to be part of the property of Kıbrıslı Mansion.

A visit to the Kıbrıslı Mansion would suffice to have an idea of the traditional "winter gardens" owned by wealthy families: the light emitted by large windows, the greenery outside, the fountain in the middle, and the sofa in the middle all remind that we can have serenity with traditional materials as well.

The adjacent neighbor of this mansion is a large apartment. The Ismail Pasha Waterfront Mansion used to be there for many years and was even used as the summer residence of the author's family. In 1972 a fire completely burnt it down and later it was replaced by this apartment. The mansion is part of the memories of the Bornovalı family with a *hagiasma* (holy spring) in its garden and a *serdab* (half buried, relativey cool room for summer months) like structure which was turned into a shelter during World War I.

The next mansion is named after a prominent Late Ottoman figure, Abud Efendi. The mansion has recently become famous as the set of a TV series. The Abud Efendi Mansion was actually built in the middle of the 19th century as a property of the Altunizade family. This family reminds us of another marriage between people of "different worlds" as seen in the marriage of Halet Çambel and Nail Çakırhan which we mentioned in Arnavutköy. The dissident communist poet Nazım Hikmet (1902-1963) was married with Piraye "Altınoğlu" the granddaughter of the Altunizade family; and though they did not live in this mansion, he spent a long time with her in their mansion in the Altunizade neighborhood (an entire neighborhood still carries the family's name).

We next see the Kont Ostrorog Waterfront Mansion, which begins with a large garden. Since there is open space here, we can see the terraces in the background, which are actually part of every mansion. Looking a bit further, it is possible to notice that the terraces are decorated with stone artifacts from the

Kıbrıslı Mansion with
Adile Sultana's Palace (on the hilltop)

Abud Efendi and Ismail Pasha mansions

archaeological collection of the owner. This, of course, cannot be related to tradition, but still, they look stylish.

On the coastal part of the garden, there are three ancient-looking marble columns again part of the same collection. Under normal circumstances, they would carry something, but there is nothing on them. Their function might not be obvious

Here once was the Ismail Pasha mansion

Count Ostrorog and Hadi Bey mansions and the hillside pavilions

when seen from the sea. Those who will pass by on the right day can observe that they are used for flying a flag on national holidays.

The section on the property of the mansion is used as a large seaside garden. This is quite an unusual situation as no such gardens existed on the Bosphorus. Actually, old photographs show that there used to be housing in the area. Although the family living in the mansion could easily get legal permission to reconstruct it, it seems they prefer not to build anything here. This is very different from the general tendency to squeeze as many buildings as possible to every square meter of the Bosphorus.

Just above, on a terrace there is a mansion with the same color. We know that it was entirely renovated in concrete and then arranged in line with traditional forms by the architect Dr. Sinan Genim. An example of the use of shutters that we see in this mansion and its pavilion as well as in the next mansion was always common and necessary for the residences along the Bosphorus. It is difficult to imagine a mansion without shutters: the drizzle from the sea and the harsh weather conditions in winter would certainly damage these summer homes if the windows were not properly sealed. They also function as screens blocking the sun when pulled up at the desired level. On the other hand, we observe that the shutters of this mansion are almost always closed. It is evident that it is not inhabited frequently.

After the Kont Ostrorog Mansion comes the Hadi Bey Mansion. The residence which was demolished was entirely accurately rebuilt. McCurdy & Co., the company that also rebuilt the "Shakespeare Globe Theater" produced all the timber pieces of the buildings with different types of oak trees in England and then the building was assembled on the land on the shore. For some reason, the lantern that we see in old photographs, was not added to its top. Yet we can appreciate the indispensable shutters in this mansion as well.

Remembering Cemile Sultana

As we move toward Kanlıca Pier there is a road winding up the slope. The area covering the hill is the Cemile Sultan Woodlot.

The name of Cemile Sultana, daughter of Sultan Abdülmecit, has many connections to the Bosphorus: she had a palace in Fındıklı (currently Mimar Sinan Fine Arts Faculty). She also lived in the huge İsmail Pasha Palace (now destroyed) in Emirgan and bought the Hüseyin Avni Pasha waterfront palace in Paşalimanı.

Her woodlot on the slopes of Kandilli is currently used as a facility of Istanbul Chamber of Commerce. The woodlot named after Cemile Sultana has had a more fortunate fate than the similar ones covering the other side of the hill. As it is the property of Istanbul Chamber of Commerce, there is limited housing there.

As might be guessed, she had a splendid palace on the shore, connected to this upper side of the hill and it can be noticed in all its glory in a panoramic photograph of Boğaziçi (Bosphorus) University.

There is a pedestrian road between the homes and the sea, which is unusual for the Bosphorus, starting from the pier and continuing up to the cape. Thus, it is possible to have a walk – albeit a short one – along the shore in front of the houses here. If you walk until the Edip Efendi Mansion on the cape, you can have a very extended view of the Bosphorus. This line is often used by those who come for fishing. The dock has been slightly damaged by the rough waves of the Bosphorus. Walking here also gives us an opportunity to inspect the Edip Efendi Mansion more closely.

The mansion is divided into two almost symmetrical halves on a line very close to its middle. The park overlooking the Black Sea direction is a little bit bigger and was built as the harem; the part on the Marmara side is the *selamlık* (quarters reserved for men). Its boathouse on this end is still highly distinct. Just behind the mansion is an unseemly radar tower.

Edip Efendi Mansion, clearly divided into two parts (Harem and Selamlık)

A virtual line from this mansion to Aşiyan is the shortest distance between two continents on the Bosphorus. The width is less than 700 meters. As might be understood from the narrowing of the distance, Kandilli is a protruding cape with houses all around it. There are many apartments and a few noteworthy reconstructions among them.

We know that during World War I, a vessel loaded with oil crashed into the shore and burnt down 11 of the mansions on this line. Edip Efendi Mansion, due to its high and durable firewall, was the only mansion that survived the fire. There is more than one mansion along the slope which has been reconstructed according to old photographs. The most striking example of reconstruction on the shore is the timber building known as the Clifton Mansion. Until a few years ago, there was a low quality two-floored concrete building where a garden is now located. With the help of visual documents, the mansion was given its old appearance and rebuilt on the vaults of a stone boathouse as it was before.

Following this, we see the largest building in the area, an apartment which is one of the works of Sedat Hakkı Eldem.

Kandilli High School for Girls as an Alternative to American College for Girls

The building at the very top of the Kandilli Cape is named Adile Sultana Palace. It attracts attention with its large size. The edifice was first used as a school for girls ("*inas mektebi*" in Ottoman Turkish) It burnt down in 1986 and was totally renovated. A school with the name of Kandilli Kız Lisesi still exists,

The recently rebuilt Clifton Mansion, an unusual style for the Bosphorus

but not in this building, it functions in the newer buildings built on a lower elevation. Since it was allocated as a school campus, it was not subdivided into parcels and zoned for housing. Therefore, it still has the appearance of a woodlot.

The main building of Adile Sultana Palace, which was reconstructed and flamboyantly decorated, now serves as an events venue. It dominates the view of almost all corners of the Bosphorus.

Adile Sultan İnas *Mektebi* (Adile Sultan Imperial School for Girls) was founded shortly after the foundation of the American College for Girls on the opposite coast of Arnavutköy in 1907. Although on opposite shores, they are almost directly across from each other. This could well be a coincidence, but it would not be unrealistic to assume that this was a counter step taken by the Ottomans so as not to be overshadowed by such a comprehensive initiative of education taken by a foreign country, recruiting local youth to its education system. As a matter of fact, we do not have to look far in the past, as such competition still continued until the 1950s. When the mother of the author of these lines was a successful student at Kandilli High School for Girls, she was invited by an American committee to their school, and she was educated there and graduated from the American College for Girls.

It is not possible to see it from a boat, but it is reassuring to see a pristine example of civil architecture located along the hill at the level of Adile Sultan Palace on Sıraevler Street.

There is more than one reconstructed mansion on the terraces between the narrow front façade of the palace and the shore. Thanks to low-density housing and with buildings likened to old structures, they are still preserved in their natural and historical appearance.

Next along the shore are several more apartment mansions. We come across zoned areas where numerous villas with pinnacles brought together. Sometimes we see buildings with two pinnacles. Based on the information given by the property owners, these attics are not used in daily life, but rather function as storerooms.

These tower–like houses are actually not only the part of the fate of the Bosphorus; they also reflect a trend which is seen in the suburban houses of the American middle classes, which is often deemed a "McMansion" in the States, as they are ostentatious houses with no cultural background. We frequently come across such buildings of the Bosphorus. The same style might be seen not only in residences but the public buildings of the Bosphorus as well.

From Eastern Turkey Down to the Bosphorus

On the opposite shore, we see a line, used sometimes as a car parking area and sometimes as a park with plants which does not suit the past of the Bosphorus. This is followed by a series of privately-owned mansions.

The first residence we come across reminds us of some good deeds done along the Bosphorus. The building, which used to belong to the Recaizade family, was used as an oil factory for a long period with an additional waterfront industrial building in its current garden. It was eventually turned into a house of a family. The additional structure was demolished, and a peaceful garden was built instead. The owner of the factory adds an even odd elements to this strange past: the Süleymangil family. Yılmaz Güney (1937-1984) a Palme d'Or winner actor and movie director, devoted almost all his works to the plight of ordinary, working class people in Turkey but found the love of his life Fatoş Güney in this family; during summers she used to spend a lot time here in the summer residence of her grandfather in Vaniköy. This is actually another love story between a rich girl and poor boy. Actually, two wealthy women: the late Yılmaz Güney's former wife Nebahat Çehre, as well still lives in a waterfront home in Yeniköy on the Bosphorus.

Following the first timber-like mansion in this series, there are two red mansions, one tall and the other with a single floor. The building, which was a gift to one of the wives of Sultan Reşat (r.1909-1918), still commemorate this history as the Kadın Efendi Mansion.

From here we continue with a series of Vaniköy mansions. Most of these are properties that frequently change hands among very few wealthy families of different eras.

In this series, we remember a fire which burnt down two mansions at the beginning of the 1990s. One of them was rebuilt in its original form. The adjacent mansion was not reclaimed. Its ruins stand in a marshy garden with lots of plants in it.

Vaniköy Mosque is in the middle of this residential line of continuous mansions. Both the mosque and the neighborhood are named after Vânî Mehmet Efendi (d.1685), who came from Eastern Turkey and was bestowed these lands by the sultan of the period, Mehmet IV. This is not a big gift for a *Hâce-i Sultani* (tutor of the sultan). Actually, Mehmet Efendi is not from central Van, but from the town Hoşap, thus he was also known as as Hoşabî. However, since he was educated in Van, this was a more direct association. (He is not to be confused with another Mehmet Efendi from Van (d.1592) who is known for his dictionary "*Vankulu Lugati*"). Mehmet Efendi rapidly had a successful career; when the Yeni Cami Mosque in Eminönü was completed and opened after almost one hundred years of construction time, he was appointed as its imam. He had the honor of teaching the princes. His sermons influenced a wide range of individuals including the sultans.

Vânî Efendi played an important role in the decision for the Second Siege of Vienna (1683) by Mehmet IV, who was actually against war. Mehmet Efendi, who participated in the siege to offer religious service for the military, continuously motivated

Kandilli Observatory (1920s)

the soldiers. When the siege failed, the *Hodja* (teacher), too, fell from grace and died shortly afterwards during his exile.

The adjacent neighbor of the mosque, the mansion of the Kıraç family, is another work by Sedad Hakkı Eldem.

If viewed at a distance from the shore, on the hill, the tower of the Kandilli Observatory (which for some unknown reason it is located not in Kandilli, but in Vaniköy) can partially be seen.

There used to be an artillery unit of the Command of Straits and fire watchers of the Municipality of Istanbul on this hill until 1910. After these were closed out, the foundations of the observatory ("*Rasathane-i Amire*"), which is currently affiliated with Boğaziçi (Bosphorus) University, were laid. Just three years after the declaration of the Republic, in 1926, the foundation of the telescope building, which can be defined as the symbol of the current observatory, was laid. It was opened for service in 1936. We have no documentation about the architect of the building which is characterized by the First National Architectural Movement. As part of the Boğaziçi University, the building is not part of tour routes. Although its existence can be noticed from a great distance, we cannot discern its details because of dense forestation.

Mahmut Nedim Pasha's mansion with one of the well-preserved woodlots

Towards the end of the series, we see the Mahmut Nedim Pasha Mansion. We know that the novelist Sami Paşazade Sezai (1859-1936) lived in this mansion for many years, but there are no documents showing that part of his literary production was done here.

Its *harem* and *selamlık* quarters changed hands several times. The selamlık section belonged to the Red Crescent for a time. Later, it was acquired by a single family and used as the different units of the same property. The units were arranged so that their façades kept their original forms. The property of the Mahmut Nedim Pasha Mansion's woodlot on the slope was subdivided. The pavilion on the hill is named after Eymen Topbaş, who was an important figure of Turkish politics in the 1980s.

Great Elegance in Great Size: Kuleli Military High School

After the series of mansions and cape ends, we can see the beginning of the Kuleli Street along the shore and parks. As the street name suggests, the façade of the Kuleli Military High School dominates the opposite side of the road.

There are many people who think that this building is named after its towers (*"kule"* means "tower" in Turkish), but this is misleading. When the neighborhood was not yet named Vaniköy after Vânî Mehmet Efendi, the name of the area was Kuleli. This is most probably related to a tower built by Sultan Suleiman the Magnificent: Evliya Çelebi describes the structure as a tower with nine floors.

The main building of the Kuleli Military High School and its adjacent wing bring about a very long façade for the Bosphorus. The structure reflects the characteristics of the architecture of large barracks built during the Late Ottoman Era with a courtyard in monumental proportions.

Rows of windows with a monotonous rhythm, the highlighting of the two corners and the central entrance area are some of the leading characteristics of this tradition. In some other examples the corners are accentuated with lower units of buildings, but here, the towers and cones add originality to the façade.

The structure has a depth which is hard to perceive by the eyes of the viewer conditioned by the splendid façade. The part between the two towers on the shore is actually the short side of the rectangular body of the building that moves inland from the sea.

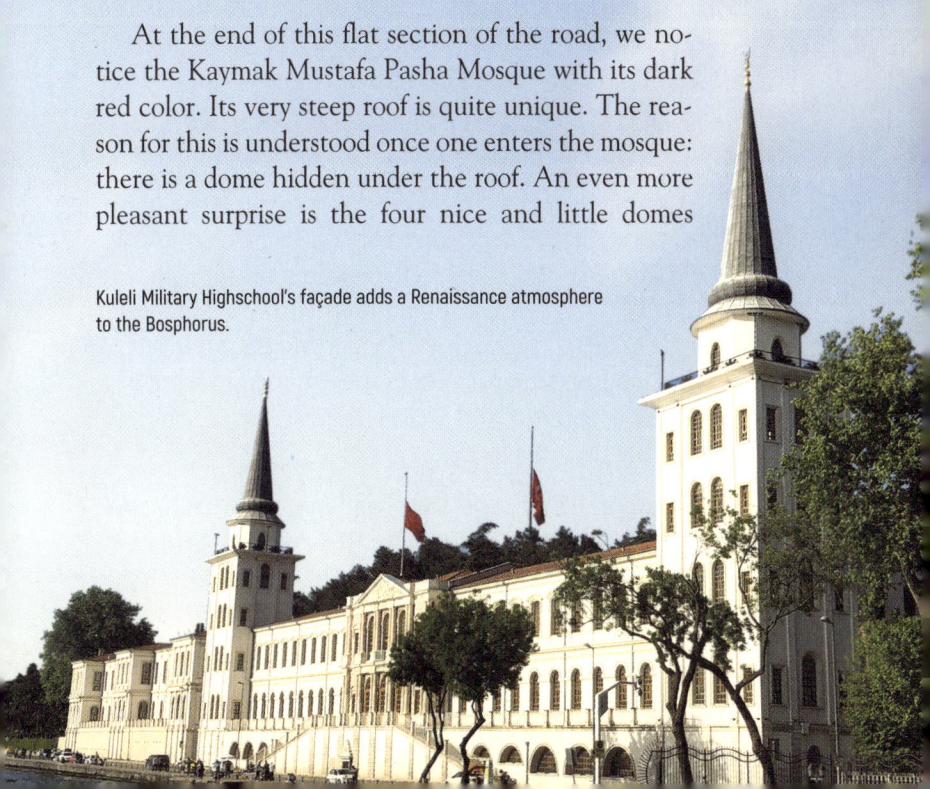

At the end of this flat section of the road, we notice the Kaymak Mustafa Pasha Mosque with its dark red color. Its very steep roof is quite unique. The reason for this is understood once one enters the mosque: there is a dome hidden under the roof. An even more pleasant surprise is the four nice and little domes

Kuleli Military Highschool's façade adds a Renaissance atmosphere to the Bosphorus.

Kaymak Mustafa Paşa's mosque and its unexpected dome

filling the empty spaces towards the corners on four sides of the main dome. One should take the chance to climb up the stairs to enter the building. After all, this is a *"fevkani"* style mosque (two-storey mosque). In other words, its main space is positioned a bit higher than ground level.

Unlike those who prefer being buried along the Bosphorus, the Pasha was buried in the cemetery of the Beyazıt Merzifonlu Kara Mustafa Pasha Madrasah in the city center, most probably because it was deemed more prestigious. However, he was not lucky, and in 1956, his tombstone was broken into two pieces when his tomb was being transferred after the expropriation of the cemetery.

Following this, there are many parks along the coastline. Then there are some industrial buildings, first on the opposite side of the road along the parks and then both on inland and along the coast. The buildings on the shore were arranged as hotels, cafes, and restaurants. Once these buildings start, the road goes inland, and it is no longer a coastal road. Definitely, it is best to view this area by boat.

On this line, there are the Köçeoğlu and Vahdettin pavilions on the top of the hill. This group of structures was enlarged inland, and after comprehensive arrangements, they began functioning as the Prime Minister's Anatolian Office.

The buildings we see are first the Köçeoğlu Pavilion, the Vahdettin Pavilion in the middle with its bulbous dome and the twin pavilions of *Kadınefendi* and *Ağavad*. The existence of these last two was known, but their exact locations could not be determined. They were reclaimed on the same line with the others, most probably to make the best use of the view.

The Vahdettin Pavilion is particularly impressive with its dominating position over the Bosphorus. It announces that it is not a mansion, but it still has a light architecture as might be seen in summer resorts, like on the Princess Islands. It shines out with its asymmetrical body, its part with the Baroque eaves and especially with its elegant tower on the corner. It should be stated that it could easily be a "subject for a landscape painting" when it is integrated with the accompanying trees.

It is interesting to consider the childhood of Şehzade (Crown Prince) Vahdettin who was later to become the last sultan of the Ottoman Empire (r. 1918-1922) as we mention the *Kadınefendi Dairesi* (Lady Governess' apartments). His mother Gülistû Hanımefendi passed away when the prince was a baby. He was only six months old when he lost his father Sultan Abdülmecit.

Villas on the slopes (80s) and a hotel housed in a former factory

Kemalettin Tuğcu, a very prolific novelist, published more than 200 books in his 94-year lifetime.

The mansion is a sign of loyalty to the "*kadınefendi*" the Governess who raised him.

There is a large cemetery behind the large grounds of the mansion. The most famous resident is the author Kemalettin Tuğcu, after whom the street going towards the center of Çengelköy is named.

Returning back to the shore, we will soon have a direct view of the Çengelköy ferry pier. We observe that some of the

Bostancıbaşı Abdullah Ağa Mansion was recently rebuilt as well.

One of the jewels of the Bosphorus: Sadullah Pasha Mansion, an extremely well-preserved Ottoman home

long-gone buildings were reconstructed from the port onwards. Among these, the most striking one is the Abdullah Ağa Waterfront Mansion, which is currently painted in yellow and whose careful reconstruction was made by Architect Dr. Sinan Genim, who also restored the Vahdettin Pavilion. The wide platform added in its front as part of its modern function is absolutely not part of the Ottoman tradition.

One of the most precious witnesses to the history of Çengelköy and the whole Bosphorus is the Sadullah Pasha Mansion that we see just after the Abdullah Ağa Mansion. It was once talked about much in the media because of some famous persons who rented it. The *selamlık* quarter of the mansion which is among the few examples that survived from the 18th century no longer exists, only the harem quarter has survived.

One of the nice surprises of this mansion, which appears to be covered with a roof from outside, is its dome over the hall room which is hidden under the roof. We just saw a similar example in Kaymak Mustafa Pasha Mosque. This type of dome, which is called as "Çârpuşta" ("with four veils" in Persian, that is to say, "roofed") was a quite typical component of the Ottoman civil architecture that we are used to seeing now.

The survival of the mansion in such good condition with its well-kept garden was made possible thanks to the diligent restorations it went through and the meticulous protection of the Tek Esin Foundation. Architects Turgut Cansever and Cahide Tamer, whom was mentioned in reference to the restoration of Rumelihisarı, assumed active roles in the restoration of this mansion, whose value was understood much earlier than many other buildings.

تُورْكَ ائِلْغَتِى

تُورْكْ دِيلْلَرِنِكْ اشْتِقَاقِى وَأَدَبِى لُغَتْلَرِى

Hüseyin Kazım Kadri's Ottoman/Turkish dictionary and his waterfront residence

We again come across a sequence of waterfront apartments. The next ten buildings or so are not much pleasant to see (they might probably be a bit pleasing for their residents), whereas there are a few excellent examples of cultural heritage, such as the pink Hüseyin Kazım Kadri Mansion on the shore. Hüseyin Kazım Kadri was known for his political personality and his pro-sultanate writings during the first years of the Republic. He stood out with his rather skeptical and even negative attitude toward Atatürk. His memoirs make this very clear. He wrote other works under the nickname Sheikh Muhsin-i Fânî ez-Zâhirî. His most well-known work is "*Türk Lûgati, Türk Dillerinin İştikakı ve Edebî Lûgatleri*" (Turkish Dictionary, The Etymology of Turkic Languages and Their Literary Dictionaries"). He started writing this work just before the Alphabet Revolution (1928) and finished afterwards. The first two volumes were printed in the Arabic alphabet and the other two in the Latin alphabet.

Later, Fahrettin Kerim Gökay (Long term Governor of Istanbul 1949-1957), bought the Hüseyin Kazım Kadri Mansion from his heirs but never lived in it. Currently, it is used as a fish restaurant.

Next is a residence designed in the 1970s. The mansion is the work of Architect Utarit İzgi and his colleagues. Although it does not make any direct references to traditional forms, it

Not a traditional building but it clearly respects the traditional architecture (70s).

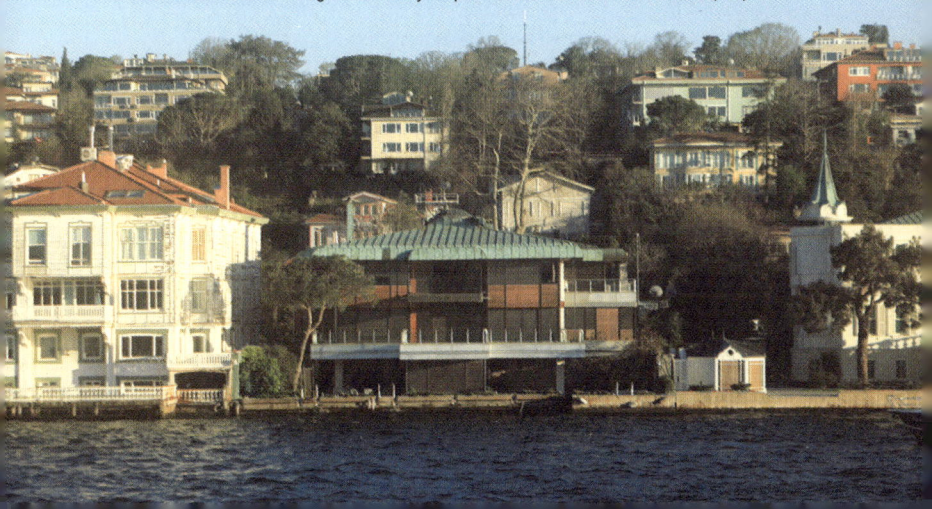

proves that its designer is in full command of the tradition and also an intellectual representative of contemporary architecture.

The base floor of the three-storied composition is comparatively light and hollow. The design is balanced with the proper distribution of materials used on the upper floors and the calm lines of the balcony and the terraces. The copper coated roof adds a modern elegance and architectural mastery beyond the aesthetics of tiled roofs.

It is also important to mention the *Haydarabad Nizamı* (Hyderabad Rajah) Mansion with two towers. We should at least remember that the members of the Ottoman Dynasty had surprising marriages with the Hyderabad rajahs, the richest Muslims of the period, and how the rajahs gained some nobility through these marriages. The mansion was used as a film set for the "Topkapı" movie (1964, with Melina Mercouri and Peter Ustinov). Being a rather old movie, perhaps it has been already forgotten by most. This is the rearranged architecture of the *selamlık* quarter of the Hasip Pasha Mansion.

The residence which is presently known as the Hasip Pasha Mansion is actually the *harem* quarter and it is next to this *selamlık* quarter with two towers. It burnt down completely and was later reconstructed on the same plot of land, but a little bit further from the sea. It should be seen as a successful reconstruction. It is only incoherent in one way: Since it was built a

Hasip Paşa Mansion was totally swept by fire.

little set back from the shore with a dock area left in its front, the eaves, cornered on the sides and convex in the middle, no longer stand above the water. Thus, the thin line between an architecture that overflows above the sea and a residence overlooking the sea is crossed in this example.

We are approaching a mosque. The mansion, which was designed by Vallauri for İsmail Bey, the member of parliament from Debre, was adjacent to the mosque, and it burnt down (the identical mansion which was built in its place is used as a hotel and a restaurant). One of the repurposed boathouses of the Bosphorus belongs to this mansion. The terrace formed on the boathouse was used as a basement floor. The opening of the boathouse in the façade was covered with glass for receiving light and insulating it from the sea. The restaurant part of the building is here, where one feels no detachment from the sea, at all.

A Peaceful Dock in Beylerbeyi

Beylerbeyi Mosque was designed as a "waterfront mosque". Architect Sinan's Şemsi Pasha mosque complex and the "New Mosque" (*Yeni Cami*), embracing the Golden Horn as a monumental example, are part of this tradition as well. Beylerbeyi Mosque also exhibits some components of palace applications beyond mosque architecture. It faces the sea with a symmetrical body. The dynamism of the building, however, is weak and the simple row of windows are not much different from palace-mansion architecture. The upper floor was reserved for the sultan's visit, and this builds a direct relation with residential architecture. The basement lightened with porticos, and the timber-look felt in the upper floors despite the windows set an example of how the Ottoman architecture approaches balance.

Despite all this solemnity, a bitter experience revealed that the mosque's lead coated dome was actually made of timber instead of the same material as the remaining of the structure, which is stone. The dome was entirely burnt down in a fire. After the mosque stayed uncovered for a short period of time, it was revived with a diligent restoration.

Later on, along the shore of Beylerbeyi, there is a work of Sedad Hakkı Eldem, which was for many years known as the Pink Waterfront Mansion (*Pembe Yalı*). Since the building quietly changed color, it was erased from our memories. Its sea façade is shadowed by the additional spaces of glass and polymer, required by restaurant architecture. Therefore, it is not possible to feel the real Münevver Ayaşlı Mansion, a 1930s work of Eldem.

Since we have come to her house, we can say a couple of words about its owner. While she was the bride of Sadullah Pasha whom we mentioned earlier, she was actually more famous for the books she wrote. In one of them, in 1975, she talks about Bosphorus mansions' restorations, as well reporting Albert Gabriel's words: "When I hear the words restoration in Turkey I shiver with fear, because I know from earlier examples that the restoration will certainly sweep away the authentic and real identity of the historical and beautiful building and instead there will be an undefined identity and meaning deprived of any style." Ayaşlı is still present on the Bosphorus as she rests in the Aşiyan Cemetery.

Beylerbeyi Mosque stands still since the 1770s.

Beylerbeyi Palace: Resort and Exile on the Bosphorus

The shore now brings us to Beylerbeyi Palace (1865). Like many other splendid buildings of the Bosphorus, this place should undoubtedly be extensively studied. What we can see as we pass by on a boat can only give us some hints.

The construction of Beylerbeyi Palace with timber material dates back to the reign of Mahmut II. Surely, its land was much larger in its time. The area it is located is referred to as İstavroz Bahçesi ("Cross Garden"). There are baseless arguments about the origin of this name. Most probably it is named such because it has the *Cihar Bağ* (four gardens") form with its distinct paths drawing a + ("plus") sign. The name İstavroz ("Cross") is regularly used in historical documents.

The present state of the palace reflects the period of Abdülaziz. We also remember Beylerbeyi as the palace where Abdülhamit II spent his last years (1912-1918).

When we talk about the size of its land, we mean a much larger area than we can think of today: it becomes easier to perceive that the former size of the land cannot be compared with its current size if we think of the fact that one part of the land was separated for deer where they could walk about freely. Together with the First Bosphorus Bridge and the planning of surrounding roads, dozens of decares were allocated to the Directorate General of Highways. The Non-Commissioned Officers School also rests on dozens of acres of land which was part of this property.

Beylerbeyi Palace, main building (1860s)

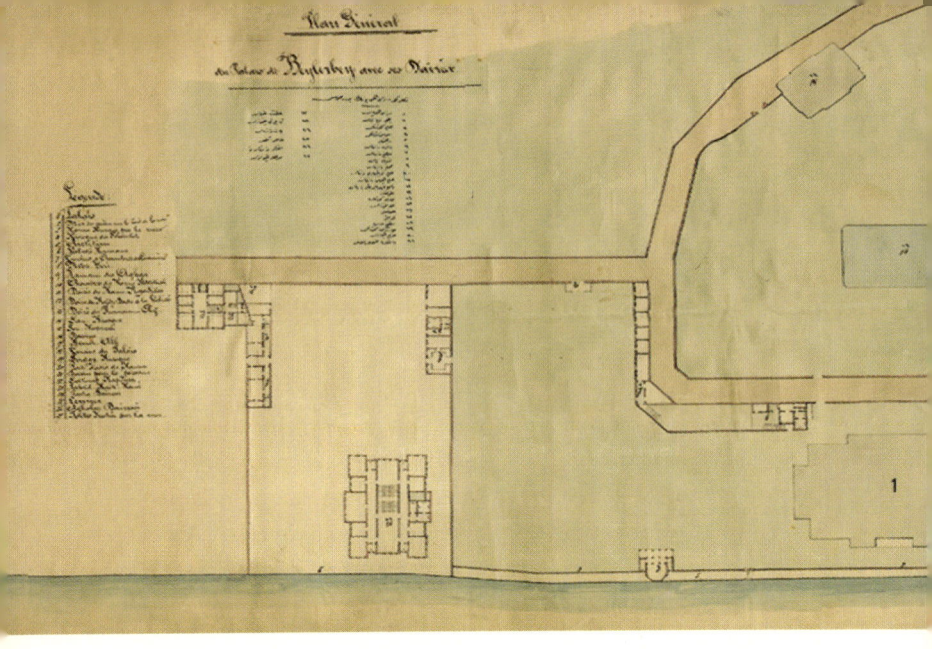

We know that the gardens of the property spread on the hills and extended up to the *Millet Bahçesi* public garden, that is to say to almost Altunizade. One of the units here is presently in use as the Presidential Office on the Asian side.

As we pass by the shore, we notice the sea kiosks on the dock in front of the main building. These are elements close to the picturesque-exotic structures in Europe. The shape of their main body and roof could well be seen almost as reflecting a tent effect. The building has many Western influences and the positioning of these sea kiosks, one towards the harem and the other towards the *selamlık*, is again part of the Turkish house tradition. Unfortunately, the series of small domes above the entrances cannot be noticed from the sea, because, although the kiosks were designed to contemplate the Bosphorus, they do not offer any access to or from the sea. The sea can only be discerned through an opening on the wall which completely cuts the garden's connection to the sea.

The terraced gardens of private residences were mostly subdivided into parcels and used with different functions by their owners, or they were destroyed completely. Hence, although many of the terraced gardens have lost their integrity, they were partially preserved (actually despite some serious losses) on the

Plan of the Beylerbeyi Palace compound (1888)

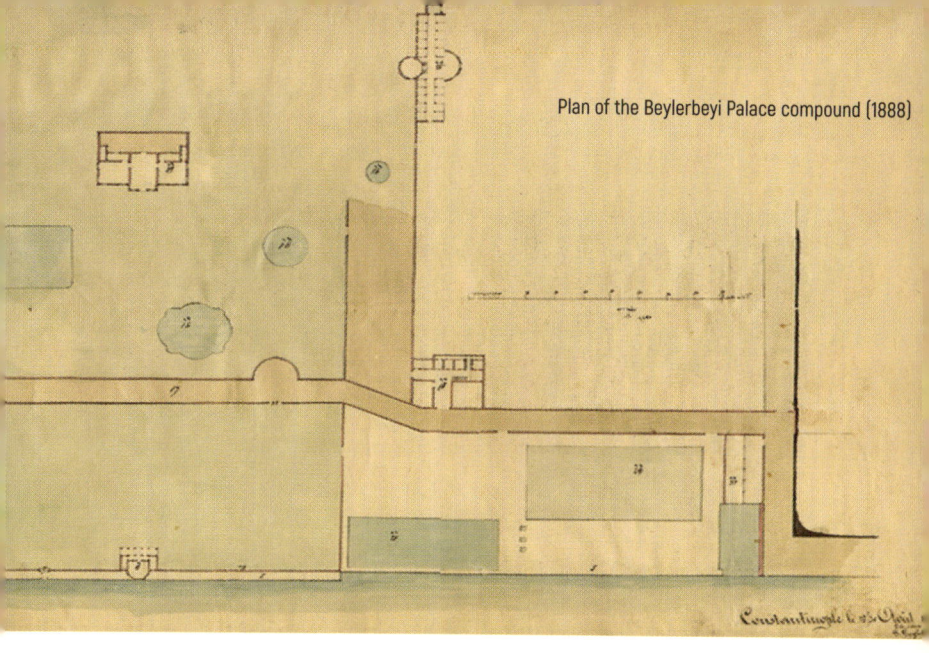

grounds of this palace. Developing a tour route that would make it possible to dig deeper to this area would be a good idea.

There is also the tunnel which passes under the bridge leaving behind the military facilities. It was once open for motor vehicles, and many of them have passed through it. This is no longer possible.

As we pass by on our boat, we can admire the terraces even from a distance. We find consolation in the fact that the tunnel was anyhow not visible and we regain our good spirits when we see two adjacent mansions just after the military facilities following the bridge. They are not in very good condition, but both of them are high-quality buildings. Halil Haşim Bey (whose architect was Vallauri) and Kâmil Pasha mansions.

As we look towards the slope, we can see that the buildings named Cemil Molla Pavilion dominate the whole slope. There was a mention of the Italian Alberti as its architect, but we do not have any clear evidence to substantiate it. The Üryanizade Masjid, a charity building of the same family, is on the shore. It is a complete timber structure. When looked closely, it is seen with great pleasure that the minaret is no exception to this. The mansion of the family used to be located next to the masjid, but the masjid was preserved, and the mansion was replaced by an apartment.

The shore with many car parking areas continues without any mansions again. There is the Nakkaştepe Cemetery on the slopes just above. The headquarters of Koç Holding is in Nakkaştepe.

Üryanizade Mosque's wooden minaret

Kuzguncuk

We are now in Kuzguncuk, where there are residences again, and the road is again behind the mansions, hence cannot be seen from the sea. Up there we have the Marko Pasha Mansion, which is currently used as a school. As we get closer to the dock, we notice the domes of the two adjacent and popular religious buildings of Kuzguncuk behind the mansions and the road. One is Kuzguncuk Mosque and the other Surp Kirkor Lusavoriç Church.

Kuzguncuk has resisted against high-rise buildings; its timber buildings, or at least the timber-covered ones, were protected when the roads were widened. The texture of the neighborhood deserves a visit on foot, rather than just viewing it from the sea. You can even see synagogues and a Greek church if you walk inland.

Speaking of synagogues, İnciciyan, who wrote about Kuzguncuk in 1794, states that "the Jewish people believe the soil of this place is holy for burial" (160).

As we turn back to the shore, in contrast with the other piers of the Bosphorus where timber is the main material, we notice the timber Kuzguncuk Pier. This piece by Architect Talat Bey was demolished. After serving in an anonymous state for a long time, it was transformed into its present condition through a diligent reconstruction under the responsibility of Architect Barış Han. In its present state, the Kuzguncuk Pier is also a product of the architectural conception of the early 20th century, which is referred to as "national movement". Its land façade with three arches was designed in likeness of a classical mid-size Ottoman mosque. The tile-covered surfaces which are unusual on mosque doors have almost accentuated the "Ottoman feel" of the structure. The towers on the upper part, on the other hand, bear traces of the Art Nouveau architecture seen in Central and Western Europe in the same period. Thus, the "national" lines of the dock are combined with an "international" dimension.

Although Kuzguncuk goes on pleasing the eyes with the series of mansions that continue after the dock, the greater gift of this area is surely the Fethi Ahmet Pasha Mansion. The grounds of the mansion, whose *selamlık* has survived, used to cover the woodlot that covers the slope behind the road. The woodlot which is currently a recreational area is named after the Pasha.

The Pasha is usually remembered in Turkey for his foundation of the *Asar-ı Atika* (Antiquities) Museum inside the Hagia Eirene Church and excavating the Byzantine Hippodrome. His fame can be seen in the fact that some European composers, Johann Strauss (Op.96) to begin with, dedicating some of their waltzes to him. Fethi Ahmet Pasha is also directly related to the places we mentioned on our route along the Bosphorus: he got married to Atiye Sultan, sister of Sultan Abdülmecit who commissioned the construction of Dolmabahçe Palace. Fethi Ahmet Pasha was appointed as the Grand Master of Artillery, and he took an active role in the furnishing of Dolmabahçe Palace. He managed the Beykoz glass factory, contributed to the popularization and development of Çeşmibülbül. He also managed the Şirket-i Hayriye Company, which ran the ferries of Istanbul until 1945.

Paşalimanı

Following the mansions on the shore, there is a wide park. As we mentioned earlier, this area is not originally intended to be used as a park. The reason why a place which is remembered as Öküz (ox) port area is called Paşalimanı is that *Sadrazam* (grand vizier) Hüseyin Avni Pasha's mansion used to be here. Part of the woodlot between them belonged to this mansion. A kiosk, inside which was also named after the Pasha, recently burnt down (162).

Just across the road, we can notice a fountain, which is visible from the sea as well (if the parked cars in front of it would allow). It is one of the most splendid fountains of the Ottoman Era with its ten basins. Looking at the fountain, it is not difficult to imagine the splendor of the mansion. The structure combines many characteristics in itself; it is different from the classical and post-classical compositions in Ottoman

The monumental Hüseyin Avni Pasha Fountain

Hüseyin Avni Pasha's tomb behind the Süleymaniye Mosque

art. Actually, the central composition is conventional, and the arrangement is one that became dominant after the mid-18th century. However, both sides of the center were extended with four marble covered surfaces, and a large and horizontal façade was created.

It consists of a central part where water comes out, a midsection with Rococo touches, and landscape architecture that surrounds it. The arches expressed in concave and convex lines widen towards the upper section. The design is accompanied by two thin columns on both sides and the volutes supported by them. The upper part has a wavy surface that both houses the inscription and crowns the structure. The elevated mid part of the façade joins the side units with an elegant wave motion. The whole composition is monumental as is enriched with exquisite details and assumes a Baroque character with this movement. We should definitely consider Hüseyin Avni Pasha, who had this fountain built, an animal lover: there are basins without taps, but with holes beneath them so that they are filled with water. This suggests that there were basins reserved for animals.

We know that the splendid mansion, whose fountain was only a detail, was used as a tobacco storehouse during the Republican Era. A couple of years ago the newspapers wrote about the municipality's intention to rebuild the mansion here. There

The Paşalimanı Storehouses nearby a historic mill, now house a theater.

will be those who still remember the Pasha with the critical role he played in the coup which dethroned Sultan Abdülaziz and declared Murat V as the new sultan. His splendid tomb at the burial grounds of Süleymaniye Mosque is also worth remembering.

As soon as we leave the park behind, we see large warehouses on the opposite side towards the road. Now they are allocated for theatre activities. Next, to it, there is a mill which lost its floors except for the four walls and its chimney. The mill was built in 1858. It has a special value within industrial heritage as one of the oldest mills in Istanbul. There was a thesis which was about its reuse as a public building. However, it was sold to a group of construction companies by a family in the textile business who owns the land on the slope behind it. Most probably this building will be used as an office like the tobacco warehouse we will see soon. The news about its sale was heard long ago, but there is still no action.

The Paşalimanı Tobacco storehouse houses a large enterprise's offices.

The land on the slope we mentioned above is separated from the Fethi Ahmet Pasha Woodlot in a vague manner. It is the woodlot of Nuri Demirağ, whom was mentioned in connection his "aircraft workshop" in Beşiktaş. It is also named after Halide Edip Adıvar, who lived in the mansion here.

Looking back to the shoreline, we see the multi-storyed Şark *Tütün Deposu* (Tobacco Warehouse) designed by the Architect Vedat Tek. It is also known as the Nemlizade Tütün Deposu. It stands out as a highly diligent design compared with the warehouse function ascribed to it. It is presently used as the headquarters of a private group of companies. The old photographs show that there was a miniature pinnacle tower on one of its corners. However, this unit was not rebuilt because it has no function today.

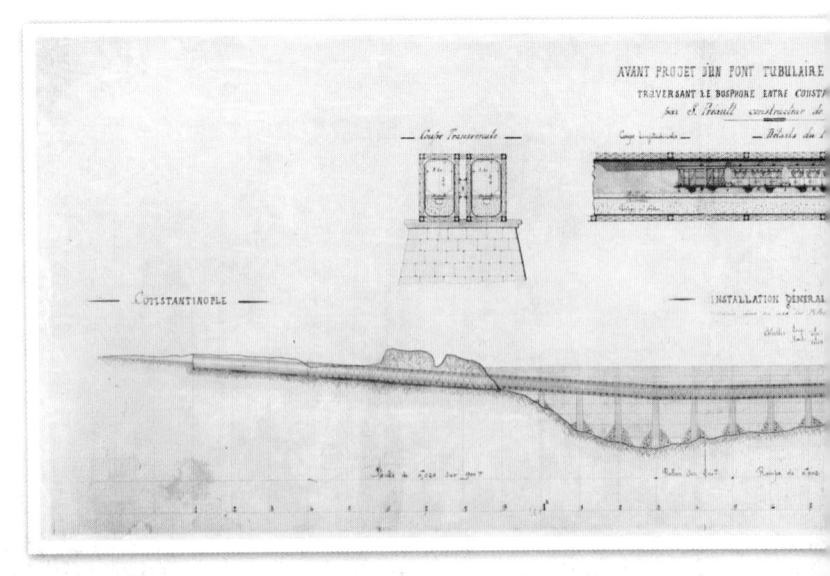

The first project for the Eurasia Tunnel (1891)

Dream City Üsküdar

We are finally approaching the Üsküdar Square. We notice the somehow hidden Mihrimah Mosque Complex among the chaos of the area. Even the fountain which was positioned as a kiosk looking towards the sea instead of being squeezed in a covered courtyard by Architect Sinan is hard to notice. The dome of the fountain is unexpectedly painted in green. The fountain and another one added to the wall below provide a lovely view when looked carefully during the sunset.

Then we greet the square fountain of Ahmet III. It is a simpler example of the fountain, which is named after the same sultan, located just in the Topkapı Palace, in front of Bab-ı Hümayun (The Imperial Gate). The one in the Topkapı Palace is a square fountain with the same design on all of its façades, the one in Üsküdar has an arch on its sea façade only. This wide arch covers the fountain and on both sides of the fountain two splendid niche arrangements still survive. It is clear that it was intended as a single-sided waterfront fountain instead of a square fountain. Currently, it is difficult to define it as a square fountain because it is surrounded by city traffic and also because physically there is no square.

We observe that the integrity of the square was entirely lost due to numerous metro superstructures.

This could have been the entrance for the metro even in 1891: There is a detailed drawing about this in the State Archives, and it was published by several researchers. As far as understood from the drawings the tunnel which was planned to be built 130 years ago would have impacted the surface less in Üsküdar.

Behind the modern and (un)designed, random forms arranged for Marmaray, we see another structure that also failed in creating the desired visual impression. This is the Valide-i Cedid Mosque, a sort of *selâtin* (imperial) mosque.

Thankfully, the Şemsi Pasha Mansion still preserves its mansion characteristics. It is adjacent to the mosque on the sea direction. It is an unusual building with its tomb placed by the waterside. The Şemsi Pasha Mosque Complex is not usually cited when listing the masterpieces of Architect Sinan. However, this design is like a lesson that teaches us how a group of small-sized structures can be arranged in harmony with one another and how they can be integrated with the sea. Actually, the volume of the bodies of buildings, their height, and the accompanying domes form the main architectural idea are in line with the classical Ottoman architecture. The porticos also function as the main source of harmony for the relation between full and void. Here the architect balances the building not only in relation to water, by the sea, but also to the landscape on the hill and the structures on the slopes, hence, creates a visual extension of the Rum Mehmet Pasha Mosque that rises in the background. Thus, Şemsi Pasha complex are able provide good lessons.

An articulated religious complex in a limited plot of land, Şemsi Pasha by Sinan (circa 1580)

However, this small mosque complex, placed on land surrounded by other buildings, is currently isolated. It is easy to guess that there used to be waterfront mansions on both sides of it. Today, it is difficult to believe that there used to be another tobacco warehouse and factory adjacent to it on the opposite side of the road until the 1980s. It was much larger than the other tobacco warehouses along the Bosphorus, and it was a tasteful work of design. However, unlike the others that were repurposed, it was regrettably demolished in favor of a coastal road and a never-built square in Üsküdar. It was a construction led by Victor Adaman, whom we mentioned in reference to the tobacco warehouse in Beşiktaş.

Finally, we can have a quick look at the Maiden's Tower that we pass by: it is not easy to place the architectural characteristics of the Maiden's Tower within the traditional lighthouse architecture. The Maiden's Tower evolved into an independent image due its location, size, and forms. It is actually a lighthouse. The ground floor, reserved for administrative work, give horizontality to the building and it also accentuates the section which rises up in a tower form. A prismatic main body and the recessed upper part with windows and the cover are the main components. As the style and construction techniques of Ottoman architecture have changed throughout centuries, the Maiden's Tower was restored accordingly. The distant relationship with the Beyazıt Tower or the relative similarity with the sliced dome of Alay Köşkü, for example, are all related to the chronological synchronicities of past interventions.

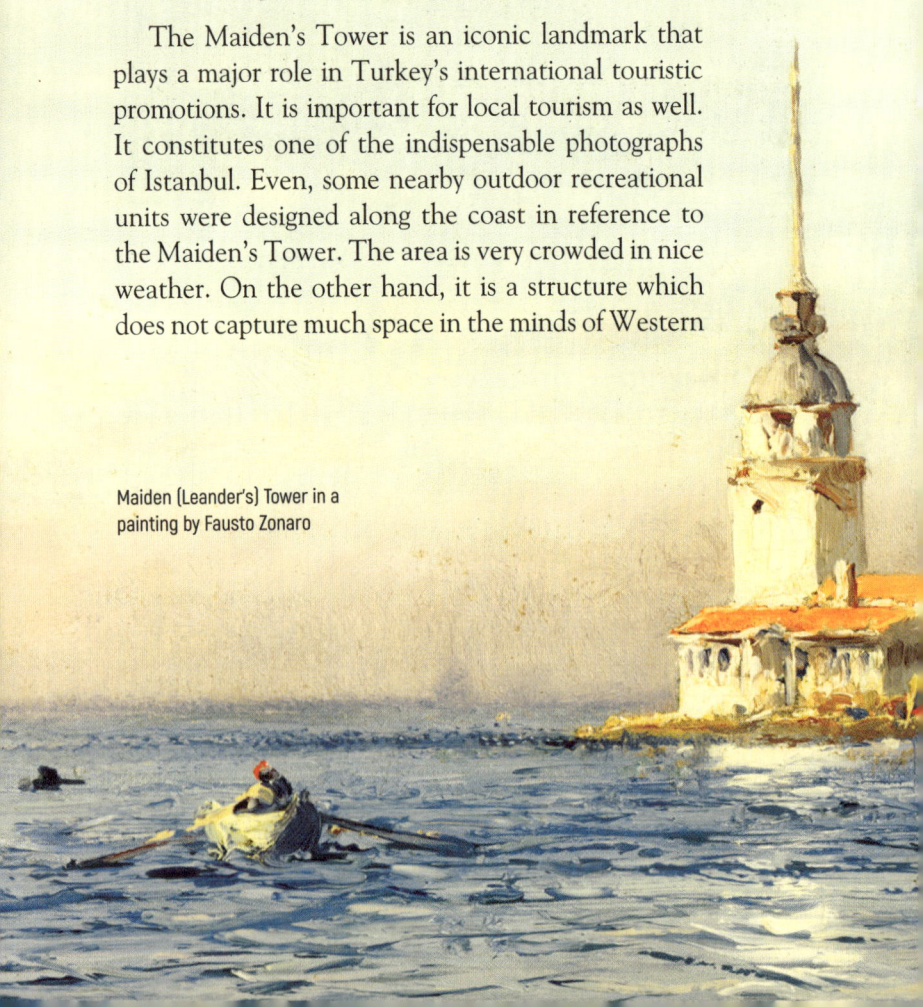

The Maiden's Tower is an iconic landmark that plays a major role in Turkey's international touristic promotions. It is important for local tourism as well. It constitutes one of the indispensable photographs of Istanbul. Even, some nearby outdoor recreational units were designed along the coast in reference to the Maiden's Tower. The area is very crowded in nice weather. On the other hand, it is a structure which does not capture much space in the minds of Western

Maiden (Leander's) Tower in a painting by Fausto Zonaro

tourists when they think about Istanbul. The Western world showed the greatest interest in this building, which is actually a rock with a small hut-like tower on it, in the 19th century in Orientalist compositions.

We stated in the beginning that "the Maiden's Tower marks a sort of a beginning line" of the Bosphorus. With this in mind, we are once again passing under the Galata Bridge and headed towards the Golden Horn. We could recite the poems of Yahya Kemal Beyatlı, who is deeply associated with many places along the Bosphorus. Lines from one of his most famous poems were inscribed on the Barbaros Monument in Beşiktaş just across Üsküdar. *"Süleymaniye'de Bayram Sabahı"* (The Morning of a Holiday, in Süleymaniye). And we now raise our eyes slightly and once again approach the Yemiş Pier under auspices of the indelible seal impressed on the silhouette of Istanbul by the Mosque of Süleyman the Magnificent and thus conclude the story of several thousands of years, just at the very point where we had departed from.

ILLUSTRATION ACKNOWLEDGEMENTS

3	Voyage pittoresque de Constantinople et des rives du Bosphore, Antoine Ignace Melling	118	Boğaziçi Lisesi Yıllığı, 1936
		119	Dumbarton Oaks Research Library and Collection
10	BNF Gallica	128-129	Library of Congress
12-13	BNF Gallica	133	Erol Makzume Image Archive
15	Bosforo Tracio, Luigi Ferdinando Marsili	134	BOA PLK_p__00603_0001
		136-137	Erol Makzume Image Archive
21	Private Collection	138-139	Châteaux turcs du Bosphore, Albert Gabriel
32	Erol Makzume Image Archive		
34-35	Erol Makzume Image Archive	141	Hayri Fehmi Yılmaz
37	Salt Research	144-145	The Engineer, 13 Eylül 1867
38	Salt Research	145	Neues System für Eisen-Brücken grosser Spannweiten, Karl Ruppert
42	Hydrodynamica, Daniel Bernoulli		
42-43	Voyage pittoresque de Constantinople et des rives du Bosphore, Antoine Ignace Melling		
		151	H. Demet AKSU
		155	BOA PLK_p__3566_0001
		155	BOA PLK_p__3580_0001
44	Arolat Mimarlık	155	BOA PLK_p__3593_0001
46	Hüseyin Özkan	156 üst	Nevzat Sayın
48 alt	Salt Research	157 üst	Nevzat Sayın
52-53	The J. Paul Getty Trust	176 üst	Garbis Özatay
54	Library of Congress	178 ve 179	Austrian State Archives
58	Erol Makzume Image Archive	180	Dennis Jarvis
61	BOA PLK_p__3109_0001	183	Alataş Mimarlık
64	BOA PLK_p__01091_0001	186	Alataş Mimarlık, Photo Gürkan Akay
64 alt	Ministry of Foreign Affairs Archive - Rome - Italy		
		190-191	BOA PLK_p__3500_0006
66	Turkish State Archives 59 - 397 - 6	193-194	BCA 230-0-0-0 / 61 - 27 - 1
66 alt	Teğet Mimarlık; Photo Alican Aktürk	195 üst	Garbis Özatay
		200	Master and Fellows of Trinity College Cambridge
67 üst	Teğet Mimarlık; Photo Alican Aktürk		
		202	BOA PLK_p__00685_0001
72	İstanbul Arkaeological Museums	204-205	Voyage pittoresque de Constantinople et des rives du Bosphore, Antoine Ignace Melling
77	BOA PLK_p__2993_0002		
78	BCA 30 - 52 - 3		
85	Vakıflar Genel Müdürlüğü, Murat Sav		
86	Vakıflar Genel Müdürlüğü, Murat Sav	206 üst	Barış Han
		225	Şerif Yenen
91	Salt Research	229	Erol Makzume Image Archive
94	BOA PLK_p__00375_0001	234	Library of Congress
96	Garbis Özatay	235	Alexxx Malev
97	Önder Kaya	236-237	Sinan Genim
98-99	BNF Gallica	238 üst	Sinan Genim
102-103	Voyage pittoresque de Constantinople et des rives du Bosphore, Antoine Ignace Melling	253	Alexxx Malev
		259	Hüseyin Özkan (Timaş archive)
		258	BOA PLK.p..3002
		266-267	BCA 95 - 40 - 2
106	Salt Research	271	depositphotos.com
111	Önder Kaya	272-273	Erol Makzume Image Archive
112-113	BOA PLK_p__2925		
113	Alataş Mimarlık, Photo Cemal Emden		

BIBLIOGRAPHY

Adil, S. (1980). *Hayat Mücadeleleri Selahattin Adil Paşa'nın Hatıraları*. (E. Koray, Ed.). İstanbul.
Akozan, F. (1991). *Sait Halim Paşa Yalısı*. Ankara: Türkiye Kalkınma Bankası A.Ş.
Akpınar, İ. Y. (2013). *Boğaziçi Emirgan Atlı Köşk: Sakıp Sabancı Müzesi'nin 10 yılı*. (A. Anadol, Ed.). İstanbul: Sakıp Sabancı Müzesi.
Alpagut, L. (2012). *Cumhuriyetin Mimarı Ernst Arnold Egli*. İstanbul: Boyut Yayınları.
Altıntaş, S. (2016). *Boğaz'ın Dört Muhafızı*. İstanbul: Destek Yayınları.
Anderson, M. S. (2001). *Doğu Sorunu - 1774-1923 Uluslararası İlişkiler Üzerine Bir İnceleme*. İstanbul: Yapı Kredi Yayınları.
Arslan, M. (2010). *İstanbul'un Antikçağ Tarihi klasik ve Hellenistik Dönemler*. İstanbul: Odin Yayıncılık.
Asan, Ü. (2010). *Boğaziçi'nde Yaşayan Tarih Zamana Tanıklık Eden Anıt Ağaçlar*. İstanbul: İstanbul Büyükşehir Belediyesi Ağaç ve Peyzaj Müdürlüğü.
Aslanoğlu, İ. (1983). 1936-1938 Yılları Türkiye'sinde Eğitici ve Mimar Olarak Bruno Taut. In *Bruno Taut, 1880-1938 : Türkiye'de Mimar ve Öğretmen, 1936-1938*.
Ayaşlı, M. (2014). *İstanbul Dersaadet*. İstanbul: Timaş.
Aydemir, O. (2010). Beşiktaş Şeyh Yahya Efendi Külliyesi Onarım Çalışmaları. *Vakıf Restorasyon Yıllığı*, 1(1), 33–44.
Bachmann, M. (2012). *Boğaziçi'nde Yazlık: Alman Büyükelçisinin Tarabya'daki Yazlık Rezidansının Tarihçesi ve Gelişimi*. Almanya Federal Cumhuriyeti Büyükelçiliği-Deutsches Archaologisches Institut.
Balmumcu, Ş. (1948). Victor Adaman. *Arkitekt*, 1948(193–194), 46–47.
Barbaro, N., & Diler, Ş. T. (1976). *Kostantiniyye Muhâsarası Ruznâmesi*. İstanbul: İstanbul Fetih Cemiyeti.
Barillari, D. (2010). Modern Kozmopolit Mimariler: Raimondo D'Aronco'nun İstanbul'daki Eserleri. In *Osmanlı Mimarı D'Aronco 1893-1909 İstanbul Projeleri*. İstanbul: İstanbul Araştırmaları Enstitüsü.
Barillari, D., & Godoli, E. (1997). *İstanbul 1900: Art-Nouveau Mimarisi ve İç Mekanları*. İstanbul: Yapı Endüstri Merkezi.
Batur, A. (1998). Katafalk Ölümün Draması Duygusal ve Zarif. In *Atatürk İçin Düşünmek İki Eser Katafalk ve Anıtkabir İki Mimar Bruno Taut ve Emin Onat*. İstanbul: İstanbul Teknik Üniversitesi Rektörlüğü.
Batur, A. (2003). *M. Vedad Tek Kimliğinin İzinde Bir Mimar*. İstanbul: Yapı Kredi Yayınları.
Batur, A. (1968). *Yıldız Serencebey'de Şeyh Zafir Türbe, Kitaplık ve Çeşmesi*. İstanbul.
Batur, A. (ed.), (2015). *İstanbul Mimarlık Rehberi: Boğaziçi ve Asya Yakası C.3*. İstanbul: TMMOB Mimarlar Odası İstanbul Büyükkent Şubesi.
Bayat, A. H. (1988). *Hekim Devlet Adamı Keçecizade Mehmed Fuat Paşa'nın Nesirleri Şiirleri Nükteleri Hakkında Yazılan Şiirler*. İstanbul: Türk Dünyası Araştırmaları Vakfı.
Biasi, A. (1995). *Villa Tarabya*. Ankara: İtalyan Kültür Merkezi.
Byzantios, D. (2010). *Boğaziçi'nde Bir Gezinti*. (M. F. Yavuz, Ed.). İstanbul: Yapı Kredi Yayınları.
Çelik, G. (2012). Prens Mehmed Ali Hasan Köşkü (Atlı Köşk), Sabancı Üniversitesi Sakıp Sabancı Müzesi, Emirgan. In *Değişen Zamanların Mimarı Edoardo de Nari 1874-1954* (pp. 182–193).
Çelik, H. (1991). *Ali Suavî Hayatı ve Eserleri*. İstanbul Üniversitesi.
Çetintaş, M. B. (2009). *1453'ten 1928'e Kadar İstanbul'da Gömülmüş Türk Denizcilerinin Mezar Taşları*. İstanbul: Deniz Kuvvetleri Komutanlığı Kültür Yayınları.
Civan, C. (2013). *İstanbul'un 100 Türbesi*. İstanbul: İstanbul Büyükşehir Belediyesi Kültür A.Ş. Yayınları.

Derman, M. U. (2014). Büyük Mecidiye (Ortaköy) Camii'nin Kitabesi, Hat Levhaları ve Bunların Hattatları. In *Büyük Mecidiye Camii ve Ortaköy* (pp. 345–365).
Derman, M. U. (2013). Yesarizade Mustafa İzzet Efendi and his Contributions to Ottoman Architectural Calligraphy. In M. Gharipour & I. C. Schick (Eds.), *Calligraphy and Architecture in the Muslim World* (pp. 326–345). Edinburgh: Edinburgh University Press.
Dizer, M. (1973). *Kandilli Rasathanesi*. İstanbul: M.E.B.
Doğan, O., & Tunç, S. (2011). *Bir Zamanlar Boğaziçi- 1851*. İstanbul: Çamlıca.
Doğan, R. (söyleşi). (2010). *Toplarönü: (İstanbullu Doğan Kuban ve Boğaziçi)*. (E. Metin, Ed.). Heyamola Yayınları.
Dördüncü, M. (2015). Sadrazam İbrahim Hakkı Paşa'nın Hayatı ve Avrupa Seyahati. *Afyon Kocatepe Üniversitesi Sosyal Bilimler Dergisi*, *17*(1), 7997.
Dursun, H. (2010). *Boğaziçi'nde Kırk Yılım*.
Dursun, H. (2009). *Boğaziçi'nde Kırk Yılım*. İstanbul: Heyamola Yayınları.
Eğecioğlu, Ö. (2010). Strauss ve Lanner'in Fethi Ahmet Paşa'ya İthaf ettiği Valsler. *Sanat Dünyamız*, (118).
Egli, E. (2009). *Osmanlı Altın Çağının Mimarı Sinan*. İstanbul: Arkeoloji ve Sanat Yayınları.
Egli, E. A. (2015). *Atatürk'ün Mimarının Anıları Genç Türkiye İnşa Edilirken*. (E. Yalçın, Ed.). İstanbul: Türkiye İş Bankası Kültür Yayınları.
Ekdal, M. (2008). *Kapalı Hayat Kutusu Kadıköy Konakları*. İstanbul: Yapı Kredi Yayınları.
Eken, G., Bozdoğan, M., İsfendiyaroğlu, S., Kılıç, D. T., & Lise, Y. (Eds.). (2007). *Türkiye'nin Önemli Doğal Alanları*. Ankara: Doğa Derneği.
Eldem, S. H. (1993). *Boğaziçi Yalıları*, İstanbul: Vehbi Koç Vakfı.
Eldem, S. H. (1971). Akbank Genel Müdürlük Binası. *Arkitekt*, 112–114.
Eldem, S. H. (1977). *Köçeoğlu Yalısı, Bebek Boğaziçi le yali de Köçeoğlu, à Bebek sur le Bosphore*.
Eldem, S. H. (1971). Uşaklıgil Köşkü. *Arkitekt*, *1971*(3–343), 109–111.
Erdenen, O. (2007). *Boğaziçi Kendini Anlatıyor*, Kitabistanbul.
Erdenen, O. (2006). *Boğaziçi Sahilhaneleri: Avrupa Yakası*. İstanbul: İstanbul Büyükşehir Belediyesi Kültür A.Ş.
Erdoğan, S. (2011). *Kandilli Rasathanesi Yerleşimindeki Korunması Gerekli Kültür Varlıklarının Envanteri ve Dürbün Binası Restorasyon Projesi*, İstanbul Teknik Üniversitesi.
Erkoç, E. (2004). *Beşiktaş Muhafızı Yedi Sekiz Hasan Paşa*. Çorum: Pegasus Görsel İletişim Hizmetleri.
Eyice, S. (2007). *Bizans Devrinde Boğaziçi*, Yeditepe Yayınevi.
Femir, H. (1944). "Lido" Yüzme Havuzu. *Arkitekt*, *1944*(11–12), 155–156.
Fındıklı, E. B. (2005). Bir Mekânın Yeniden Üretimi: Park Otel. In B. Kaya (Ed.), *Dolmabahçe Mekanın Hafızası* (pp. 427–438). İstanbul: İstanbul Bilgi Üniversitesi Yayınları.
Franck, O. A. (2010). Bir Modernlik Arayışı: Emst Egli ve Türkiye (1927- 1 940). In E. A. Ergut & B. İmamoğlu (Eds.), *Cumhuriyet'in Mekanları, İnsanları, Zamanları*. Ankara: Dipnot Yayınları.
Gabriel, A. (1970). *İstanbul Türk Kaleleri*. İstanbul: Tercüman.
Girardelli, M. A. (2013). Léon Parvillée's Early Years in Istanbul: Cezayirlioğlu Mansion and the Church of Surp Krikor Lusavoriç in Kuzguncuk. In F. Hitzel (Ed.), *14th International Congress of Turkish Art Paris, 19-21 September 2011, Paris, Collège de France* (pp. 89–95). Paris.
Gölpınarlı, A. (1992). *Melamilik ve Melamiler*. İstanbul: Gri Yayın.
Göncü, C. (2011). Belgelerle Milli Saraylar. *Milli Saraylar Dergisi*, (7), 169–174.
Göncü, C. (2014). Büyük Mecidiye (Ortaköy) Camii'nin (Eser-i Cedîd-i Bî-Bedîl) İnşa Sürecine İlişkin Yeni Belgeler ve Tespitler. In *Büyük Mecidiye Camii ve Ortaköy* (pp. 245–265). İstanbul: Kuveyt Türk.
Göncü, C. (2006). Modernleşme Sürecinde Muayede Törenleri ve Dolmabahçe Sarayı'nda Uygulanışı. *Milli Saraylar Dergisi*, (3), 37–56.
Grant, R. G. (2008). *Battle at Sea: 3000 Years of Naval Warfare*. DK Publishing.

Gülersoy, Ç. (1985). *Hıdivler ve Çubuklu Kasrı*. İstanbul: Türkiye Turing ve Otomobil Kurumu.
Gülersoy, Ç. (1985). *Küçüksu: Çayır, Çeşme, Kasır Meadow, Fountain, Palace*. İstanbul: Türkiye Turing ve Otomobil Kurumu.
Güleryüz, A., & Yüce, H. (2002). *Şirket-i Hayriye'nin Boğaziçi Vapurları*. İstanbul: Denizler Kitabevi.
Güleryüz, N. (1992). *İstanbul Sinagogları*. (O. Duru, Ed.). İstanbul.
Hamlin, C. (1893). *My Life and Times*. Boston: Congressional Sunday School and Publishing Society.
Hamlin, C. (2012). *Robert Kolej Uğrunda Bir Ömür*. İstanbul: Dergah Yayınları.
Hasol, D. (2017). *20. Yüzyıl Türkiye Mimarlığı*. İstanbul: YEM.
Hellier, C. (1993). *Splendours of the Bosphorus: Houses and Palaces of Istanbul*. London: Tauris Parke Books.
Hepgüler, M. (1968). T. Sınaî Kalkınma Bankası U. Müdürlük Binası. *Arkitekt*, 1968(329), 12–15.
Herodotos. (1973). *Herodot Tarihi*. (A. Erhat, Ed.). İstanbul: Remzi Kitabevi.
Hızlı, K., & Kılınç, S. (2013). *Sultan Abdülaziz Han'ın Yadigârları Aziziye Camileri*. İstanbul: Çamlıca Basım Yayın.
Holmes, D. N. S. (2012). *The Independently Fortified Tower: An International Type in Ottoman Military Architecture 1452-1462*. Princeton University.
İhsanoğlu, E., & Kaçar, M. (Ed.). (1989). *Çağını Yakalayan Osmanlı: Osmanlı Devleti'nde Modern Haberleşme ve Ulaştırma Teknikleri*. İstanbul: İslam Tarih, Sanat ve Kültür Araştırma Merkezi (IRCICA).
İnalcık, H. (2015). *Tarihe Düşülen Notlar I*. İstanbul: Timaş.
İnalcık, H. (2011). *Rönesans Avrupası Türkiye'nin Batı Medeniyetiyle Özdeşleşme Süreci*. İstanbul: Türkiye İş Bankası Kültür Yayınları.
İnciciyan, G. V. (1998). *Boğaziçi Sayfiyeleri*. İstanbul: Eren Yayıncılık.
Irmak, E. (2012). *İstanbul Naval Museum*. İstanbul: Deniz Müzesi Komutanlığı.
Irmak, S. (2009). *Bahçesinde Deniz Olan Okul 100 Yıllık Eğitim Çınarı Kabataş Erkek Lisesi 1908/2008*. (M. Altun, Ed.). İstanbul: Kabataş Erkek Lisesi Eğitim Vakfı.
Jamgoçyan, O. (2014). *Osmanlı İmparatorluğu'nda Sarraflık: Rumlar, Museviler, Frenkler, Ermeniler (1650-1850)*. İstanbul: Yapı Kredi Yayınları.
Kadri, H. K. (2000). *Meşrutiyet'ten Cumhuriyet'e Hatıralarım: İstanbul/Trabzon/Selanik/Suriye*. (İ. Kara, Ed.). İstanbul: Dergâh Yayınları.
Kahraman, S. A., & Dağlı, Y. (Eds.). (2003). *Günümüz Türkçesiyle Evliya Çelebi Seyahatnamesi*. İstanbul: Yapı Kredi Yayınları.
Kamhi, J. V. (2007). In N. M. Cengizkan (Ed.), *Haluk Baysal - Melih Birsel* (p. 95). Ankara: MMOB Mimarlar Odası.
Kancan, S. (2009). *Unutulmuş bir Boğaziçi Yerleşimi: Beykoz*. (C. Özbatak, Ed.). İstanbul: Heyamola Yayınları.
Kaya, H. (2014). *Adalet Partisi ve Ragıp Gümüşpala (1961–1965)*. T.C. Ankara Üniversitesi.
Kayra, C. (1993). *Bebek Mekanlar ve Zamanlar*. İstanbul: Akbank.
Kayra, C., & Erol, Ü. (1993). *Kandilli Vaniköy Çengelköy Mekanlar ve Zamanlar*. İstanbul: İstanbul Büyükşehir Belediyesi.
Koçak, C. (2011). *Geçmişiniz İtinayla Temizlenir*. İstanbul: İletişim.
Koçak, M. H. (2014). *Camın İşçileri: Paşabahçe İşçilerinin Sınıf Olma Öyküsü*. İstanbul: İletişim Yayınları.
Kona, S. (2015). *Paşalimanı Un Fabrikası ve Yeniden İşlevlendirme*. Maltepe Üniversitesi.
Kostandov, P. G. (2011). *İstanbullu Bulgarlar ve Eski İstanbul Geçmişten Günümüze Osmanlı Bakiyesi Bulgarlar Üzerine Bir Araştırma 1800-2000*. İstanbul: Sanat Dükkânı Yayıncılık.
Kuban, D. (2007). *Osmanlı Mimarisi*. İstanbul: YEM Yayın.
Küçükerman, Ö. (2002). *Beykoz Camları: 200 yıllık Boğaziçi Camcılık Mirası içinde*. İstanbul: Türkiye Şişe ve Cam Fabrikaları A.Ş.

Kuran, A. (2002). *Bir Kurucu Rektörün Anıları: Robert Kolej Yüksekokulu'ndan Boğaziçi Üniversitesi'ne*. (G. Danışman, Ed.). İstanbul: Boğaziçi Üniversitesi.
Kuran, A. (1986). *Mimar Sinan*. İstanbul: Hürriyet Vakfı Yayınları.
Kuruyazıcı, H. (Ed.). (2011). *Batılılaşan İstanbul'un Ermeni Mimarları*. İstanbul: Hrant Dink Vakfı.
Kut, G., & Eldem, E. (2010). *Rumelihisarı Şehitlik Dergahı Mezar Taşları*. İstanbul: Boğaziçi Üniversitesi Yayınevi.
Loud, G. A. (2010). *The Crusade of Frederick Barbarossa: The History of the Expedition of the Emperor Frederick and Related Texts*. Routledge.
Makzume, E., & Trevigne, C. M. (2011). *Twenty Years Under the Reign of Abdülhamid The Memoirs and Works of Fausto Zonaro*. İstanbul: Geniş Kitaplık.
Marsili, L. F. (1681). *Osservazioni intorno al Bosforo Tracio overo Canale di Costantinopoli, rappresentate in lettera alla sacra real maesta di Cristina regina di Svezia*. Roma: Nicolò Angelo Tinassi.
Mazlum, D. (2008). Sadullah Paşa Yalısı'nın Onarım Öyküsü. In D. Mazlum (Ed.), *Sadullah Paşa ve Yalısı Bir Yapı Bir Yaşam* (pp. 177–192). İstanbul: YEM.
Melling, A. I. (1819). *Voyage Pittoresque de Constantinople et des Rives du Bosphore*.
Naskali, E. G. (2003). *Tütün Kitabı*. İstanbul: Kitabevi.
Okan, N. (2003). Heyelanlar. *Mavi Gezegen*, (7), 14–17.
Orlandi, L. (2011). Istanbul Contemporanea. *L'Architetto Italiano*, VIII(42), 31–74.
Örs, H. (Ed.). (1969). *Moltke'nin Türkiye Mektupları*. İstanbul: Remzi Kitabevi.
Özgentürk, N. (2004). *Bir Yudum İnsan* (4th ed.). İstanbul: Alfa Yayınları.
Özgüven, B. (1997). *Barut ve Tabya: Rönesans Mimarisi Bağlamında Fatih Sultan Mehmed Kaleleri*. İstanbul Teknik Üniversitesi.
Pamuk, Ş. (2007). *Osmanlı'dan Cumhuriyet'e Küreselleşme, İktisat Politikaları ve Büyüme*. İstanbul: Türkiye İş Bankası Kültür Yayınları.
Paşa, A. C. (1980). *Ma'ruzat*. (Y. Halaçoğlu, Ed.). İstanbul: Çağrı Yayınları.
Patrick, M. M. (2001). *Bir Boğaziçi Macerası İstanbul Kız Koleji (1871 - 1924)*. İstanbul: Tez Yayınları.
Pazarbaşı, E. (1998). Vani Mehmed Efendi, Hayatı ve Eserleri. In A. H. Köker (Ed.), *Vani Mehmed Efendi 17 Mart 1998 Kayseri*. Kayseri: Erciyes Üniversitesi.
Pinardi, N., Özsoy, E., Latif, Mohammed, A., Moroni, F., Grandi, A., Manzella, G., … Lyubartsev, V. (2018). Measuring the sea: Marsili's oceanographic cruise (1679-1680) and the roots of oceanography. *Journal of Physical Oceanography*, 48 (April), 848–860.
Ramazanoğlu, F. S. (2017). *Kanlıca - Boğaziçi'nde Bir Köy*. İzmir: İon Mimarlık Yayınları.
Saner, T. (1998). *19. Yüzyıl İstanbul Mimarlığında "Oryantalizm."* İstanbul: Pera Turizm ve Ticaret A.Ş.
Saner, T. (1993). 19. Yüzyıl Osmanlı Eklektisizminde "Elhamra'nın Payı." In Z. Rona (Ed.), *Osman Hamdi Bey ve Dönemi Sempozyumu 17-18 Aralık 1992*. İstanbul: Tarih Vakfı Yurt Yayınları.
Saner, T., & Keskin, Ç. (2014). Büyük Mecidiye (Ortaköy) Camii'nin Mimarisi. In *Büyük Mecidiye Camii ve Ortaköy* (pp. 267–307). İstanbul: Kuveyt Türk.
Şehsuvaroğlu, H. Y. (1986). *Boğaziçi'ne Dair*. İstanbul: Türkiye Turing ve Otomobil Kurumu.
Şener, B. (2014). Türk Boğazları'nın Geçiş Rejiminin Tarihi Gelişimi ve Hukuki Statüsü The Historical Evolution and Legal Status of the Passage of the Turkish Straits. *Tarih Okulu Dergisi*, 7(17), 467–493.
Somel, S. A. (2009). Gölgede Kalmış Bir Osmanlı Devlet Adamı Şeyh'ül-Vüzerâ Namık Paşa. *Toplumsal Tarih*, (186), 60–67.
Tamer, C. (2001). *Rumeli Hisarı Restorasyonu (Belgelerle-Anılarla) 1955-1957*. İstanbul: Türkiye Turing Otomobil Kurumu.

Tanman, B. M. (2008). Sadullah Paşa Yalısı'nın Geç Dönem Osmanlı Mimarlığındaki Yerine İlişkin Bazı Gözlemler. In D. Mazlum (Ed.), *Sadullah Paşa ve Yalısı Bir Yapı Bir Yaşam* (pp. 123–142). İstanbul: YEM.
Tanman, B. M. (Ed.). (2011). *Nil Kıyısından Boğaziçi'ne: Kavalalı Mehmed Ali Paşa Hanedanı'nın İstanbul'daki İzleri*. Suna ve İnan Kıraç Vakfı İstanbul Araştırmaları Enstitüsü,.
Tanman, M. B. (2014). Osmanlı Dönemi Boğaziçi Uygarlığı. In M. B. Tanman (Ed.), *Büyük Mecidiye Camii ve Ortaköy* (pp. 12–59). İstanbul: Kuveyt Türk.
Tanman, M. B. (1998). Durmuş Dede Tekkesi. In N. Akbayar (Ed.), *Dünden Bugüne Beşiktaş*. İstanbul: Beşiktaş Belediyesi.
Tanman, M. B. (Ed.). (2014). *Büyük Mecidiye Camii ve Ortaköy*. İstanbul: Kuveyt Türk.
Tanman, M. B. (1998). Tekkeler. In *Dünden Bugüne Beşiktaş*.
Tanyeli, U. (2007). *Mimarlığın Aktörleri Türkiye 1900-2000*. İstanbul: Garanti Galeri.
Tanyeli, U. (Ed.). (1994). *Doğan Tekeli Sami Sisa Projeler Yapılar 1954-1994*. İstanbul: YEM.
Tcholakian, H. J. (1998). L'Eglise Armenienne Catholique en Turquie. İstanbul.
Tekeli, D., Sisa, S., & Hepgüler, M. (1960). Rumelihisarı Bahçesinin Tanzimi. *Arkitekt*, 1960(299), 61–67.
Tugay, E. Ç., & Tugay, M. S. (2007). *İzzetabad Kasrı Akıntıburnu'ndan akıp geçen zaman*. İstanbul: H. Bayraktar Holding Kültür Yayınları.
Türker, O. (2004). *Nihori'den Yeniköy'e Bir Boğaziçi Köyünün Hikayesi*. İstanbul: Sel Yayıncılık.
Tyrrell, H. G. (1911). *History of Bridge Engineering*. Chicago: University of Chicago Press.
Ünal, F. (2013). Ruslar Tarafından 1833'de Beykoz /Selvi Burnu'na Dikilen Kaya Anıtı "Moskof Taşı" (Камень Московитовъ). *Türkiyat Mecmuası*, 23(3), 187–206.
Ünver, S., & Eldem, S. H. (1970). *Anadoluhisarı'nda Amucazade Hüseyin Paşa Yalısı*. İstanbul: Türkiye Turing Otomobil Kurumu.
Ural, M. (1998). Anıtkabir'de Sanat Büyük Acıyı Estetiğe Dönüştürmenin Bilinci Yalın ve İnsani. In *Atatürk İçin Düşünmek İki Eser Katafalk ve Anıtkabir İki Mimar Bruno Taut ve Emin Onat*. İstanbul: İstanbul Teknik Üniversitesi Rektörlüğü.
Uras, B. (2012). Park Otel, Gümüşsuyu. In *Değişen Zamanların Mimarı Edoardo de Nari 1874-1954* (pp. 154–161).
Uras, B. (2014). Taşlık. *İstanbul Art News*.
Uras, B. (2014). Abraham Paşa'dan Edoardo de Nari'ye İstanbul'un Unutulmuş Eğlence Merkezi Büyük Beykoz Parkı. *İstanbul Araştırmaları Yıllığı*, 3(3).
Yavuz, M. F. (2014). *Byzantion: Byzas'tan Constantinus'a Antik İstanbul: Antik Edebi Kaynaklar*. İstanbul: Pera Müzesi.
Yıldırım, N. (1990). Karantina. In *İstanbul Ansiklopedisi C.3* (pp. 459–460).
Yılmaz, Ö. F. (2010). *Boğaziçi'ne Tüp Geçit: Sultan İkinci Abdülhamid Han'ın tüp geçit (tünel-i bahrî) projeleri*. İstanbul.
Yorulmaz, N. (2014). *Arming the Sultan: German Arms Trade and Personal Diplomacy in the Ottoman Empire*.
Yücel, U., Bekiroğlu, E. H., Oktay, Ö., & Boran, A. T. (2012). Küçük Mecidiye Camii Kubbe Künk Sistemi ve Uygulama Süreci. *Vakıf RestorasyonYıllığı*, 4(8), 6–14.
Yusufoğlu, N. T., & Pilehvarian, N. K. (2017). Beşiktaş Tayyare Fabrikası. *Megaron*, 12(2), 249–262.
Hayalet Yapılar. (2010). İstanbul: Pattu.
Boğaziçi'ne İki Köprü: Sultan ikinci Abdülhamid Han'ın "Cisr-i Hamidi" (Hamidiye köprüleri) projesi. (2009). İstanbul: Çamlıca.
T.C. İstanbul Vilayeti Büyükdere Bahçe Kültürleri istasyonu fidan satış kataloğu, 1958-1959. (1958). İstanbul.
Gölge Boğaziçi Lisesi Yıllığı. (1936). İstanbul: Maarif Matbaası.

TURKISH STATE ARCHIVES (BOA & BCA)
MINISTRY OF FOREIGN AFFAIRS ARCHIVE - ROME - ITALY